DATE DUE

FE 5 '99			

DEMCO 38-296

DREISER'S
RUSSIAN
DIARY

The University of Pennsylvania
Dreiser Edition

THOMAS P. RIGGIO
General Editor

JAMES L. W. WEST III
LEE ANN DRAUD
Textual Editors

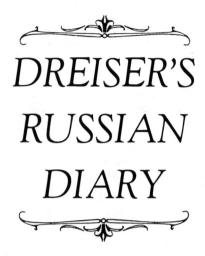

DREISER'S
RUSSIAN
DIARY

Edited by
THOMAS P. RIGGIO
JAMES L. W. WEST III

PENN

University of Pennsylvania Press

Philadelphia

on Data

P. Riggio, James L. W. West, III.
reiser edition)

2. Dreiser, Theodore, 1871–1945—Journeys—
West, James L. W.   III. Title.   IV. Series: Dreiser,
Theodore, 1871–1945. University of Pennsylvania Dreiser edition.
DK27.D73   1996
914.704′842—dc20   96-20778
                                                                            CIP

Research for this publication was supported by a grant from the International
Research and Exchanges Board, with funds provided by the U.S. Department
of State (Title VIII) and the National Endowment for the Humanities. None
of these organizations is responsible for the views expressed.

Printed in the United States of America

For
Anna, Tommy, and Rob

CONTENTS

ILLUSTRATIONS

PREFACE

On 3 October 1927, Theodore Dreiser received an invitation from the Soviet government to travel to Moscow for the celebration of the tenth anniversary of the Russian Revolution. On that day he began writing a diary that he would finish on 13 January 1928, when he had come to the end of a lengthy tour of Russia. In Moscow he met Ruth Epperson Kennell, who, as his secretary and companion for the trip, contributed significantly to the composition of the diary.

Dreiser's careful preservation of his papers makes possible this first publication of the Russian Diary of 1927–28. It is a document that will be of special value to anyone interested in American and Russian history in the twentieth century. During his stay in the former Union of Soviet Socialist Republics, Dreiser kept the diary to provide a record of the conversations he had with many of that country's most famous cultural and political figures: Sergei Eisenstein, Konstantin Stanislavsky, Anastas Molotov, Vladimir Mayakovsky, Karl Radek, Nikolai Bukharin, and Archbishop Platon, among others. These exchanges and Dreiser's firsthand account of conditions in the Soviet Union during the pivotal years of the late 1920s make the diary an important primary source and among the last such historical documents from this era.

This volume continues the Pennsylvania Dreiser Edition's tradition of publishing authoritative texts of writings that either survive only in manuscript or are otherwise inaccessible to both the specialist and the general reader. Such an undertaking would be unimaginable without the goodwill of the administration and the special training of the staff at the Van Pelt–Dietrich Library Center of the University of Pennsylvania. Paul H. Mosher, Director of Libraries at the university, has provided continuing support to the Dreiser Project. Michael T. Ryan, Director of Special Collections at the library, has generously devoted his own time and the resources of his staff to facilitating the work of the Dreiser Edition. The reorganization of the Dreiser Collection by Curator of Manuscripts Nancy Shawcross has made easier the preparation of this book and of others in progress.

Together with the Pennsylvania Edition of Dreiser's *American Diaries, 1902–1926* (1982) and *An Amateur Laborer* (1983), this edition of the *Russian Diary* is one of a projected series of volumes that will provide scholarly texts of Dreiser's private papers. Because Dreiser never prepared this diary for publication, it has been presented in conformity with widely accepted principles governing the editing of private documents. The editors, Thomas P. Riggio and James L. W. West III, conceived the volume and shared equally in the verification of the text and the writing of the annotations and identifications. Riggio provided the Introduction and West the Editorial Principles and apparatus. The editors, and associate editor, Lee Ann Draud, proofread the text and verified the contents at each stage of preparation.

THOMAS P. RIGGIO
General Editor
The University of Pennsylvania
Dreiser Edition

ACKNOWLEDGMENTS

For permission to publish the text of Dreiser's Russian Diary, the editors are grateful to the Trustees of the University of Pennsylvania, who hold copyright on Dreiser's unpublished writings. The editors thank Arthur D. Casciato, who produced an initial transcription of the diary that was a helpful starting point for our work. Thanks also to Stephen F. Cohen and Rosemarie Reed for their generosity in providing information about and photographs of Nikolai Bukharin.

Professor Riggio wishes to thank Jay West and Marina Tchebotaeva for help in verifying Russian spelling and identifying Russian place names, events, and geographical features. He would also like to acknowledge Irena Kutkina, whose aid as translator and guide in the Russian archives, as well as at the sites that Dreiser had visited, made his stay in Russia both more profitable and more enjoyable. Special thanks also to Drs. Eleonora A. Kravchenko and Alexandro Kutkina of Moscow for their generous hospitality and aid in matters large and small. Professor West thanks LaVerne Kennevan Maginnis for assistance with the textual chores; he is grateful to Flora Buckalew, Kim Fisher, and Suzanne Marcum for much help with the annotations.

INTRODUCTION

> Russia would make a most delightful socialistic community if the Emperor could be suddenly done away with and the people as suddenly educated. The Government controlling everything, it would only be necessary to transfer the control to the people's choice and you would have a kind of Utopia. The thing might be worked inversely and a fine socialistic community transformed into the most despotic form of government, with the reins all in one man's hands, but that would not be likely to happen where people have once gained any kind of an intellectual status.
>
> —Dreiser, at age 22, in the *St. Louis Globe-Democrat*,
> 2 January 1893

On 10 January 1928 Theodore Dreiser found himself making his way through the cold of a Russian winter day in the Ukrainian city of Odessa, an industrial center on the Black Sea near the mouth of the Dnieper River. He was ending a strenuous two months' visit to the former Union of Soviet Socialist Republics and was having difficulty getting a visa to travel through Poland to western Europe. To his dismay, customs agents told him that he needed special permission to take manuscripts and printed matter out of the country. He was most concerned about a diary that he had kept since 3 October 1927, when he first learned of the Soviet government's offer of an all-expenses–paid trip to Moscow. On that day he began his handwritten diary as a record of his experiences and reflections, beginning in New York and continuing aboard ship, and while traveling through Europe—first to Paris, then to Berlin and Warsaw, and finally into Russia.

He was invited initially, along with some fifteen hundred other international celebrities, for a week-long observance of the tenth anniversary of the October Revolution. When he requested that the government extend the invitation and finance him to a longer tour of the country, he was quickly obliged. He wanted, he told the Russian representative, "to see the real, unofficial Russia—the famine district in the Volga, say" (p. 29). The request seems not to have fazed the envoy. Dreiser was clearly a valuable commodity to a government that understood the value—and vanity—of artists and intellectuals. "The Soviet believes you to be the outstanding literary intelligence of America" (p. 28), he was informed, and preparations were speedily made for his trip.

By early November he was in Moscow and had hired a private secretary, Ruth Epperson Kennell. A thirty-four-year-old American expatriate who had been living in Russia for more than five years, Kennell made a living by translating and editing so-called anniversary editions of American writers, including Dreiser, for the government publishing house.

Shortly after their first meeting, she and Dreiser became lovers. When the American socialist Scott Nearing nominated her to be the novelist's secretary for the extended trip, Dreiser jumped at the suggestion: "Since we are already so close," he wrote in the diary, "it strikes me as almost an ideal choice" (p. 66). Because Kennell was not a party member, local bureaucrats objected, but when Dreiser angrily threatened to return home, a deal was struck that allowed her to stay on at his expense. Of course the government sent along with them an official guide provided by VOKS, the agency responsible for cultural relations with foreigners. Kennell followed Dreiser everywhere, made shorthand notes of his reactions and conversations, at times took dictation, and each evening reorganized her notes in the form of a typed diary.

Years later, Kennell recalled her unusual arrangement with Dreiser: "He had instructed me to use 'I' to mean himself in writing the diary. But he left the writing entirely to me, except for an occasional reminder to be sure to make a note of this or that."[1] (In practice Kennell sometimes strayed from this routine and lapsed into her own voice to describe Dreiser's actions or to address brief asides to him.) Dreiser also requested that she make a carbon copy for herself, since he expected her to help him later in mining the diary for various publications. Kennell worked diligently at her task for sixty-eight days. She typed her text each evening, straining her portable Corona until a cable snapped, which sent Dreiser on a frenzied hunt for a repair shop in the port town of Batum on the Black Sea. At times she needed the better part of a morning to transcribe the previous day's copious notations. At the journey's end, she later recalled,

1. Ruth Epperson Kennell, *Theodore Dreiser and the Soviet Union* (New York: International Publishers, 1969), 49. Dreiser later added Kennell's text to the diary he had written in his own hand; moreover, he cut, arranged, revised, and augmented her notes to suit his own ends.

there was a scramble "to finish typing my daily notes in order to hand over the complete diary of the tour to my employer at the border."[2]

The writing of a second, secret diary of her own added to Kennell's workload. In it she recorded conversations and events not included in the text that Dreiser carried away with him. For the book she later wrote about the novelist's stay in Russia, *Theodore Dreiser and the Soviet Union* (1969), she turned to these pages for scenes that, as she observes, are "based on my own, not the official, notes."[3] Kennell's "notes" have not survived, but they probably contained an account of her more private moments with the man she called her "dear boss."

What does survive, at The State Archives of the Russian Federation in Moscow, is a copy of the parts of the diary that she typed for Dreiser. Accompanying it is a letter to the head of VOKS' Foreign Affairs Department, Yaroshevsky, in which Kennell explains the nature of the document: "You will see the order is like a diary— the last pages are the first and the notes should be read from the bottom to top, beginning November 8 to November 30. Some pages are missing of the first two days." She promises to "finish typing from my notes when I return and will give it to you."[4] She made good on her promise; without informing Dreiser, she delivered the greater portion of the diary to the VOKS home office.

Kennell's leaking of the diary to the Russians seems to have been an act of self-protection. As an American given an unusual position at the insistence of a foreign celebrity, she naturally felt the need to prove her loyalty to her superiors. She must have suspected that VOKS was getting letters about Dreiser's unflattering views of the country from its appointed guide, Trevis, and from Dr. Sophia Davidovskaya (the "Davi" of the diary), a physician who was sent along by VOKS to look after Dreiser's health.[5] Kennell's awareness

2. Kennell, 183.

3. Ibid., 109. For an example of the differences between the two texts, see the interview Dreiser had with Archbishop Platon in the diary entry for 30 November 1927 and compare it with Kennell's version in *Theodore Dreiser and the Soviet Union*, 109–12.

4. Kennell to Yaroshevsky, undated, The State Archives of the Russian Federation, Moscow. The diary and letters, which I discovered in the Russian archives, provide an added dimension to the complex relationship between Dreiser and Kennell.

5. The letters from Trevis and Davidovskya that survive at The State Archives of the Russian Federation show this to be the case. The letters are particularly critical of what was considered Dreiser's unfriendly attitude toward the customs and people of the Soviet Union.

that she too was being watched may be the reason she made a point of occasionally distancing herself from Dreiser by commenting on his behavior in the diary itself. The government's knowledge of the diary may also explain the difficulty Dreiser had in leaving the country with his manuscript.

In any case, Dreiser eventually disentangled himself from the bureaucratic red tape at the Russian border and carried the "official" diary to America, where he brought it to the state in which it now exists. He edited Kennell's typescript, cutting and pasting together various portions of it and expanding and altering the text in longhand throughout. Certain entries in the diary suggest that Dreiser began this revision in Russia, but by 18 November he was already ten days behind schedule (see p. 108), and he appears to have stopped emending the text altogether as the trip increasingly drained his strength.

When Dreiser completed his work on the diary in New York, it ran to 424 leaves, 134 of which are in his own hand exclusively and 290 of which are edited portions of the document Kennell turned over to him at the Russian border. The final product is a complex document, more objective than a private diary and, at the same time, more self-consciously subjective in its desire to clarify and correct.[6]

What were Dreiser's intentions in all this? Why did he keep such a "personal" diary? Why didn't he tell Kennell about the alterations he made to her text? And why did he edit it so extensively?

Even before he left New York he seems to have conceived of the diary as something more than a private journal. His initial entries give details and information that suggest he had an audience in mind: for example, he identifies his dog as "Nick (the Russian wolf-hound)" and his upstate New York home as "Iroki (the country place)" (p. 31). In addition, the early sections contain extended segments of carefully wrought dialogue between himself and others. This is very different from the staccato, summary-style entries of his other surviving diaries and travel notes. In the past, each of his travel diaries was written mainly as an aide-mémoire for projected

---

6. Arthur D. Casciato, in the only study of the diary to date, has pointed to what he calls the "textual intersubjectivity" produced by Kennell's and Dreiser's joint participation in the writing of the text: "Neither his nor hers but rather theirs, the Soviet diary records and reproduces that intersubjectivity." Casciato, "Dictating Silence: Textual Subversion in Dreiser's Soviet Diary," *Papers on Language and Literature* 27 (Spring 1991): 187.

magazine articles or a travel book. In them he mainly jotted down impressions and half-lines—as in the travel notes that served as the raw data for *A Traveler at Forty* (1913) and *A Hoosier Holiday* (1915).[7] Later, when he began writing these books, he turned to his notes and let memory and invention do their work.

One of the odd features of the book that he wrote about his Russian experience, *Dreiser Looks at Russia* (1928), is its minimal reliance on the structure or contents of this diary. It might be that Dreiser was saving the Russian diary to publish as a travel memoir, a genre that was becoming popular among political pilgrims. If he did, he gave up the idea after revising Kennell's text. *Dreiser Looks at Russia* probably would have been a better book had he followed his usual method of building a narrative around selected portions of his travel diaries, which he arranged chronologically and linked together with anecdotes and personal reflections. Instead he opted for chapters with impressive-sounding titles—"The Current Soviet Economic Plan," "Communism—Theory and Practice," "The Present-Day Russian Peasant Problem"—on subjects he was not well qualified to discuss.

Consequently, the Russian diary is far more instructive and colorful than the travel book. What they have in common is the uncertainty over the Soviet experiment that Dreiser shared with many American intellectuals in the 1920s. By 1927 little was left of the uncritical enthusiasm over the new Russian order that had led Lincoln Steffens to declare "I have been over into the future, and it works."[8] Such early hopes for a new political mecca at Moscow were clouded by the world war. The Red Scare further polarized Americans. Moreover, the Bolshevik heroes of 1917 seemed all too human after the ravages of the Russian civil war. And in the mid-twenties the Soviet adoption of the New Economic Policy appeared to many, including Dreiser, to be a shift from democratic socialism toward something closer to American capitalism. In addition, by the time Dreiser arrived in Russia, many of the earlier revolutionaries had already come to sorry ends. John Reed was buried in the Kremlin amid rumors of his final disillusionment; Emma Goldman,

7. Dreiser's unpublished travel diaries are in the Dreiser Collection, Special Collections Department, Van Pelt–Dietrich Library Center, University of Pennsylvania.

8. Quoted in John P. Diggins, *The American Left in the Twentieth Century* (New York: Harcourt Brace Jovanovich, Inc., 1973), 90.

very much alive, had written eloquently of her disenchantment after Lenin squelched the anarchists at Kronstadt; and the diary itself records Dreiser's memorable picture of the pathetic last days in Moscow of the exiled labor leader, Big Bill Haywood.

By the time Dreiser traveled to Russia, only diehard radicals, such as Scott Nearing, Joseph Freeman, and Michael Gold, were still publicly expressing their early faith in the Soviets. Others, including Max Eastman, John Dos Passos, and Goldman, had already reversed themselves and publicized their negative conclusions about the aims and future of the Communist state. A large body of liberals in America had, however, continued to give lip service to the "great experiment," on which they projected their own dissatisfaction with American bourgeois values. But their lack of actual contact with Russian life, and their own comfortable middle-class lifestyles, resulted in ambivalent responses to Soviet policies. Even the Americans Dreiser met in Moscow did little to dispel his own ambivalence. Although he spoke to pro-Soviet activists such as Nearing and the journalist Anna Louise Strong, Dreiser spent as much time with Sinclair Lewis and Dorothy Thompson, hardly ardent supporters of the new order.

The Russian diary, then, is a product of the years before American progressives such as Dreiser turned with any real fervor to the Soviet Union as a model for a just society. This alone, however, does not explain its tone and character. Dreiser's uneasiness about the Soviet system also reflects some basic and enduring aspects of his own thinking. Even in his Russophile phase in the 1930s, his political position could be summed up best in his words to the novelist Evelyn Scott: "I am not an exact Marxian by any means, and while I was in Russia, I was constantly threatened with being thrown out for my bourgeois, capitalistic point of view. My quarrel is not so much with doctrines as conditions. Just now, conditions are extremely badly balanced."[9]

Conditions at home looked pretty good to Dreiser in 1927. He had finally published a best-seller, *An American Tragedy* (1925), and this, along with a lucrative film contract, had allowed him to share in the short-lived prosperity of Coolidge's America. Consequently, his inclination was to praise capitalism at the expense of the Russian

---

9. Dreiser to Evelyn Scott, 28 October 1932. In *Letters of Theodore Dreiser*, ed. Robert H. Elias (Philadelphia: University of Pennsylvania Press, 1959), 2:615.

system. He argued that "American workers are the best off in the world," boasted of "the unselfish work of scientists in America and the achievements of American financiers in building up industry, [the] 50% income tax, gifts of rich men to [the] country, improvement of social conditions to a high point"—and then he added, in a giant leap of economic illogic, "And perhaps the next step . . . will be the Soviet system, and I believe if this system were put to the masses in America, they would accept it" (p. 156).

The diary contains a number of such erratic conclusions. Dreiser was capable of swinging pendulum-like from an "ugly American" stance of smug nationalism to a naively idealistic view of Soviet goals and programs. But he was a good observer, particularly of official policies and the living conditions of the common people. Kennell, who frequently crossed ideological swords with her "boss," remarked shrewdly, "I had the feeling always that he was arguing with himself, not me."[10] The same may be said for the often charged exchanges recorded in the diary between Dreiser and notable figures such as Nikolai Bukharin, Sergei Eisenstein, Vladimir Mayakovsky, Konstantin Stanislavsky, Karl Radek, and Archbishop Platon.

These conversations, along with the vivid pictures Dreiser supplies of life under the ten-year-old regime, give the diary a privileged place among social documents of the time. It belongs on a short list of important American records of life in Russia in the 1920s—a list that includes the accounts found in Eastman's *Since Lenin Died*, Freeman's *American Testament*, Goldman's *My Disillusionment in Russia*, and the journalism of Walter Duranty, the English-born correspondent for the *New York Times*.

More than any of these writers, Dreiser was an enigma to his hosts. By 1927 the fifty-six-year-old novelist was regarded highly in Soviet circles, and his works were being translated by the state press. His books offered sympathetic portraits of proletarian characters such as Jennie Gerhardt and Clyde Griffiths, who surely could be viewed as victims of capitalism. Yet he also had aggrandized a predatory robber baron in the two Cowperwood novels—*The Financier* (1912) and *The Titan* (1914)—that he based on the career of the Chicago traction king Charles T. Yerkes. While in Russia his comments in praise of American individualism led Kennell to conclude, with some justice, that "At the time of his pilgrimage to the first socialist

10. Kennell, 200.

country, the author's challenging approach reflected a sympathetic identification with his hero Cowperwood."[11]

Kennell's observation captures one side of Dreiser. But his political allegiances, always hard to gauge, were more complex than she suggests. Strongly influenced by the Progressive movement of the 1890s, he was nevertheless distrustful of reform. In the nineteen-teens, he befriended political rebels such as Daniel DeLeon, Eugene Debs, and Reed; but he never expressed any of the fervor found in, say, Reed's prose epic of the Revolution, *Ten Days That Shook the World* (1919). Dreiser's writing appeared in radical magazines such as *The Masses* during the same years he was allying himself in literary battles with the political Tory H. L. Mencken—who by 1917 had already begun to worry in print that his friend was becoming a "professional revolutionary."[12] On the day the novelist left for Russia, his Marxist-leaning friends Freeman, Diego Rivera, and Joseph Wood Krutch were among a small group that gave him a farewell party, at which Dreiser reportedly became nostalgic over monarchy and expressed sympathy for the czar's family.[13]

What could the Russians have expected of such a visitor? The young Soviet critic Sergei Dinamov, who figures prominently in the diary, had written Dreiser a year earlier, asking him what solution he had to the economic and political problems facing the world. Dreiser responded: "Life, as I see it, is an organized process about which we can do nothing in the final analysis. . . . Until that intelli-

11. Ibid., 80.

12. H. L. Mencken, "The Dreiser Bugaboo," *The Seven Arts* (August 1917); rprt. in *The Correspondence of Theodore Dreiser & H. L. Mencken, 1907–1945*, ed. Thomas P. Riggio (Philadelphia: University of Pennsylvania Press, 1986), 2:773.

13. Daniel Aaron, *Writers on the Left* (New York: Discus Books, 1969), 159. Daniel Aaron stated that he recalls this story's being told to him by Mike Gold but that after so many years he cannot be certain (Aaron to Riggio, 21 September 1994). It is worth noting that in the diary Dreiser shows no such sentiments; in speaking of Czar Nicholas II and his family, he says, while visiting one of the royal palaces outside Leningrad, "I could understand quite clearly why it was necessary to get rid of these people" (26 November 1927). As early as 1896, when Dreiser was editor of *Ev'ry Month* magazine, he placed the following under a photograph of Nicholas:

> Practically the arbiter of Europe and, as director of all the energies of the Russian horde, a menace to civilization, he is anything but a brilliant man. He confers and decides in affairs that may affect ages and peoples most remote, and yet, to such a pass has the iniquitous inheritance system arrived, the wildest, most crack-brained heirling can by birth inherit such power and estate. (1 December 1896)

For Dreiser's thought during this period, see Nancy Warner Barrineau (ed.), *Theodore Dreiser's Ev'ry Month*. Athens: University of Georgia Press, 1996.

gence which runs this show sees fit to remould the nature of man, I think it will always be the survival of the fittest, whether in the monarchies of England, the democracies of America, or the Soviets of Russia."[14] Despite a long history of such statements, he was clearly someone on whom the Russians were willing to take a chance.

Although his thinking led him to emphasize "the nature of man" at the expense of national differences, Dreiser experienced culture shock when he arrived in Russia. The diary shows that his first response was to settle for easy stereotypes. He exhibited the traveler's natural tendency to compare the customs of a new country with those of his own land. More often, however, Dreiser thought in literary rather than ethnocentric terms. He immediately projected images from his readings onto the undecipherable human mass before him: "In so far as I can see these are the true people of Russia's great writers—Tolstoy, Gogol, Turgeniev, Dostoievsky, Saltykov. One sees their types everywhere" (p. 59). Only as Dreiser gradually worked his way through the new landscape did it come alive for him and yield at times to his feel for place, mood, and detail.

Even after adjusting to the new sights and sounds, he found it hard to warm up to his hosts. The feeling was mutual. Some sense of the unofficial Soviet response to Dreiser can be found in the letters at Moscow's State Archives. They suggest, as does the diary, that he was not the easiest guest to please. On meeting the famed Marxist theoretician Bukharin, Dreiser immediately "began my attack without delay" (p. 184). This appeared to Kennell as a supreme act of arrogance. But the interchange (one of the highlights of the diary) was not simply the product of hubris on Dreiser's part. His attitude toward Bukharin was not without precedent, even among political radicals in America. Eastman, for one, had written in 1925 that although Bukharin was being praised for "a supposed theoretic mastery of the Marxian philosophy," he had in fact "written a book about Historical Materialism, which is at once so scholarly in appearance, and so utterly undigested and confusing to the brain, that most people are willing to concede his mastery of Marxism in order to avoid having to read and study this book. What Lenin said about Bukharin is that he 'does not understand the Marxian dialectic.' "[15]

---

14. Dreiser to Sergei Dinamov, 5 January 1927, in Elias, *Letters*, 2:450.

15. Max Eastman, *Since Lenin Died* (New York: Boni & Liveright, 1925), 30. For another, less polemical, view of Bukharin's intellectual abilities, see Stephen F. Cohen, *Bukharin and the Russian Revolution* (New York: Alfred A. Knopf, 1973).

The contentious Dreiser certainly did not need any such precedent to take on the various Russian dignitaries who crossed his path.
Unable and, to some extent, unwilling to control the headstrong
novelist, Kennell put her job in jeopardy by supporting Dreiser's un-
orthodox requests. Despite her attempt to head off trouble by offering VOKS a copy of the diary, her relationship with Dreiser, both
public and private, probably accounts for her own permanent departure from Russia shortly after he left.

After Kennell began transcribing the notes and relaying them
to VOKS, all mention of her intimacy with Dreiser disappears. She
did, however, write a curious postscript to the diary, which she sent
to Dreiser in America. It is part love letter and part continuation of
the polemic they engaged in throughout the trip. "And now farewell,
a long farewell to my dear boss. I hope I can live down my loneliness, but if I don't, won't that prove the endurance of human affections—once in a while at least? . . . Your overpowering personality
still envelops me. No one has ever so completely absorbed my individuality. . . . Just the same, I think you are wrong in your ultimate
conclusions about life and specifically about the social experiment
in Russia" (pp. 283, 281).

Kennell probably deserves more credit for influencing Dreiser's
long-term thinking about Russia than she has hitherto received. Her
multiple roles—as private secretary, guide, translator, collaborator
on the diary, lover, and later as correspondent and editor of *Dreiser
Looks at Russia*—placed her in a privileged position during the time
Dreiser was beginning to shape his ideas about the Soviet Union.
As Dreiser's first and chief antagonist in the debate over the authen-
ticity of the Soviet experiment, she helped him formulate opinions
on both sides of the question.

This was, of course, not a debate that Dreiser or Kennell origi-
nated. Dreiser did not have to read all the books and articles by
those who had visited Russia to know the terms of the argument.
In New York he had read Walter Duranty's vivid reports in support
of the new government.[16] He also knew of the less sanguine conclusions reached by Goldman. Deported by the U.S. government for
her anarchist views at the time of the Red Scare, Goldman arrived in

---

16. Duranty's newspaper articles are collected in Gustavus Tuckerman (ed.), *Duranty
Reports Russia* (New York: The Viking Press, 1934).

Moscow with far greater hopes than did Dreiser. By 1922, however, she was issuing broadsides on the flaws of the Soviet system and the shortcomings of Russian heads of state. "Obsessed by the infallibility of their creed, giving of themselves to the fullest, they could be both heroic and despicable at the same time. They could work twenty hours a day, live on herring and tea, and order the slaughter of innocent men and women."[17] Because Goldman had many close contacts among the Russians and could speak the language, she was attuned to social nuances that Dreiser missed. Nevertheless, many of Dreiser's conclusions in 1928 echoed her convictions. Both deplored Soviet terrorism, arguing that, in Goldman's words, "the Communists believed implicitly in the Jesuitic formula that the end justifies *all* means."[18] Dreiser sensed, as Goldman had, that "the Bolsheviki were social puritans who sincerely believed that they alone were ordained to save mankind."[19]

Unlike Goldman, however, Dreiser was in many ways attracted to Soviet dogmatism, notwithstanding his repeated outbursts against it. It was in his nature to be as absolutist and puritanical in his beliefs as any party member. One can sense this in the diary, particularly in his dialogues with Russian leaders. There is something close to a willingness to be converted beneath the heated exchanges, a desire to believe that an ideal society is possible, if only someone could answer his questions and quiet his vast skepticism about human nature.

In the late 1920s Kennell came close to being that someone. Among other things, she succeeded in getting Dreiser to rethink his prejudices. To her credit, she confronted him more honestly than she needed to. She seems, in fact, to have had nearly as many divided impulses as he. Dreiser sensed this in her, if we can trust the portrait of Kennell entitled "Ernita," which he published in *A Gallery of Women* (1929). There he concluded that when he last saw her in Russia, she was "still strong in the Communist faith and all that it meant in the way of freedom for women, [but] she was no longer one who was convinced that it was without faults."[20] Dreiser's position as her employer, as well as their romantic involvement, naturally complicated

17. Emma Goldman, *My Disillusionment in Russia* (New York: Doubleday, Page & Company, 1923), 111.
18. Ibid., 110.
19. Ibid., 112.
20. Theodore Dreiser, *A Gallery of Women* (New York: Horace Liveright, 1929), 1:357.

matters for her.[21] Nevertheless, she remained, for all her friendship with Dreiser, ideologically committed to the Soviet experiment. On her return to America in 1928, she began a career as a writer of fiction for adolescents, most of which—from *Vanya of the Streets* (1931) to the stories she continued to write until her death in 1977—sought to challenge the stereotypes about Russia that Americans absorbed at a young age. Even as late as the 1960s, after the idealism over the Soviet Union had long been shattered by the horrors of Stalin's reign and by post–World War II realities, Kennell remained an unreconstructed advocate for Russia. Her 1969 book on Dreiser in the Soviet Union often takes him to task for what she considered his obtuse resistence to what is best in Russian life. This was, to be sure, an extension of the program of educating him that she had begun forty years earlier, only now she was using the medium of a memoir to speak to a larger audience. In retrospect it is clear that this was a long-term project for her. As early as the diary, we find her planting ideas for Dreiser's later consideration; even her asides—such as "I didn't say all this but I thought about it afterward" (p. 230)—show the ways in which the diary took on the character of an instructional manual in her hands.

Her lessons were not wasted on Dreiser. Although he opened his book on Russia by announcing that "I am an incorrigible individualist—therefore opposed to Communism,"[22] he had mainly good things to say about the Soviet state. Kennell's resistance to his ideas also had a long-range effect on his positions in the thirties, when he made use of many of her arguments in public pronouncements. During that decade, Dreiser was one of many Americans whose idealization of the Soviet Union was stimulated by the economic

21. After reading the story of "Ernita" in manuscript, Kennell wrote to Dreiser that

The story wouldn't be complete if it didn't tell how Ernita, after a series of painful personal experiences at the hands of individuals in the cause she had given herself to, met a certain great man, and came to know him very intimately and with deep, almost maternal, affection, and how they battled over principles and theories of society until he gradually broke down her philosophy and her faith, and some of her most cherished principles in regard to her sex. This sounds as though he might be a villain, but he isn't at all. Quite the contrary.

Kennell to Dreiser, 9 June 1928, Dreiser Collection, Special Collections Department, Van Pelt–Dietrich Library Center, University of Pennsylvania.
22. Theodore Dreiser, *Dreiser Looks at Russia* (New York: Horace Liveright, 1928), 9.

breakdown and social malaise of the depression years. In effect, the Russian diary bears witness to one of the major historical ironies of these decades. In the 1920s, when Russia was going through a relatively democratic and orderly phase, most intellectuals were either apathetic or, like Dreiser, divided in their opinions about the Communist system, whereas in the 1930s, they projected their utopian ideals onto the most repressive regime in Soviet history.

The ambivalences in Dreiser's pronouncements about Russia sent mixed messages to his readers. On the basis of Dreiser's public statements, Mencken concluded that his old friend had been brainwashed by the Russians.[23] When Dorothy Thompson accused Dreiser of plagiarizing from her book *The New Russia* (1928), Mencken judged that the Russians had fed her the facts for the book and that "Dreiser also went to Russia and was taken for the same ride and loaded with the same material."[24]

The diary, however, tells a different story. The situation was more complex than Mencken understood. It is difficult, even with the evidence of the diary before us, to determine the extent to which Dreiser's travels were controlled. He was obviously treated to the royal "guided tour" whenever possible—including the standard visits to model prisons, schools, and housing complexes for workers. And he was supplied with a state guide, whose duty was to keep him away from any kind of spontaneous contact with the natives.

But Dreiser was more difficult to brainwash than either Mencken or the Soviets supposed. He was always suspicious of dogma of any kind, even dogma he wanted to believe in. Kennell

23. Other critics have followed Mencken's lead. See, for example, Aaron, *Writers on the Left*, 159. Dreiser biographer Richard Lingeman wisely concentrates on the inner debate at the heart of Dreiser's response to communism. See Lingeman, *Theodore Dreiser: An American Journey, 1908–1945* (New York: G. P. Putnam's Sons, 1990), 289–310.

24. H. L. Mencken, *My Life as Author and Editor*, ed. Jonathan Yardley (New York: Alfred A. Knopf, 1993), 337. There are a number of more likely explanations. One is offered by the journalist Anna Louise Strong, who said that she had given Dreiser and Thompson the same notes "which both of them used in undigested form." Quoted in Mark Schorer, *Sinclair Lewis: An American Life* (New York: McGraw-Hill Book Company, Inc., 1961), 495. Some support for this is found in the diary, when Dreiser is noted listening attentively and at length to Strong's ideas about Russia (see entry for 17 November 1927, p. 107). Another possibility was provided by Louise Campbell, who typed and helped edit the manuscript of Dreiser's book. She told Dreiser biographer W. A. Swanberg that Dreiser instructed her to use Thompson's newspaper articles to pad *Dreiser Looks at Russia*. Swanberg speculates that Dreiser might have asked others who helped him put together the book to do the same thing. See Swanberg, *Dreiser* (New York: Charles Scribner's Sons, 1965), 343.

understood this. She knew that her charge was not duped by the ploys of his hosts, and as a result she tended to go along with his attempts to dodge governmental restraints. Years later she recalled that, "alert to propaganda, he was suspicious of the Russians."[25] The diary shows Dreiser complaining constantly about the official line he was being handed. "There are so many fixed things the Soviet is determined the foreigner must see—usually (always, I might say) things which reflect glory on the Soviet labors. In consequence I am hauled here & there all to speedily. As for touching or sensing the intimate, commonplace life of the city—not a taste" (pp. 161–62). Dreiser looked to his secretary to help him contact some of the commonplace life of the country. Sometimes that meant merely getting a good local meal. Even in this, Dreiser was aware of the standard policy: "I tried to persude someone to take me to a simple Russian restaurant in Leningrad—but no—foreigners must see only granduer" (pp. 163–64).

Kennell, to be sure, conspired with Dreiser to undermine what Paul Hollander has called the "techniques of hospitality" that are employed by governments to win over foreign visitors.[26] This was not always an easy task. The tour organizers hoped that she would work with the VOKS agents to keep Dreiser in line during the trip. When, for instance, they were about to leave Moscow for the first time, the interpreter Trevis turned to Kennell and in a confidential tone said, "We'll be traveling together for several weeks, I hope. Between us we ought to be able to manage the old man—right?"[27]

Kennell resisted all such overtures. More than once the diary shows her leaving behind the appointed guides and sneaking away with Dreiser on unauthorized excursions. She oversaw the meeting between him and Radek, who, as a friend of Trotsky, was being watched and therefore had to slip past the guards at his Kremlin office to talk politics with Dreiser at a hotel. At times Kennell uses the diary to expose the darker side of life under the Soviets. For example, when they met a local priest in a small village, Dreiser plied him with potentially embarrassing questions. The priest responded vaguely and with apparent untruths. In the diary account of this event Kennell includes the priest's parting words, whispered to her

25. Kennell, 22.
26. Paul Hollander, *Political Pilgrims: Travels of Western Intellectuals to the Soviet Union, China, and Cuba, 1928–1978* (New York: Oxford University Press, 1981), 16–21.
27. Kennell, 88.

in secret: " 'Please explain to the gentleman that I would gladly have answered his questions, if we had been alone, but before a Jewess, and the government representatives and a newspaper correspondent! If I had given my opinions—' He drew his finger across his throat" (p. 205).

Kennell trusted Dreiser with such information because she believed that the unvarnished truth was enough to convince him that the Soviet state was the best hope for the future. (She seems to have assumed, somewhat naively, that her reader at VOKS would understand her intentions as well.) Moreover, for all her complaints, she evidently took pleasure in Dreiser's habit of playing devil's advocate, his often perverse disposition to oppose and contradict. Her parting words to him acknowledged the "tremendous intellectual stimulus" (p. 281) he had been for her, although she evidently admired him more for his questioning mind than for the consistency of his ideas. Lastly, she realized how much a creature of moods he was. She reminded herself and others along the way that "When Mr. Dreiser was feeling tired and miserable, he always took a gloomier view of conditions."[28] Not a systematic thinker, Dreiser held "views" that reflected his deepest prejudices, many of which were not altogether conscious. Among the most obvious was his suspicion that the Soviets were dogmatists in the manner of his bête noire, the Catholic church.

Churches and religious services drew Dreiser like a magnet throughout his travels. He noted with interest that a great number of Russians had continued to take the "opiate of the people." At any moment he would turn to the question of religion, as he did in the middle of an economic discussion with the vice president of the All-Russian Cooperatives: "Does not the Soviet Govt. try to educate the children to be adherents of the Soviet Govt? just as the Catholic Church educates the children to be Catholics?" (p. 125). Unhappy memories of a Catholic childhood had led Dreiser to adopt exaggerated nativist fears about the power of the Roman church in America. He believed the church engaged in a secret program of international expansion, a form of spiritual imperialism that matched the political aspirations of many Soviet leaders. In pessimistic moments these fears surfaced, and he projected his worst nightmares onto the Soviet regime: "Your program . . . is exactly that of the Catholic Church or

28. Ibid., 147.

the Greek Church. . . . & it's policy toward the young—its desire to color permanently the psychology of the same. I have said—and repeat—that the Soviet Central Committee got rid of one iron dogmatic faith only to erect a second & to me more dangerous one in its place" (pp. 188, 173–74).

Although Dreiser's was not an uncommon view of Soviet dogmatism, his intense outrage sprang from other than political causes. He might have been less troubled on this account had he been aware of the full force of the Soviet campaign against organized religion: in 1927–28 alone the authorities closed more than 270 churches, eighty monasteries, fifty-nine synagogues, and thirty-eight mosques.[29] Dreiser, however, focused less on such political events than on the nature and function of religion in society. After returning to America he wrote to Kennell, chiding her for mistaking his position. His great enemy, he said, was not religion but religious dogma: "There is, for instance, the religion which is a response to as well as awe or reverence before the beauty and wisdom of creative energy. Many people—free of any dogma—enjoy it."[30] What finally overrode many of his scruples about party dogmatism was his gradual awareness (and strong approval) of the Soviet aim to destroy the patriarchal structures of old Russia—including those relating to the church, family life, marital bonds, and the role of women in society.

Although Dreiser was deeply concerned about such social issues, the political infighting that intrigued most of his contemporaries did not engage his energies or attention. He seems barely aware of the momentous struggles for power that were taking place in Russia, resulting soon after his departure in the emergence of Joseph Stalin as absolute dictator. Other than a few vague references, there is no mention of Leon Trotsky's dramatic revelation of Lenin's *Testament* in October 1927. Nor does Dreiser reflect on the historic events that occurred during his visit: the consolidation of Stalin's power through the expulsion of prominent Bolsheviks from the party in November and December and the exile of Trotsky to Central Asia in January 1928.

He was equally uninformed on matters that had a more di-

29. See Basil Dmytryshyn, *USSR, a Concise History* (New York: Charles Scribner's Sons, 1984), 131.

30. Dreiser to Kennell, 5 September 1928, Dreiser Collection, Special Collections Department, Van Pelt-Dietrich Library Center, University of Pennsylvania.

rect impact on him as a writer. He surely would have been unhappy to learn that the state publishing house, Gosizdat, which he courted while in Russia, refused to publish the works of some of his intellectual heroes: Herbert Spencer, Schopenhauer, Tolstoy, Nietzsche, and Dostoevsky. Or that, along with Nadezhda Krupskaia's infamous Committee for Political Enlightenment, Gosizdat conspired to remove such writings from the libraries.[31] Dreiser did, however, experience firsthand the government's censorship of Russian theater and film productions. He laughed off a socialist dramatic version of *Uncle Tom's Cabin*. But the joke turned sour when it came to his own work: he walked out on Stanislavsky when the director was ordered not to produce a play based on *An American Tragedy* because censors found the "religious sections" and the relations between employers and workers to be presented too sympathetically. He was followed out of Stanislavsky's office by the director's secretary, who placed her hand in his arm and said gently, "Perhaps in another five years we might be permitted to produce it."[32]

By 1928 such antagonisms and disappointments were already beginning to take second place to what proved to be the major factor in Dreiser's response to Russia: the issue of what he called "equity," by which he meant social and economic parity for all. What unifies Dreiser's point of view in the diary is a cast of mind that habitually led him to question the integrity of any purportedly humane economy. Dreiser has often been accused of being, to borrow William Dean Howells's characterization of Mark Twain, a theoretical socialist and a practical capitalist. Unlike later critics, Howells recognized this as a typically American paradox, not a character flaw. And in any case, it applies more aptly to Dreiser's posture in the thirties than to the voice we find in the Russian diary. While in Russia, Dreiser knew that the figure he cut was mainly that of "a materialistically infected bourgeois—or blood-sucker, not fitted to either grasp or sympathize with the ills of the underdog" (p. 178).

There's a mixture of disingenuousness and assertive pride in this statement. Dreiser took obvious delight in arguing what Kennell called his favorite thesis: that the big, naturally endowed individual gets ahead, and the little, incompetent mind falls behind in

31. Richard Pipes, *Russia under the Bolshevik Regime* (New York: Alfred A. Knopf, 1993), 295–96.
32. Kennell, 43–44.

the struggle of life. He repeated this like a mantra, to the point that Kennell began to suspect that the gentleman was protesting too much. Put another way, he was straining, as he had done most of his adult life, to identify himself with the uncommon man. His comments throughout the diary reveal a good deal about the unspoken drives behind his "thesis." A few examples will suffice. Of Bukharin, he belligerently asks, "Can you mention a great mind from the proletariat?" (p. 190)—a strange challenge coming from a world-famous writer who had himself risen from proletarian origins. Or take the incident aboard ship at Gagri on the Black Sea, where the second- and third-class passengers produced in him a strong visceral reaction: "The huddled masses of them gave me a sense of nausea" (p. 264). One need not be a devout Freudian to appreciate such a verbal "slip" from the pen of this American son of an immigrant. In the same vein, he defends American justice in the Sacco-Vanzetti case: "I tried to explain the attitude of the American public to foreigners who had not been naturalized" (p. 239).

Not many years later, Dreiser would do an about-face on these matters. He could then, for instance, write to Mencken, justifying his allegiance to the Soviet agenda on the grounds of his proletarian beginnings: "I know you have no use for the common man since he cannot distinguish himself. But I have. . . . You see, Mencken, unlike yourself, I am biased. I was born poor."[33]

Actually, this personal element appeared in a muted way among his first newspaper articles after returning from Russia. He speculated that in the new Russia it might "be possible to remove that dreadful sense of social misery in one direction or another which has so afflicted me in my life in America ever since I have been old enough to know what social misery is."[34] This side of his feelings about Russia emerged more clearly in the 1930s, when widespread economic problems in America encouraged Dreiser to contemplate the social and political roots of his childhood deprivations. In the process of doing so, he revised backward his earlier experiences: "As for the Communist System—as I saw it in Russia in 1927 and '28— I am for it—hide and hoof."[35]

33. Dreiser to Mencken, 27 March 1943, in *Dreiser-Mencken Letters*, 2:689.
34. Quoted in Lingeman, 309.
35. *Dreiser-Mencken Letters*, 2:690.

The Russians have always appreciated Dreiser's good will, keeping his books in print and even, in 1968, naming a street after him ("Dreiser Street") in the Ukrainian coal-mining center of Stalino, later called Donetsky. But while Dreiser was still in Russia, he was noticeably less elated by the system, as he made clear when he took leave of Kennell: "I'd rather die in the United States than live here," he grumbled (p. 276). By this point the great champion of individualism had been exhausted by the rigors of the trip. Kennell later recalled his state: "How pitifully altered was the American delegate! His smart light-gray topcoat was grimy, his scarf bedraggled, his suit untidy, his bow tie missing, and he himself unwashed."[36] He sat waiting for his train, his bronchitis aggravated by the damp Russian winter, his chest wracked with pain, and his handkerchiefs filling with phlegm faster than Kennell could have them washed.

Kennell feared that the trials of his final days in Russia would color his report to America. But a letter written to her on 24 February 1928 made her hopeful that he had recovered from his last ugly mood. He assured her that his book would "not seriously try to injure an idealistic effort." He also commented on a new fact of life in America that dramatically altered his analysis of Russia: "Besides, learning that there were bread lines here—the first since 1910—I became furious because there is too much wealth wasted here to endure it. Hence, while I am going to stick to what I saw favorable and unfavorable I am going to contrast it with the waste and extravagance and social indifference here. I may find myself in another storm. If so, well and good."[37]

For better and worse, this "contrast" became the standard by which he conducted his ongoing critique of American life for the remainder of his days. And, as he predicted, the storms did come.

THOMAS P. RIGGIO

36. Kennell, 184.
37. Dreiser to Kennell, 24 February 1928, Dreiser Collection, Special Collections Department, Van Pelt–Dietrich Library Center, University of Pennsylvania.

Dreiser's Russian diary is both a *private* and a *collaborative* document. Its printed rendering in this edition reflects both of these characteristics. The diary is *private* in that it was not finished for publication. A scholarly text of such a diary should therefore preserve its preliminary, personal nature, insofar as that is possible in a typeset medium. Public documents (novels, stories, essays) usually appear in public dress, with misspellings corrected, grammatical errors rectified, and slips of the pen set right. In private documents, these same features are usually preserved unless they interfere seriously with comprehension. Accordingly, nearly all misspellings, grammatical mistakes, and other idiosyncrasies—in both Dreiser's and Ruth Kennell's sections of the diary—are preserved. Substantive emendations have been introduced only to clarify confusing passages, and some minor punctuation has been added to assist in readability.

This diary is *collaborative* in that it is the product of two hands: Dreiser writing as himself and Kennell writing both in her own persona and in Dreiser's. This collaboration, essential to an understanding of the diary, is signaled by the use of differing typefaces. Dreiser's handwriting is rendered in an italic face; Kennell's typing is printed in a roman face. The majority of the entries in the diary are entirely in one face or the other, but many are genuinely collaborative, with Dreiser revising and augmenting the typed entries that Kennell produced. The alternating faces always signal this collaboration to the reader.

The diary is presented almost entirely in clear text, with no symbols, diacritics, or other barbed wire. No effort is made to render excised words. A few illegible readings are indicated by "[unreadable word]." Blank spaces that appear when Dreiser could not recall a name or a term are printed as ⌞   ⌟. All underlinings in the original diary are printed as underscores, not italics. The diary has been divided editorially into six sections in order to reflect the stages of Dreiser's journey: "En Route," "Moscow," "Leningrad," "Return to Moscow," "Through Russia," and "Farewell."

Annotations are supplied throughout the diary for persons, literary works, journalistic writings, and public buildings and establishments. The minor Soviet officials whom Dreiser met and interviewed are not identified, nor is an effort made to gloss the names of all towns and communities that he visited in Russia. Well-known figures such as Tolstoy, Turgenev, and Kerensky are not annotated. A few confusing readings in the text are clarified in the notes. When necessary, words in other languages (principally in Russian) are defined, and the most serious of the misspellings in Russian are corrected. If no note appears, then the person or place is unidentified or has been judged not to require annotation.

Many of the place names recorded in the original diary are misspelled. Dreiser and Kennell often made their notes several hours after passing through train stops or villages, and they did not always spell the names of such places correctly. In the Russian sections of the diary there was the added problem of rendering the Cyrillic characters into the Latin alphabet. The errors in these place names do contribute to the private character of the diary, but from a practical viewpoint they might confuse biographers and scholars. Place names have therefore been corrected, whenever possible, by reference to maps and guidebooks of the 1920s.

There are some small problems with dates. Both Dreiser and Kennell occasionally lost track of the day of the week or entered an incorrect year. Dreiser would sometimes compound such errors by figuring the date of the next entry from the erroneously dated previous entry, thus carrying forward the mistake. There seems to be no good reason to preserve such errors; they are rectified here, and the emendations are recorded in a separate table in the apparatus.

The original diary is a part of the Dreiser Collection (MS Collection 30, Box 222) in the Special Collections Department, Van Pelt–Dietrich Library Center, University of Pennsylvania. The diary began as a volume of blank paper, 150 × 228 cm, bound in unstamped dark blue imitation leather. Archivists, in processing the diary, added folio numbers in pencil to each leaf. The diary text covers leaves 1–424 of the volume; the remaining leaves are blank. One leaf, between 20 and 21, has been razored out, removing the final page of Dreiser's discussion with Helen Richardson about whether she will accompany him on the trip. The diary was in Helen's possession for several years after Dreiser's death, before it came to Penn. It is likely that she excised the page, perhaps to remove some personal or intimate reference. The entry breaks off during a discussion about a pair of Russian boots ("red ones, maybe") that Dreiser is to bring back for her. It is now beyond our ability to know whether she received the boots.

Dreiser made nearly all of his holograph entries on the rectos of the leaves, using a variety of ink and pencil colors—blue, blue-black, purple, red. Kennell typed her entries (in an elite face) on separate leaves, rectos only. Most of the copies that she gave to Dreiser were carbons, in purple. Later, back in New York, Dreiser cut up her typed leaves, emended and augmented them in his own hand, and pasted them onto the rectos of the bound volume, thus swelling its bulk considerably.

Other surviving travel diaries kept by Dreiser are filled with interesting detritus from his trips—photographs, postcards, receipts, menus, maps, telegrams, and letters. Surprisingly, the Russian diary contains almost none of this kind of material, although it does preserve several pencil sketches by Kennell—of Dreiser and of persons whom they met and interviewed. Two of these sketches are reproduced in this edition.

The textual apparatus at the rear of this volume is a selective record, listing only emendations that affect meaning. A full record of emendation is on deposit in the Dreiser Collection, along with other materials gathered during the preparation of this volume.

James L. W. West III

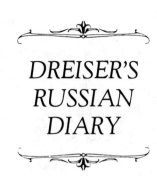

DREISER'S
RUSSIAN
DIARY

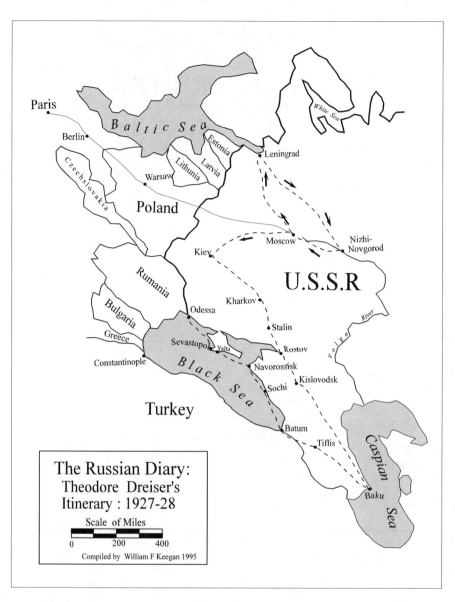

The Russian Diary:
Theodore Dreiser's
Itinerary : 1927-28

Scale of Miles

0   200   400

Compiled by William F Keegan 1995

Map illustrating Dreiser's itinerary. The solid line on this map shows Dreiser's route from the time of his arrival in Paris to his travel by train to Berlin, Warsaw, and finally to Moscow. The broken lines follow his movements within the Soviet Union. At first Dreiser was centered in Moscow, from which he traveled to Leningrad and Nizhni-Novgorod. Afterward, he began a more extensive tour of the country, beginning with a trip to the Ukrainian center of Kiev, and then on to other major Ukrainian, Caucasian, and Georgian cities. The last lap of his journey took him to port cities along the Black Sea. He concluded his tour at Odessa, from which he took a train back to Paris. Not shown on the map are occasional stopovers at small towns and the one special visit he made to Tolstoy's home at Yasnaya Polyana, which is located one hundred miles south of Moscow.

EN ROUTE

To Russia
October–1927

From a Russian Soviet Banner

"Life without labor is robbery.
Labor without art is[1]

Oct 3rd 1927– I am apprised by a telephone call from Pell[2] that some representative of the Soviet Russian government is seeking my address in order to lay before me an offer of a free trip Russia—the object being to show me truthfully what has been achieved by the Soviets or their representatives in the 10 years in which USSR has been functioning. I suggest that he furnished the gentleman with my address.

Oct 7–1927. I receive a telephone call from an individual who says he is Mr. Royce of the International workers Aid and that he wishes to make an appointment for F. G. Biedenkapp, Executive Secretary of that organization. That Mr. Biedenkapp speaks for the official Soviet regime in Moscow and wishes to explain the nature of an invitation he is charged to extend to me. I appoint the following morning at 10 A.M.

Oct–8–1927– Mr. Biedenkapp does not appear. Instead a telephone call from Mr. Royce. Mr. Biedenkapp has been called to Chicago but will reappear presently and lay the matter before me as planned. I am curious as to the validity of all this.

Oct 11–1927– Tuesday. N.Y. City
No further news of Russia until today when I am called on the telephone again. It is Mr. Biedenkapp himself. He is back from Chicago & leaving

---

1. The incomplete quotation is likely from John Ruskin, *The Crown of Wild Olive* (Lecture 2): "Life without industry is guilt; industry without art is brutality." The slogan was adapted for early Soviet propaganda; Dreiser apparently saw it, in Russian, on a banner. It would have been translated for him approximately as he has it here. On the verso of a letter sent to Dreiser in Moscow by Otto Kyllmann of Constable and Company, Dreiser's British publisher, the following is written in pencil in an unidentified hand: "Life without labor is robbery, / Labor without art is barbarity."
2. Arthur Pell was treasurer of Boni & Liveright, Dreiser's publisher at the time.

soon for Russia. Would it be possible for him to see me today. I appoint
3 PM. Punctually he appears—a small, dark self-impressed man—and fortunately over-impressed by me. He begins rather unnecessarily with things
about himself,—his pressing duties, trip to Chicago, delays. An automobile which he was driving recently came to grief. It overturned, crushing
for a second time his left hand which had been crushed by another accident
years before. I thought that sad & most strange—lightning in the same
place,—and said so. Now here, however, was his mission. The International Workers Aid was after its fashion a Russian Red Cross. Its plan was
to aid workers in all countries (I wondered just how) and it was now rapidly
being organized in as many countries as possible—Germany, France, England, America.

"Just how many workers in America do you represent?"

"About 300,000."

"And you seek to do what for them"

"Furnish them relief in distress due to strikes, et cetera. Furnish them
life-insurance at a low rate; legal, medical & other aid in a crises."

Can this be the Soviet entering through the door of charity I pondered.
But said:

"And what does the International Workers Aid want of me?"

"Nothing that will cost you any money. We have been authorized by
the Soviet Government at Moscow to extend to you a personal invitation
to visit Russia at its expense".

"Yes. And what for?"

"To witness for yourself what has been accomplished for Russia by
the Soviet Union in the ten years of its existence".

"But why me"

"The Soviet believes you to be the outstanding literary intelligence of
America and it would like to convince you, among others, of the meaning
& value of its existence

"What others"

"Well here is how it is. The Russian Goverment is planning a decen-
nial celebration of its reign which begins Nov. 3$^{\underline{rd}}$ and ends Nov. 10$^{\underline{th}}$. It
wishes to show its economic and cultural developments. There will be pag-
eants, exhibitions and entertainments. You personally will have an opourtunity to meet the leading government and art figures and forces in Russia
and learn for yourself how things stand."

"In a single week?"

"No. In your case the time is to be extended. You may stay a month or

six weeks if you wish, go where you will, accompanied or un-accompanied
by Russian officials, and judge for yourself what has been and what is hap-
pening."

"And to what end."

"Well, your opinion in America, should it chance to prove favor-
able—and we think it will be favorable—would have weight here"

"The Russian Goverment is seeking recognition by the American
Govt."

"It is"

"But supposing my opinion should prove unfavorable?"

"We will risk that"

"But suppose it should"

"We—or rather the Soviet Govt, reserves the right to argue your con-
clusions"

"After I return to America."

"Yes"

"And who is to pay for this long stay"

"The Russian Goverment"

"All of my expenses to & fro?

"All of your expenses"

"And who is to guarantee me this?"

"Well, I will tell you how that is. The majority of those invited—
some 1500 in all, are not going to be re-imbursed for anything but their ex-
penses after they cross the Russian frontier. Some few, like yourself, are to
be guaranteed all their expenses.

"By whom."

"The Soviet Goverment"

"And how am I to know that"?

"We will bring you official cables from Russia, if you choose.

"Well, I so choose. I have important work in hand. Under no circum-
stances would I trouble to travel to Moscow to see a pageant that endured
for a week. My only object would be to see the real, unofficial Russia—
the famine district in the Volga, say.[3] Some of the small towns and farms
in Siberia & the Ukraine, some of the rivers and fisheries and then—the
principal engineering and manufacturing feats or features introduced or

3. In the early years of the Soviet regime, the system of collective farming did not function efficiently. The famine to which Dreiser refers caused despair and starvation during the
winter of 1920, especially in the Volga River region, and brought about major agricultural reforms.

achieved during the life of this goverment. If you can bring me letters and cables guaranteeing me my time, expenses & personal freedom I will go, but otherwise not."

"And how soon could you go?"

"Why should I need to go soon?"

"The official celebration. The Soviet Goverment would like to be able to announce that you are coming to that."

"But I am not interested in any celebration or convention"

"But you could meet many distinguished people who talk English & discuss with them their views. You would be entertained and learn maybe—(I do not mean to influence you in any way) of some things which you yourself might choose to see. After the celebration you proceed at the goverments expense"

"And you will confirm this by letter & cable"

"Yes".

"Well, then how soon would I have to go.

"To reach Moscow in time for the celebration you would have to leave here by the 20ᵗʰ at the latest."

"In nine days!"

"Yes".

"Well, bring me your letters and cables at once. Until I see them I will not feel justified in preparing"

"I will send you a letter from myself in the morning." Today yet we will begin cabling & show you our replies as quickly as they appear." (See letter file marked Russia) Mr. Biedenkapp bustled out.

Oct. 11–1927– Tuesday, 5 PM.

Just now I talked to Helen about this.[4] She looks upon it as flattering and yet to the advantage of the Russian Goverment. "Oh, you do not know what it means to them here. Your name attached to a favorable opinion. You do not see yourself as you are—but I do." And then—

"But I hate to see my Dody go so far away. All the nights! All the days! Could I go long"

"Now, Babes—haven't I just described how I would like to travel in Russia—3ʳᵈ class maybe. How free I would like to be. It will be cold there. I am told that winter begins about Nov. 1."

4. Helen Patges Richardson, Dreiser's distant cousin with whom he began a relationship in New York in September 1919 and who eventually became his second wife.

"Yes, I know—but if my Dody can stand it cant I"

"Maybe—but I think best not. I think it best to go alone"

"Will you sure be back in two months

"Not sure, no; likely, if I have luck."

"You gonto fall in love with one of those Russian girls and get yourself all tangled up again—and run down too, maybe, and not come back."

"Who, me? Russian girls! Those wild Bolsheviks? Aren't these American girls bad enough? No Bolsheviks."

"Oh, yes—thats the way you always talk. But just let one come along. Dont I know and then get sick, maybe. Can I come over and meet you on your way back—London or Paris".

"No meeting me in London or Paris. Never."

"Why not"

"Because."

"Why not"

"Cant I have two months of spiritual peace. The ascetic life."

"The ascetic life. Yes. You"

"The ascetic life. That's what I said. No girls. No fol-de-rol. All earnest observation & meditative travels in the snow. Long talks with learned officials & wild theorists. You dont speak Russian anyhow."

"Neither do you"

But I'll have translators—scribes and emmissaries."

"Please, Dody"

"No London; no Paris. I must have rest and peace"

"Oh, yes. dont be so mean. How can you be so mean. I'll be so lonely by then, too"

"Well, think of all the things to be done. That property at Mt Kisco; my letters and affairs here. Whose to take care of Nick (the Russian wolfhound)" [5]

"Ill get Marion up at Iroki (the country place) to look after him."

"Oh, well, dont pester now. I cant say any how. I may not go."

"Well, if you do—can I?

"I wont say"

---

5. Dreiser's country retreat at Mt. Kisco was called Iroki (Japanese for "beauty"). It was designed primarily by his friend Ralph Fabri. A painting by Fabri of Helen with Nick, the Russian wolfhound, hangs in the Special Collections Department of the Van Pelt–Dietrich Library Center; it is reproduced in Helen's My Life with Dreiser (Cleveland and New York: World, 1951), preceding 249.

"And when you come to London will you bring me a cute little pair of Russian boots? red ones, maybe. Oh, wouldn't I look smart in those."

"God—I am to travel six or seven thousand miles to find a pair of red Russian boots. That's what the revolution was for. So that I could go and find red boots. Well, any how, if they have 'em—I will. But I hope the Russian goverment doesnt find out about it"[6]

New York Oct 12–1927: Wednesday

Saw B____ at office at one P.M. today.[7] She was troubled at news of my going. The long distance: The misery of waiting. I would not come back the same. There would be some other girl before then. Was Helen going. ("No") Was I telling the truth? Supposing she came over in December—would I meet her some where. B____ might let her. He had said he would let her go with a girl friend. I countenance it as a possibility. But really see no hope for it. Because of the likely departure, though, a strong evocation of passion. I think to myself after we have wearied ourselves,—that I shall miss this intense zest. Her eager devotion has brightened my days not a little. I promise to look for a Russian bracelet for her. And to write—as often as possible. But I see no great possibility of that. Return to the studio (200 West 57$\underline{th}$ St) and begin calculating things to be done in my absence & things to be taken care of before I leave.[8] Brandt & Brandt.[9] Articles for Bye.[10] Articles for Elser (Metropolitian Syndicate).[11] A letter from Kyllmann (Constable & Co. London) desiring an introduction to "The Road to Buenos Aires."[12] A telephone message from Robin saying he will have the "Genius"—(allegory form) ready for final reading on Saturday.[13] I arrange for him to come

6. A page has been removed from the diary at this point, between leaves 20 and 21 of the original document. See Editorial Principles, pp. 21–22.

7. B____ is unidentified.

8. In 1926 Dreiser had moved to an apartment in the Rodin Studios building at 200 West 57th Street.

9. Brandt & Brandt, a prominent literary agency in New York that handled some of Dreiser's work.

10. George Bye, a literary agent through whom Dreiser sometimes placed articles.

11. Max Elser, an editor at the Metropolitan Syndicate in New York, which distributed articles to various newspapers and magazines throughout the country.

12. Otto Kyllmann, director of the London firm of Constable, Dreiser's British publisher at the time. For The Road to Buenos Ayres, see note 33.

13. James G. Robin, businessman and playwright who began a friendship with Dreiser in 1908. The central character in "'Vanity, Vanity,' Saith the Preacher" in Twelve Men is modeled after Robin. Dreiser supplied the introduction for Robin's verse tragedy Caius Gracchus, which Robin published under the pen name Odin Gregory in 1920.

to 200 West & go with us from there to Mt. Kisco (Iroki) in the car—over Sunday. Then work on "Rella"—for Bye—and later to bed.[14]

N.Y. Oct. 13- 1927. Thursday.

Am somehow in the thick of things—feeling that I am going. Ed Royce— (in some way connected with the International Workers Aid—telephones to say that Mr. Biedenkapp is going to leave for Russia on Friday and that he has delegated him (Royce) to carry out arrangements with me. He has been cabling and has two messages from Moscow, one from Maxim Litvinov, assistant commissar of foreign affairs. I am to come to Russia as a guest of the goverment. Another from Olga Davidovna Kameneva—(Trotzky's sister and the wife of Kamenev, Minister of ⌊   ⌋. She heads the Soviet Society for Cultural relations). For the Soviet Govt—(through her husband) I am invited to come—and all obligations undertaken by International Workers Aid will be fulfilled. I agree to recieve Ian Gileadi—of the foreign department of the Amalgamated Bank of N.Y. (the Soviets Bank in New York) who is to bring the cables and arrange all my affairs. I appoint Friday morning at 10. At the same time I am asked if I cannot sail Wed. Oct 19th since on that day the Mauretania leaves and the bank can obtain for me a large room on it.[15] I agree that I can and inform Helen, B_____, Esther, Louise, and Ch_____ of my proposed departure.[16] Esther, with whom I spend the evening, wants to know if she cant come to London and return with me!

N.Y. Oct 14- 1927. Friday

200 West 57th St. Mr. Gileadi arrives at 10. He looks and talks like an Argentinian but states he is an international of Tunisian origin. Has been in India, Buenos Aires, Brazil, England, France. Very affable, practical and ernest. Has the cables and a letter from the International Workers Aid containing guarantees. I am to be furnished passage on Mauretania to Cherbourg & from there to Paris. From Paris I am to pay my fare to Berlin

14. "Rella" is one of the sketches in Dreiser's A Gallery of Women (1929); the character of Rella is based on Rose White, sister of Dreiser's first wife, Sara White Dreiser. See Yoshinobu Hakutani, "Dreiser and Rose White," Library Chronicle 44(Spring 1979):27–31.

15. The Mauretania was an early twentieth-century Cunard liner, the sister ship of the Lusitania.

16. Esther McCoy performed research and editorial chores for Dreiser during this period and later in California; Louise Campbell did similar duties for Dreiser, especially on An American Tragedy. Ch_____ is unidentified.

where I am to be met by Mr. Biedenkapp, who will reimburse me and pro-
vide special transportation to Moscow. My companion—if I wish, is to be
Henri Barbusse the French author who is said to speak English. I agree. He
arranges to see me again on Saturday morning with ticket & letter of credit.
He also takes my passport in order to bring it to date. And now that I have
arranged to go, will I see reporters—and where. I agree to see a group on
Tuesday morning—the day preceding my departure. He leaves & I notify B
& L.[17] *Also Bye, Brandt & Brandt, Elser and Cerf of the Modern library.*[18]
Accept $1,000 from Elser on account and 1,000 from Cerf against a
10,000 Edition of Twelve Men in the Modern Library. Decide to clear out
office at 1819 Broadway.[19] *Have letters from Louise, Ruth, Esther, Maud*
—but cannot see any of them.[20] *Am conscience stricken about Maud.*

N.Y. Saturday–Oct 15–1927– 200 W. 57th St

Hurry through any number of things in order to recieve Robin at 3 and
hear him read the play. From one to two play with B____ in office. She
arranges for a series of letters which she is to write; and one of which I am
to read on ship board each day. Helen is all agog because of the responsi-
bilities that are suddenly to descend on her. From 2 to 3 go over finances
with Pell & set aside $8,000 in cash for use in my absence. At 3[15] *Robin*
comes to 200 West & reads play, or a part of it. We adjourn to Iroki, *stop-*
ping at White Plains for dinner. The peace of that place. The silence &
the stars. I speculate on the oddity of preparing it with so much labor only
to leave it so soon. To bed with Helen.

N.Y. Sunday – Oct 16 –1927 – Mt Kisco. (Iroki)

All day here with Robin & Helen. Boyd & Madeline come at 1 PM.[21]
We dine at the Pines Bridge inn. Boyd brings an article in the World by

17. Boni & Liveright, Dreiser's American publishers, headed then by Horace Liveright.
18. Bennett Cerf, publisher and cofounder of the firm of Random House. Cerf first encountered Dreiser in the early 1920s at Boni & Liveright, where Cerf was a junior partner.
In 1925 Cerf purchased the Modern Library reprint line from Horace Liveright and made it
into the financial cornerstone of Random House. Both *Sister Carrie* and *Twelve Men* were reprinted in Modern Library editions.
19. Dreiser kept an office at 1819 Broadway, where he wrote and played.
20. Maud Karola first wrote Dreiser in February 1924; shortly after that she became an
intimate friend. Ruth is unidentified.
21. Ernest Boyd and his wife Madeleine, who was French. Boyd, an Irish-born diplomat, writer, and journalist, was a frequent contributor to the *American Mercury,* the *Bookman,*
and *Harper's.* He was a close friend of H. L. Mencken during the 1920s and 1930s.

Alexander Harvey with a picture. The article is in Harvey's best style. Tea at 5. We ride around the lake—then back to N.Y. leaving Robin at White Plains. Nicholas & I make the best of the back seat. At 200 we get up a cold supper and talk about Boyd's article on T.R.[22]

N.Y. Tuesday, Oct 18– 1927– 200 W. 57

At 9$\frac{30}{}$ Mr. Gileadi arrives with a number of introductions to Moscow personages (1.) Serge M. Eisenstein, leading Soviet movie director. Did "Potemkin"; 2. Vsevolod Myerhold—one of the principal theatrical directors; (3) Olga Davidovna Kameneva—Trotzks sister—head of the society for Cultural relations; (4) Serge Dinamov, Russian critic, whom I know; (5) May O'Calaghan, translator—cultural relations expert; (6) Ivan Kashkin—head of the State Academy for the Arts; (7) Shura Gavrilova, conducts a salon of celebrities; (8) Ivy Litvinova, wife of Maxim Litvinov—asst commissar of foreign affairs; (9) Jackaina Tverskaia—moving picture director; (10) Jacob Doletsky, director of Tass; (11) Karl Rodek, journalist;—connected with Tass. (12) Bill Heywood, ex-American Labor Leader (I.W.W.) (12) Vladimir Mayakovsky ⌊   ⌋ (13) Constantin Sergeievitch Stanislavsky, director Moscow Art Theatre; (14) Alexander Yakovlevitch Tairoff, director Kamerny Theatre, Moscow . . . . . . He assures me that these will prove of the greatest value and that I am to present them all. At the same time a delegation of ten reporters, and I give my views—or rather my reactions, to this opourtunity. (See N.Y. morning papers for Wed. Oct 19–1927).[23] At 11$\frac{30}{}$ they leave. I have a meeting with B_____ at the office. She is upset by the change and more passionate than ever. Return and work on my Gallery of Women. At 5 PM. Robin arrives and reads some changes he has made in play. Stays for dinner. He & Helen & I go to the Venetian gardens. In spite of all my varietism I realize that I really care for Helen. It is spiritual; not material. I feel sad at leaving her.

22. The article by Alexander Harvey in the World could not be traced; Boyd's article on "T.R." [Theodore Roosevelt?] apparently remained unpublished.

23. See, for example, "Dreiser Sails Tonight for Red Celebration," New York Times, 19 October 1927, sect. 3, p. 4.

S.S. MAURETANIA

Wednesday Oct 19. 1927. N.Y. 200 W. 57
Am informed by Mr. Royce that there is to be a dinner at Sam Schwartzes
—140 MacDougall.[24] *See Mr. Gileadi once more who has another tele-*
gram. Somehow, now that I am leaving, I feel sad about Helen. She is
closest to me of any. At 1— I see B____. She has a bunch of letters
from herself which I am to read en route! Jack Powys telephones & comes
up to talk over Russia.[25] *At 4 Waldo Fawcett arrives with a word about*
my opourtunity. At 5 Helen & I leave for the Steamer. She has bought a
large bunch of Dahlias which she arranges in the cabin (57-B Dock). We
leave coats & bags & go to Schwartzes in time for the dinner. A large
company are gathered: Ernest Boyd, J. R. Smith, Hans Stengel, W. W.
Woodward, Joe Freeman, Diego Rivera, Joseph Wood Krutch, Floyd Dell;
Carl Brandt; Ernestine Evans; Lister Sharp—(a large crowd).[26] *Speeches*
by Dell, Rivera, Ed Royce, Joseph Freeman, Ernest Boyd, Mrs. Wood-
ward—and a reply by myself. Konrad Bercovici gives me a lucky Rouma-
nian handkerchief[27]*; Hans Stengel an ivory cane; Magda Johann a letter.*
At 9 it breaks up. A crowd follows to the boat. Flowers from B____.
Books from Maud. Esther and Caroline come to the room.[28] *I face more*
newspapermen; two squads of cameras. There is endless kidding until the
shore bell rings. At 11 I find myself alone. The boat is pulling out. On the
dock I see Esther waving.

---

24. Sam Schwartz was the owner of Schwartz's, a popular restaurant on MacDougal Street.

25. John Cowper Powys (1872–1963), Welsh writer and lecturer. Powys was one of Dreiser's most active supporters during the controversy over the suppression of *The "Genius"* (1915).

26. The guests are writers, artists, and activists of leftist leanings. The more important of them are identified as follows: W. W. Woodward is likely William E. Woodward, business-man, novelist, and historian; Helen worked for Woodward when she first arrived in New York in his capacity as publicity director of the Industrial Finance Co. Joseph Freeman, a young American Communist, had worked for a time in Moscow; his best-known book is *The Soviet Worker* (1932). Diego Rivera (1886–1957), Mexican painter famous for murals that reflected his Marxist ideology. Joseph Wood Krutch, journalist and critic whose reviews of Dreiser's books had appeared in the *New York Evening Post* and the *Nation*. Floyd Dell (1887–1969), nov-elist, editor, playwright, and journalist; Dell, a socialist, was active in Chicago literary circles during the first decade of the century; in 1913 he moved to Greenwich Village, wrote scripts for the Provincetown Players, and helped edit *Masses*. Carl Brandt of Brandt & Brandt, liter-ary agents. Ernestine Evans, art critic with a special interest in the work of Diego Rivera.

27. Konrad Bercovici, Romanian-born author of fiction, drama, and history.

28. Esther McCoy; Caroline is unidentified.

Sunday, Oct 23– 1927. On board SS Mauretania
*The usual ocean cruise. Up late Thursday & read articles & letters given
me to peruse. Also work on Robin's Version of The "Genius." At dinner
meet Ben Huebsch, the publisher, who comes to my table.*[29] *He speaks of
Joseph Anthony, a writer, on board.*[30] *Also of Mr. & Mrs. Ernst.*[31] *A wireless from Heywood Broun recommends them to my attention.*[32] *I promise to
come to his table on the morrow. On Friday (lunch) go to the table & meet
all—including a Judge Muller of Holland. After lunch we agree to meet
at five and visit Diego Rivera, who is travelling 3ʳᵈ. Through Mrs. Ernst
I question him as to Mexico—then bring them to dinner. He shows photos
of all his interesting work which he is taking to Russia. After dinner we
adjourn to my cabin where we talk until midnight. On Saturday read &
write—posting these notes, writing letters, finishing play. Witness a prize
fight on sun-deck at 3 PM. Talk to Anthony who represents the Hearst publications. Send wireless to Helen & Kyllmann of London. Finish reading
"The Road to Buenos Aires."*[33] *Dinner in my room. Work until midnight.
Sunday (today) sleep until noon. Talk with Muller, Mr. & Mrs. Ernst,
Anthony & Huebsch at lunch. Discuss Russia, Anarchism, Communism,
Law, the movies, drinks. I am promised more letters by Ernst. Return to
this room & bring up these notes. Begin an article for Elser.*

Monday, Oct 24–1927. S.S. Mauretania
    *By the courtesy of Judge Muller acting as translator I have just had
a long talk with Diego Rivera, the Mexican painter. He states that intellectually he is a collectivist—not an individualist—that he sees the mass
as the recipient, from superior creative powers, of quite all of the important impulses and aspirations which make for its development and so the
development of the race. (Creative Evolution after a fashion.) In this mass*

    29. B. W. Huebsch, publisher and bookman, who issued the work of Anderson, Joyce, Lawrence, Gorky, Strindberg, Chekhov, and other important writers during his most success-ful years (1902–25). Later he merged his list with Viking Press and became an executive of that firm.
    30. Joseph Anthony, a journalist who worked for the Hearst newspapers.
    31. Mr. and Mrs. Morris L. Ernst; he was an attorney with leftist sympathies.
    32. Heywood Broun, columnist and member of the Round Table at the Algonquin Hotel.
    33. Dreiser was reading bound proofs of the Constable edition of Albert Londres' book *The Road to Buenos Ayres*; these proofs survive in Dreiser's library at the University of Penn-sylvania. *The Road to Buenos Ayres* was a study of prostitution and the "white slave trade" be-tween France and Argentina. Dreiser wrote an introduction for the Constable edition, which appeared in 1928 (translated from the French by Eric Sutton). For the introduction, see "Dreiser and *The Road to Buenos Ayres*," *Dreiser Studies* 25 (2): 3–22, 1994.

the individual finds himself—in some instances, very, very low on the sensitive or mental scale—in others, as in the case of Shakespeare, Voltaire, Aristotle, Goethe, very high. But however high and however individual the individualist, still it is from the mass—his true sensitive relationship with and understanding of the same—its aspirations, impulses, compulsions, limitations, et cetera, that he draws—if he is of the creative and hence the representative type—his true significence or—at least, import. The scientist, for instance, is nothing more then a sensitive in the mass—that chances to represent and by good fortune resolve some real or occult necessity of the mass; some next step or increment in the slow change process. Ditto the artist, the statesman, the general, the poet. It is concievable, of course, that some such sensitive mass point should recieve direct from the creative impulses or forces, above or behind man, some faint intimations of things necessary to the mass—thoughts, implements—what you will—but only in so far as he subsequently identified the intimations with the needs or use or service of man would he be significant as an individual. In short he who leads most serves most. Hence his collectivism, and he feels that he is the greater artist for being a collectivist. Hence his sympathy with the communism of Russia.

I asked after his artistic history. He states that he was born in Mexico but early went to Paris to study. There he fell in with impressionists, neo-impressionists and cubists—and for a time was greatly influenced by their ideals and their technique. Later, when the great war broke out, he found himself at variance with his brothers of the brush. They felt that the new Russian revolution promised—(as a natural consequence, a complete endorsement of the cubistic idea of art. And they wanted him to go to Russia in order there to develop cubism as the great, expressive art of the future. However, with this he did not agree. Instead—being temperamentally a collectivist—he felt that art should be more directly and simply expressive, not only of the emotions and impulses of the mass but also of its understanding. To clarify himself on this point, he decided to return to Mexico where he hoped to symbolize in some fashion the dreams of the mass. And to that end he has been painting murals for the goverment. Recently, his work being fairly advanced there, and Russia appearing to offer an opourtunity for mass expression in art, he decided to go there, taking with him introductions and a large collection of photographic reproductions of his work. With these he hopes to induce the Soviet authorities to commission him to decorate Soviet Bldgs. If successful he will return to Mexico in order *to complete some work there (for a few months only) and will then return to Russia for an indefinite stay.*

x   x   x   x   x   x   x

A talk with Max Ernst the lawyer today reveals that he doubts the validity of current science as it relates to astronomy. He has (via Michaelson & Einstein) [34] *reasons to believe that the stars are not nearly so far away as the conventional statements of astronomers indicate. Also that they may not be the vast things predicated by current mathematical deductions. Another one of his thoughts is that the moon is the most powerful physical and emotional influence on man—and the earth (—the tides, menstrual periods of women, aberrating control of the insane—) and that more & more study should be given it. He also feels that the old lunar year (13 months) should be restored so as to set man mathematically in tune with his real mathematical and emotional control.*

x   x   x   x   x   x

We have a farewell party of sorts after dinner on this day—Anthony, Morris Ernst & Mrs. Ernst, her sister Mrs Epstein, B. W. Huebsch, Judge L   J *Muller, Deigo Rivera & myself. Many rounds of drinks. Ginger beer. Puns. I have a feeling that Mrs Ernst does not like me. At midnight we part. I go on the top deck for a bit of air—then to bed. Am reading* South Wind.[35]

Tuesday, Oct 25- 1927 - Plymouth, Eng. (SS. Mauretania)

Raining. The business of getting off. Papers come aboard. No auto trip to London for Ernst. I breakfast with Judge Muller. Work on article. We move on to Cherbourg. [36] *Tips—Boots $1*$\underline{00}$*. Bath Steward 2*$\underline{00}$*. Room Steward $7*$\underline{00}$*. Dining room waiter 5*$\underline{00}$*. Hat check man 1*$\underline{00}$*. Doorman 1*$\underline{00}$*. Elevator man 50*$\underline{cts}$*. Total 17*$\underline{50}$*. Lunch, and I have a talk with Judge Muller as to American and Dutch legal procedure which see below. The gulls in the rain at Cherbourg. The Cunard man who puts Muller & Huebsch in C5 at my request. The London Daily Mail man. Passports*

---

34. Albert Michelson (1852-1931), German-born U.S. physicist who established the speed of light and won the 1907 Nobel Prize for physics. His experiments laid the basis for Einstein's theory of relativity.
35. Norman Douglas's popular novel *South Wind* (1917). Dreiser mentions the book in his introduction to *The Road to Buenos Ayres* (see note 33).
36. Cherbourg is a French commercial and military port on the English Channel, some eighty miles northwest of Havre.

shown in Grand Salon. We go to the lighter[37];—then the train. The cooks man & his work for us. New tips 1^{00}. The beggars outside the train. "Mistaire". I fall for the smile of a beggar girl of twelve but find she is working for an older woman. Beggary in France. A. Dubonet.[38] Rivera goes on same train. A good French dinner. More talk of French & Dutch law. Paris. The Daily Tribune reporter I give an interview.[39] We go to the Cafe del Opera.[40] I buy a 4$\underline{th}$ of July toy. Then to the Madeline.[41] Then to the Cafe Dome (Rivera).[42] French girls. A sandwich & beer. We taxi back to hotel. Fare 15 francs.

In connection with the beggar girl—this. I never saw one before, who intrigued me. This one—age, say, 14—was obviously compelled, either by her mother or a padrone, to beg. But she had natural beauty and a most moving smile. Now this natural beauty and the smile is the point. I find myself a chronic victim of natures creative formula, as expressed in women, even at this age. Knowing this girl to be a beggar and merely using her smile for what she could get by it—still this smile—and with this knowledge in my mind at this time—this artful use of her mouth and eyes with a purely practical intent was still sufficient on the beauty or art side to sway me to throw her money. I might almost say that I could not help it. It was like electric energy or force conveyed from her to me. I must do what that paltry formula implied—an urge—give. And give. Only to see her calmly turn and allow her hag of a mother or mistress to pick up the drinks!

Wed. Oct 26–1927– Paris – Hotel Terminus

This day has been one of the most beautiful ever. The golden vintage of Paris in October. Up at 8 to breakfast with Muller & Huebsch. The usual kidding & punning. London Daily Mail & Paris Herald announces my arrival. We have an ideal French breakfast—omelettes—jelly—coffee. Then to Portier for tickets. We are promised first class to Berlin for the 3$\underline{35}$. Huebsch & I agree to go together. Then off together to see about

---

37. A lighter is a flat-bottomed barge used in transporting passengers and cargo between larger vessels and the shore.

38. Perhaps Dreiser is referring to Dubonnet, the trademark name of a cheap, sweet wine, presumably being consumed here by the beggars.

39. "Theodore Dreiser Here on Way to Study Results of Sovietism," New York Herald Tribune, Paris edn., 27 October 1927, pp. 1, 10.

40. Dreiser went to the Tavern de l'Opera, a restaurant known for its Munich beer.

41. The Church of Saint Mary Magdalene on the rue Royale is often referred to as Madeleine. This church, one of the best known in Paris, is built in the style of a Graeco-Roman temple.

42. The Dôme was a well-known expatriate watering hole in Montparnasse.

Huebsch & Mullers trunks. The depot Portier. "Ah! but that will cost you"! and "Ah, but that will cost you!" We begin to kid about "costs" in francs. "Ah—what thousends & thousends will it not cost us—francs & francs & francs to change even so much as our minds or use a public urinal. We take the trunks from the Gare del Est to the Gare du Nord. More "Ah, buts." Yet the gull-like charm of the portier is quite irresistable. The gayety of the French temperament. The lightness of its approach to life. I hear that the lowness of the franc still oppresses the French mind, but I do not see it. Such freshness. Such vivacity. Perhaps the day—but still—it is achieved. And never quite the same thing in New York, or any city that I know. Only something like it in N.Y. And the flower stands. And the aged newsboys—with their caps. (Decrepit almost.) And the uniforms & insignia—hundreds & hundreds of uniforms & insignia mingled with the smart & the shabby. On the whole France is coming back. That is evident. The French barometer is rising. We get very gay ourselves & after checking the trunks walk & then deposit ourselves in front of a cafe in the Ave Lafayette near the Magazin Lafayette. And here a gay & easy discussion of life— its meaning (The Philosophers Club) with Muller & Huebsch. Whats it all about? What the import. Muller thinks we shouldnt ask. No answer needed. We are. What is behind the arras is the same as what is before. It is beautiful or dramatic. Anyhow no one wants to die—not even the feeble or disappointed. Oh, yes, there are suicides. So are there lunatics or accidents. But in the main . . . . And then I suggest Paris—the cafe seats—as ideal perches for the old & weary who have a little money. Huebsch thinks yes. Muller—not so sure. Even the oldest should have a little something to do—not be permitted to feel that there is nothing left but to look on. He thinks that would require more courage than most old possess. I offer it, finally, as an ideal state for myself.

From thence—larking—to the Luxembourg—in an open taxi.[43] We walk & discuss flowers, artificial gardening, Napoleon, tree-trimming as practised in Europe—the French school boy in his short pants & with bare knees & the French working man with wide loose pants. We look in book stores & shops, go to an open air table in the Boul St. Michael & each eat something—I snails—with a bottle of wine. Muller & Huebsch rail at snails & frogs legs, but will eat eels which I abhor. Next to Sainte Chapelle of Louis XI[ths] day.[44] "Ah ha—6 francs more! And dont try to avoid

43. Dreiser refers to the Luxembourg Gardens, the popular Left Bank park.
44. Dreiser means Louis IX (Saint Louis), during whose reign (1226–70) the chapel to which he refers was erected. The chapel is a part of the Palais de Justice.

it. Ah no. You must pay in Paris." But the beauty of it. I am quite faint with it and sad—as before a gorgeous wax lilly in a pool under the moon. I sacrifice to the God of Beauty—the impulse to beauty in nature. Here are flowers. Here is wine spilled on the floor. I will burn incense & myrhh. I will kneel & strike my breast & touch the dust with my forehead. I will! I will! Only do not forsake me, Oh God of beauty. Touch my eyes! Incline my heart & my mind. Give me ever—sensitivity—pain at beauty. Let my heart ache! The tears flow. Bring me—oh, bring me again to Sainte Chapelle to pray as I do now.

Out & into a taxi. We have little time—only 45 minutes. But at the hotel no tickets. Ah, Mussyour, none. Non, non, non! All sold. They had said so in the morning. Ah, yes. But we had gone then. And what was a portier to do. Tell him that. But tonight. At 10. A reservé to be sure. Yes, yes. It should be ordered now. A thousand & fifteen francs & then all we would need to do. I suggest that we go to the Compagnie des Wagon Lits ourselves.[45] Why trust the damned frogs. If we come at 10 and . . . . "But oh, Mussyour—no—no—no. You misjudge us French." Still we go. And get the tickets. And get our bags & check out & take them to the Gare du Nord in order to be free of worry. And Muller, who is going to Holland, leaves to make a few purchases. But Huebsch & I, after agreeing to meet him at the Cafe de la Paix at 6$\frac{30}{}$, strike out. We pass a P.O. & I cable Helen. Then in a taxi to the Boul Mich—just to be going. And once there—near the Rue de Fous, a drink in side walk cafe—crowded. And meeting of all people—& whom I have been hoping to see, Llona (Victor Llona) in Paris for the day—(after two months in the country).[46] And with him Ernest Hemingway ("The Sun Also Rises") and some one else. Talk, talk, talk. France is still low, but . . . Art is not much now . . . . . Ludwig Lewisohn[47] . . . . James Joyce:—When I come back in January. But heavens it is 6$\frac{20}{}$. We must run. A taxi. Muller. He has just seen the mayor of Amsterdam sneaking by with a girl! Ha, ha. We are off to the Café "Au Bif ala mode" but cannot find it. Compromise on the Cafe Kobus (Restaurant Kobus) and a grand meal. Martini Cocktail; Soupe

45. Wagon lits are railway sleeping cars.
46. Victor Llona had translated An American Tragedy into French; he recalled this meeting in "Sightseeing in Paris with Theodore Dreiser," ed. Ernest and Margaret Kroll, Yale Review 76(June 1987):374–79. Llona also translated other important works of American literature into French, for example, F. Scott Fitzgerald's The Great Gatsby.
47. Ludwig Lewisohn (1883–1955), author, editor, teacher, and critic. Lewisohn wrote of Dreiser in his book Expression in America (1932) and in his autobiographical writings; he also based the character of Blaffka in his novel Don Juan (1923) on Dreiser.

Creme! Poulette Kobus, Crepes Kobus—a full bottle of Pommard—and all for one called to see how the struggling Russians are doing. We discuss the French, their cooking. This cooking! Ah, glorious! I describe a Loco father novel I could do—the Thaw-Deeming Ludwig of Bavaria, type.[48] Millions. Sexual weakness; strong sexual desire—(mental) hence beauty;—and so love defeats—and strength defeats; and commercial defeats—but with lunatic dreamers—a passion for beauty and finally suicide or death by betrayal. But heartache—amid material & even sensual splendor. Both eager to see it done . . . . . We part from Muller at 8$\frac{15}{}$. At nine Huebsch & I take a little walk through the grounds of the Palais Royale. Ah, here he stopped two years ago. And for weeks. The little shops, little restaurants, little theatre! Cafe au lait over there in the morning. Dinner at La Remi Pedoque. Drinks & talks at the Cafe Dome from 11 PM. on. Ah. We find it 9$\frac{30}{}$. Run. Run for a taxi. So to the Gare du Nord. Quick for our Bag. Ah, a communist to greet me. "I am sent by the International Workers of the World to bid you welcome to France". Very good, my friend I think but you are not a very pleasent type. I wish the I.W.W. would sent a less dubious type. You are not much—a complaining leech of sorts— I think. Still—thanks—thanks. And the talk of Russia—how welcome I will be. I sigh with relief when he goes. Into the train. We toss a coin for upper or lower—Huebsch & I. I get the lower. The rattling & bouncing train almost drives me mad. These wagons lits cars are not clean. No toilet paper in toilet. No soap. One small towel person in Wash room. Oh, that dear Pullman Co—which I have so often cursed. Pause and recieve a blessing. I take some of the curses back any how.

Thursday. Oct 27- 1927- Paris to Berlin
The Paris-Moscow express. After a wretched night we get up at 2 P.M. We are at Hannover.[49] The Germans. Some good-looking girls walking to & fro. We begin on the Germans. Clean, thrifty—the lovely, carefully gardened fields. Soon Heine, Goethe, "Have you read?" I mention Freusen.

48. Dreiser is referring here to famous murderers and lunatics. In June 1906 the eccentric and wealthy socialite Harry Kendall Thaw killed the architect Stanford White in a dispute over Thaw's wife, Evelyn Nesbit, formerly a member of the Floradora Sextette and, at an earlier time, White's mistress. Frederick B. Deeming was a con man and mass murderer in England and Australia who killed two wives and four of his own children before being convicted and hanged in May 1892. Ludwig II of Bavaria, known as the Mad King, was a patron of Richard Wagner and a morbid introvert best remembered for building extravagant and fanciful palaces. He drowned himself in June 1886.

49. Hanover is a Prussian city, the capital of the German province of the same name; it is on the Elbe, some eighty miles southwest of Hamburg.

Also trying put on Huebsch shoes for 7 minutes before deciding they were not my own. Into the dining car. A fine German dinner—excellent and with beer. I notice the large adv's of South American Steamers & begin to sense Europes new & threatening relationship to South America. We think only of North America & Europe but here now are Argentina, Brazil—Columbia—a whole new world. And appreciated & respected by Europe. And so this to talk of. Also the Uneeda Biscuit idea in Germany.—A dozen kinds of "inner-seal" cakes in a basket. "Take your choice for say 50 pfennig." "They are grabbing our ideas", I say. And so to Berlin. I think I see IWW waiting for me & slip away to the Adlon to post these notes & write letters. I get a typical German hotel room—perfect—but no bed light, no soap, no place to hang a strap—no writing paper—but fifty circulars about Germany. Oh, I will go out & have coffee & cakes. They are all I want.

Friday, Oct 28– 1927– The Hotel Adlon, Berlin[50]

On the way to Berlin Huebsch and I had a talk. The theory and philosophy of goverment. Society,—good bad or indifferent must be organized. In fact, via—Evolution—propulsion from super-directive forces it is organized—man being an implement in the hands of presumably intelligent creative energy. (Who are we—created beings that we are, to criticize Creative Energy. No Anarchy—according to its greatest expounders—is little less than—(once the act of revolution has been performed) reliance upon—or return to Creative Energy as expressed by man. And in that Energy—as in the God of the Christians or the Mohamedems, is no wrong. So regardless of experience hither to—and once the act of revolution has been performed—as in France in 1798—or Russia— 1917—the totality of mankind—or of any body of men in any country, may be left to its instincts. Without leadership, law, courts, jails or mandates of any kind from one to another, it will function as well or better than organized society as we know it. In other words the miraculous will become the real. No man will or can say to his brother thou must or thou shalt. Hence, as mankind stands, there will be—until society itself agrees with the anarchist, constant need of revolution. For the true anarchist must quarrel with and rise against all forms of human constraint or enforced human direction. Hence, if you will, the quarrel of present day anarchists with the Soviet goverment

---

50. The Adlon was one of the best Berlin hotels; it was located on Unter den Linden near the Friedrichstrasse railway station.

which, after revolution, did not contemplate miraculous instinctive directives on the part of the mass but rather an ignorant and mis-directed and non-to-instinct mass which required education—and worse,—propulsion in the direction of worth while ideals. In short that was why Alexander Berkman and Emma Goldman, while sympathizing intensely with the Russian Revolution as such and the Russian people (apart from their leaders) afterwards were still (by those leaders) driven from Russia.[51]

So far so good. On the other hand, as opposed to the Anarchists, who rely apparently on benign Creative Energy—undirected and unhindered, there stand (one) the Communists who apparently believe in direction by leadership. Yet that leadership drawn from intimate and sympathetic units of the mass—and fresh and fresh every hour or year; but also a changeful as well as sympathetic leadership—one so sensitive to the moods & the instincts of the mass that, when these same coincide with the inherent necessities for organization (as judged by experience) the moods and the instincts of the mass will be reflected in acts of goverment. And there will not be, as in the case of Moses & the Jews, any Twelve Commandments[52]; or as in the case of the United States any stiff and none-too-malleable constitution. Leadership—chameleon-wise, will reflect the best of mass mood; its real and constructive necessities. (Two) The Socialists, whose bible—an inspired and alas fixed word, is Das Kapital by Karl Marx. But here, as any one can see, is quite all law and direction. For "From each according to his capacity; to each according to his need"—is quite the first and final and iron law of Marx. But who is to interpret the capacity of each—or his proper reward; and who is to smilingly accept the judgement. Neither the anarchists or the communists as we have seen. And yet, strangely enough—and in most instances—the outstanding interpreters of these theories of goverment accept the Marxian doctrine that capital—as such—throughout the world—(the material equipment of man as he has contrived it) is the work of his hands—and these same but thinly if at all connected with that evasive and yet (to come) glorious something—mental inspiration, vision,

---

51. Alexander Berkman (1870–1936), Russian anarchist and radical labor leader. During the Homestead Strike of 1892 he attempted to murder the capitalist Henry Clay Frick; he served fourteen years in prison for the deed. He and Emma Goldman (1869–1940), also a well-known radical activist, opposed U.S. entry into World War I; both were arrested, imprisoned, and deported to Russia in 1919 for their pacifist activities. They became disillusioned with the Soviet Union and left in 1921.

52. By the "Twelve Commandments," Dreiser means the original Ten Commandments, given by Moses to the Israelites and recorded in Exodus 20:3–17; and two additional commandments, that one love God and love one's neighbor as oneself, which are found in Matthew 23:37–40.

direction, enthusiasm, which is the pride and the justification of (Three) the Capitalistic State and the Capitalist wherever he chances to be.

But the Capitalistic State, as before it the religious and the military states, each depending upon mental inspiration, vision, direction and of course organization, are things of experience—with many illustrations past and present to examine—whereas Anarchism, Communism and Socialism are, with the exception of the French Revolution (—the period immediately following the same)—and the present Soviet Experiment, without any satisfactory illustrations in history. Hence the dubiousness of the present experiment in Russia; the necessity of looking into not only its theory but its actual practise—apart from theory—and its consonance or conflict with human nature as we find it. And hence, as I said, my present trip to Russia.

"But cannot human nature be somewhat moulded—if not altered, by enforced theory—and so that same theory made to work fairly well? Especially when a given theory might agree with a particular temperament of a particular people. Not all nations are alike temperamentally. (Huebsch) "I am ready to believe. And not all temperaments could accept a [unreadable word] theory of goverment might. I have sometimes thought that some nations or races might have (as in the case of the Jews & the Slavs) a giant capacity for misery—just as some others—(the English and Americans and the Germans) appear to have a capacity for iron and almost clanking material organization—and routine. So be it. None-the-less—as one looks at life, organizations must come from somewhere—(even among the most ignorant and savage of tribes) or no life. But today—in the upward & onward push of highly organized states, is it not a question whether a relatively poor (in so far as material organization is concerned) state might not (social competition being what it is) fail? We shall see. Anyhow on this trip to Russia it is about all this I desire to learn."

After which we fell to discussing the perfectly marvellous "Crepes Kobus" we obtained of that worthy Paris restaurateur. And to wishing we had more. But Missyour Kobus is a fine illustration of inspired and yet iron restaurant organization. And supposing his restaurant an anarchist or communist affair, from whence would have come our perfect "crepes"?

Berlin. Friday, Oct 28– 1927– Hotel Adlon

I am sick this morning—not able to rise. Sore throat. Bronchitis worse than ever. I feel so poorly that I decide to call a doctor (Bernheim). As I am thinking of this the representatives of the International Workers Aid arrive. They tell me they were at the station the night before, 40-strong—and *with flowers, but that I disappeared. There intention was to escort me to the Adlon! Luckily, as I see it now, I missed them. They still have flowers and greetings. Really, I wonder at all this to do. It is so meaningless. I do inquire for a physician, and immediately Dr. Med. Felix Boenheim— a youngish dark man who does not appeal to me, is called. After they go, he arrives and makes a serious examination, deciding that it is bronchitis plus a cold. I am to fill two prescriptions and go to the turkish bath in the Admirals Palast.*[53] *My day is laid out for me by him. And I decide to go. But before that, more people—(the representative of the Hearst Papers in America—who has a cable offering me $3,600 for two articles of 3000 words each—in Russia.*[54] *I tell him to accept. Next a representative of the Berlin 8ᵗʰ hr who wants an interview.*[55] *Finally I get to the Admirals Palast and am astonished at the size of the Germans there—immense naked men who quite confound me with their enormous stomachs, shaved heads and heavy balls. And so stolid and undemonstrative as compared to the French. But the bath itself is much less attractive than almost any in New York— large—but heavy. And to me not as clean—certainly without nearly the attention bestowed upon a visitor in an American bath. I stay until six— feeling much better, and return only to find Federu (Herr Doktor) waiting. He tells me of the suicide of Scheffauer—and what was behind it—a wife of 37 and a mistress of 26. He took the young mistress with him, stabbing her three times. (Love.)*[56] *And he tells me what to do for my bronchitis. If I take* <u>Godeoment</u>, *obtainable of the Engel apotheke here in Unter den Linden, I am to be cured. I decide to get some. When he goes I work on my notes. But, a telephone call from Huebsch. He has connected with Sinclair Lewis, a Miss Thompson who represents the Public Ledger of Philadelphia in Germany,*[57] *and Frau* ⌊　　　　⌋*, the wife of the man who wrote*

53. This is the Admirals-Bad, a Russian-Turkish public bath near the Friedrichstrasse station.

54. Dreiser wrote eleven articles about his trip to Russia for the *New York World*; three other articles for 1928 issues of *Hearst's International-Cosmopolitan* became sections of *A Gallery of Women*: "Rella" (April), "Olive Brand" (May), and "Regina C____" (June).

55. The Berlin Independent Democratic newspaper *8-Uhr Abendblat* (Eighth-Hour Evening Sheet).

56. On 7 October, Herman George Scheffauer, a writer from San Francisco who was living in Berlin, stabbed and killed his secretary, Catherine von Meyer, a Russian refugee, before committing suicide by stabbing himself, slitting his wrists and throat, and throwing himself from a fourth-story window. See "Scheffauer Kills Girl and Himself," *New York Times*, 8 October 1927, p. 4.

57. Dorothy Thompson (1893–1961), writer and journalist, who would marry Sinclair Lewis in May 1928. Thompson would accuse Dreiser of plagiarizing her book *The New Russia* (1928) for his *Dreiser Looks at Russia*.

Sinclair Lewis and Dorothy Thompson. (From Yale Collection of American Literature, Beinecke Rare Book and Manuscript Library, Yale University)

Power—now a success in America.[58] *They are coming at 10 PM. since I cannot come to dinner. And when they do Frau* ⌊　　　　　⌋ *proves very charming. I suspect an affair here, if I could but stay. The smiles, giggles. And she explains that I need some one to* mother *me. I heartily agree. And at 11:20 Sinclair Lewis & his friends—a to me noisy, ostentatious and shallow company. I never could like the man. He proceeds—and at once, to explain why he did not review An American Tragedy—as though the matter was of the greatest importance. Only half of it was sent him. I smile believingly. Then beer & sandwiches & silly talk until midnight when all decide to leave. And Madame* ⌊　　　　　⌋ *indicates that she may come back tomorrow, if she can. I wonder.*

Berlin, Saturday, Oct 29– 1927– Hotel Adlon

*A bright day. More visits from representatives of the Soviet—Willi Munzenberg—for instance, the General Secretary of the Berlin Communist Workers; Frau Windmuller, a paid assistant, a French delegate to Moscow & others I do not know. The talk is meaningless. How am I getting along. Do I need anything. All tickets, passports, etc. will be arranged for me. They go . . . . . After that a telephone from Sinclair Lewis. The man is seething with an ill concealed dislike but some how feels it his duty to pay attention to me. Next a visit from Dr. Felix Boenheim whom I do not quite like. He wants to know how his cure is working out. Indicate that I am somewhat better. We talk and I find that he represents the International Workers in the free—or partially free, medical service. Yet he is not a communist—a sympathizer he calls himself. He begins to talk of my chest. He is disturbed by the state of my bronchitis. Since I am going into Russia, a cold country & where there is none too good medical service—especially in the rural districts, it might be wise, etc. A picture (X-ray) might be taken. He has a "colleague"—a "Herr Colleague" who could do it. I may say here I always dislike and mistrust medics who begin to lay plans for additional service in this manner. "How much"? I ask bluntly. The X ray will cost $12*$\underline{^{00}}$. *Oh, well. What is $12 I think. There may be something in it. I am going to a cold country. "How long will it take?" "Not more than an*

---

58. Marta Loeffler Feuchtwanger, the wife of Lion Feuchtwanger (1884–1958), a German Jewish novelist and playwright. His historical novel *Jud Süss* (1925), translated into English and published in the United States as *Power*, was a best-seller for Viking Press in 1926. The Feuchtwangers were friendly with Sinclair Lewis and Dorothy Thompson (see above, note 57). Thompson translated Feuchtwanger's satirical ballads about a booster businessman into English and had them published as *PEP: J. L. Wetcheek's American Songbook* (New York: Viking, 1929). Feuchtwanger's other success in America was the novel *Josephus* (1932).

hour I should think." I dress & go with him. He promptly climbs into a taxi for which I pay.—3 marks. Next I am introduced to Herr Dr. E. Ostwald (Kurfarstendamn 36), who is the extra man. After that I am made to wait in another room for 30 min. while they confer. Later, with great German solemnity (and the volume of it), I am called in & asked to strip to the waist. And the hardest looking girl assistant to a medic that I have seen in years stands by. Pretty but cold. Then in front of the extra.[59] And the two, beyond the plate, peer into the mysteries of my chest. Ah! "Selva schovere!" Ah. "nicht gut." "Sehen sie here. Und here." I feel fine but begin to suspect dire news. And once it is over; my blood pressure taken, & various questions asked—I am told the big news. I have an enlargement of the aorta & that is what is pressing on the left lung and producing the "broncheetus" as they call it. But worse. My state is very bad—very. Any moment I might drop. I should not think of going to Russia—or, if I do I should have some one (preferably a medical wiseacre) accompany. I see it all—they think I am a millionaire. Am I not an American! Am I not at the Hotel Adlon! I demur facially—if not otherwise. I even shake my head, if I recall aright. In any case most certainly I should not go to Russia now. Rather I should stay here and enter a sanitarium where I could be observed. After that— a month or two or three, I might return to America—never to Russia. My condition will not permit it.

"Is that so", I think. Actually I say "Gentlemen, this is all very interesting but too sudden. It comes on me too quickly. But first let me tell you I am not going into any sanitarium and I am going into Russia. My condition may be very bad but I do not happen to be afraid of death"

"Ah—but we do not predict death. No, no. Do not misunderstand us. It is not so bad as that. But you are very sick. Your condition is dangerous. Perhaps—there are other physicians. Would you like us to give you the address of another physician—perhaps call one up for you?" "No. No. I will not go to any physician but one whom I select for myself—through friends of mine. Next, if what you say should prove true I would not go into a sanitarium but would return to the United States. Even if I did enter one here, it would be one of my own personal selection." And I look at them. "Very good! Very good! It is as you wish"—but I see just the same that it is not so good. There is more talk. The pictures of the lungs are brought. "I can see for myself." But I cannot see for myself, I insist. I cannot possibly read these things with the skill which they do. Since they are so anxious I

59. Dreiser means the "extra man," Dr. Ostwald, mentioned several lines earlier.

*will do one thing. They may each write a letter explaining what is wrong
with me. Next give me a copy of the X ray. Armed so, I will look up a
physician and if he agrees I will let them know. If not—this particular case
& connection is terminated. Is that satisfactory?*

*They are compelled to agree that it is. Two letters are dictated. The
picture is to be sent to the hotel. I depart carrying the letters—and—
such is human fallibility, wondering if there is anything wrong with me. I
have been feeling pretty good—a little short of breath in the last year—but
nevertheless—come what may, they are out. I do not like their way. And
so now the bill. Remember the X ray was to have been $12$⁰⁰ but now it is
twenty. And my young doctor calmly states that his is 100 marks ($25$⁰⁰)
for two visits. I pay—and learn afterward that both fees are high for two
such young doctors in Berlin—that ordinarily Boenheim gets no more than
$5$⁰⁰ per call, if so much. 10 marks per visit should have been enough.*

*And so to the hotel. As I arrive, the bell "Klingles" and it is Lewis.
Can I come to dinner with himself and Dorothy Thompson? I cannot. I
have one with Herr Carl Federu. Well, how about tea? I begin to ask
about physicians; tell him the situation. He gets very much interested. Says
he does not know but will find out. Why not come over & talk things over.
I agree and taxi to the Hercules Hotel—13 Kaiser Freiderich Wilhelm
Strasse. He has a very large room in an old German Hotel. I state my
case. He says just what he did before. At 6$\frac{30}$ I leave & hurry back only to
find Federu. He has come with an Elsa Kaigel who is nonetheless American born & talks perfect English. She has lived in Russia. With him & her
I go to Huttes restaurant in the Potsdammer Platz—or near it—a resort
as I judge of semi-artistic—semi-literary—semi-theatrical grandees of Berlin. And presently Mrs. Federu—a sympathetic & pleasant woman. And
the director of the Elizabeth Duncan School here in Berlin. Also his star
pupil—a thin, determined & assertive looking girl. But ah, she is marvellous! marvellous! There has just been a dancing afternoon somewhere. And
there Herr Joseph [unreadable] of Munich—a critic, a humorist—and I
know not what else. We sit and dine. There are two kinds of wine. And delightful omelettes confiture.*[60] *I stay as long as I can—until about 11 & then
pay the bill & excuse myself. I am not feeling any too good. On the way I
am seized with homesickness. Here I am—nearly 4000 miles from NY. 9 or
ten days at the shortest. And I am ill—maybe seriously. Supposing I were*

---

60. An *omelette confiture* is a plain French omelet, filled with jam or marmalade, rolled
and sprinkled with sugar.

seriously ill—to die. And Helen so far away. And I have been so bad to her. I grow wretched and send a twenty word cable. If only she were here. And for hours in bed I feel like an orphan—like a cast-away in a small boat.

Berlin, Sunday Oct 30– 1927– Hotel Adlon

It is a bright morning & I feel a little better but not so much. Decide to breakfast in the hotel. I also get the N.Y. Tribune and read about Russia—the tricks of the Bolsheviks. Positively this Russian goverment mystery grows by leaps and bounds. Here I am, say—a thousand miles from the border, & all is still mystery. The peasents are starving & they are not starving. They favor the existing goverment & they do not. Moscow is a cold, unsanitary, albeit attractive city—and its climate is really no worse than that of Berlin. The water is unfit to drink—all water in Russia is— and one may get typhus, and Moscow has positively the best drinking water in the world. The Soviet leaders are liars & tricksters and they are not. They are able to borrow all the money they need & they are not. Leningrad is a cold, abandoned, malarial city and it is a grand place—like Amsterdam or Venice & with beautiful western buildings, yet the same still touched by Oriental imagination. One can live in a hotel in Moscow or Leningrad as well as one can live in New York or Berlin and one cannot! Positively I give up. There is no getting head nor tale of this thing. I can get the names of any number of people to whom to go for information. Last night at dinner Elsa Riegle—50 & agressive but still good looking and a born observer & even statistician, directed us to look up the Quaker Center in Moscow. There one might hope to get the truth, for they have workers all over Russia who speak English & who are constantly coming & going. The address is Boris Oglebsky, Perelook 15 and a Miss Annie Haines of Haverford, Pa is in charge. It would be well to write her before hand and tell her I am coming—and ask for a room. But the Soviets are supposed to look after me. Ah, but I should get where correct information will be flowing as a spring. Any how here is a good tip. I am to take all my dollar cash—some $1700 in all by the way, & buy Roubles in Berlin. Someone has just written that we can only get 2 roubles 90 kopeks for a dollar in Moscow—whereas here in Berlin, now—one can get 4 to 4$\frac{20}{}$ roubles per dollar. I decide to so advantage myself at the market—forthwith. But this being Sunday, I speculate on all I have heard & decided to finish an article for the Metropolitan Syndicate—and do.[61] Meanwhile comes Bruno

---

61. Probably "Dreiser on Matrimonial Hoboes," *New York American*, 11 March 1928, E4.

Meisels—a german critic. He wants me to come to dinner. I accept. As I do so, Lewis calls up. He has found out just the physician. It is Prof. Dr. C. R. Schlayer, chief visiting physician of the Augusta Maria Hospital. He gives me the address. Since it is so important I call up Schlayer and he asks me to come at once. He proves to be one of those really careful thinking Germans on whom one can rely—tall, blond, serious. Speaks English with a "ziss" and "zat". I show him the letters of my two doctors and the X ray. They make him serious but he makes an examination of his own. Asks after all symptoms. I tell my past. He decides at once that there is nothing wrong with my heart—or circulation. Next he examines the urine. Nothing wrong there. Finally he says that if I will come to the Augusta Maria Hospital he will make a test of blood & sputum. But he fears the Russian climate for me. Should I go? Had I better not return to America & come back in the summer? I decide to go to Russia but do not argue with him. Return to hotel and find Miesels. We discuss Berlin and a place to eat. It eventually becomes the Bedjerre—(a court dancer). Before that he calls up his wife and several people who are to act as translators. But we are getting along very well. And so another German evening—this time with young German writers. I could describe them but they do not appeal to me very much. Meisels wife is charming & he is always interesting but not so dreadfully deep. In the Bedjerre there are 10 girls frankly for hire. But not one appeals to me. We have cognac, two bottles of wine & steaks. The cost is 35 marks—practically 9\underline{^{00}}$. More talk of Germany. Literature is not much. The American movies are still the best. I am always impressed by the low state of European taste which accepts this as true. At eleven to a German Coffee House with more artistes and writers. Where do they all come from. I meet an exceedingly intelligent German who has been in Russia. He tells of the vast extent—1/6$\underline{^{th}}$ of the earth; the differences in climate; Tiflis in the Caucasus—like the Riviera; Odessa—warm like perhaps Texas. There are 61 different countries—or types. They govern themselves, but subscribe to the communist idea & use the Soviet mechanism to arrive at leadership & direction. He likes Moscow—very much, a beautiful city—but Leningrad is even more interesting, a city built by the Czars to escape, as he seemed to think, the purely Asiatic influence, strongly felt at Moscow; the buildings are western. It is laid out more systematically than Moscow. But it is very damp and therefore very cold in winter. One must be warmly dressed. No place for a person with lung trouble . . . . . Again the water everywhere in Russia is bad. One must not drink it. Typhus. But living is tolerable; the food good. One must enjoy its differences—not its comforts . . . . Then he turns to American literature. Finds it interesting from a discriptive point of view; nothing from a psychologic or spiritual side. He is thinking of the writers of the last 20 years. I agree.

*

The Russians have suffered the most from tyranny & misgoverment & so they have swung furtherest toward liberty.

Berlin, Monday, Oct 31–1927– Hotel Adlon

There are so many things about the Germans that interest me.

Augusta-Maria Hospital—to [unreadable word]. With Windmuller for breakfast, a general gloom. Drugs. I talk of MS and writing. Edward Fitzgerald calls on phone—then comes to get ms—which I edit before giving it him. Lewis calls on phone. Also Secy of Am Embassy. Federu calls to know if I can come out Tuesday night. Frau Feuchtwanger is to be there. I finally settle down & write until 11 PM. Then to a nearby restaurant for an omellette with cognac & to bed. The restaurant reminds me of old St. Louis restaurants.

Tuesday Nov 1—Write till noon. Windmuller tells me of negro & his adventures. I go for shoes & get them. Then to hotel. Fitzgerald comes. [unreadable name]. The correspondent of the London Post. Most of Russia, Europe. Fitzgerald proves most interesting. We ride out to Federus. Lost! That evening. Hotel. I revise ms. To bed. Dr. Schlayer phones to say I am OK.

Berlin Wed. Nov. 2 – 1927– Hotel Adlon

Raining. No word of going. Sinclair Lewis calls. Tells of Harris in hotel. Also Hauptmann. I go to see Harris. Then buy 200 in roubles. No word of going. Go to Workers Bdg. No [unreadable words] to be had. I telephone Am. Embassy. They get me one. Frau Feuchtwanger! Neuse calls. I pay bill. To station with Neuse. Flowers. Communists. Off in a compartment.

Thursday Nov 3–1927– En Route to Russia

The Polish plains. Like Kansas. Like Czecho Slavakia. My next door traveller. Grass covered houses. The heavy sort. Warsaw. I dont like it. Nor Poles either. Breakfast my French comrade. An artist should do well with the Polish countryside. It has a "feel". One can understand a Chopin, a Sienkiewicz, a Paderewski growing out of.[62] These long levels of green grass

---

62. Dreiser refers here to three famous Polish artists: Frederic Chopin (1810–49), com-

or black soil, bordered by black firs. The endless silver birches; the charming if—(perhaps)—unsanitary farm houses or hovels with their green sod roofs. The wide flat marshes—rivers & lakes. The rounded, sturdy girls & women & the stodgy & yet somehow picturesque men. An ideal land for a temperament such as Turgenev to contemplate. Hay cocks; hay covered shelters or bins And now—here & there good white stucco one story houses & fair roads[63]. . . . . . Bialystok. Ice on the ground. Many new bldgs. The swaggering officers & policeman in apparently warm & comfortable uniforms swaggering here and there—mere ragbags of conventions, notions and sex. And a girl or two in smart clothes, silk stockings & slippers and heavy, many skirted peasants women with bundles & cheap bags. The roads are mostly mud & very bad. Judging by what I see the whole world is trying to catch up on the housing problem—Poland among others. Beyond Bialystok—snow—the 1st I have seen this year. These little groups of grass or mud thatched houses—huddled so closely together—on these great plains—and at such long intervals. Forrests—open spaces, flat, dreary rivers, more forrests & then some where one of these. But how lonely. Not a soul in sight. A horse, maybe a cow or two. A few rooting pigs. Perhaps within huddled about a fire in this cold are the laborers with their closely woven loves hates ambitions, —and mostly of the soil. And these far, far off cities, —Berlin, Paris, London. And the integrated, intense life of them— millions and millions of swarming and equally meaningless—if not more so—souls, but not lonely. Even in train as I pass I shiver. I am cold with loneliness of country life—their life here. I am glad I am going by Walkowysk—a white station, as usual. Why do the Poles & Czechs love white stations? Nearly all the houses are new, long & yellow—harboring perhaps two or three families. Somehow it all reminds of Missouri, Iowa, Kansas . . . . . . These very little wagons with horses. Well, the horses will never die of hard work . . . . . . Clouds of crows flying over the snow. I think of the retreat from Moscow . . . [unreadable word]. A long procession of farm wagons returning from the fields at dusk—hundreds of them. For the first time I see the Troika—and sense the reality which the Russian novelists have pictured.[64] Yet this is Poland. Tea & cake offered at 5 PM. More new stations. At supper—close to the Russian frontier. Dining car refuses

---

poser and pianist; Henryk Sienkiewicz (1846–1916), novelist who wrote *Quo Vadis?* (1896) and won the 1905 Nobel Prize for literature; and Jan Paderewski (1860–1941), pianist and composer who was briefly prime minister of Poland in 1919.

63. Dreiser drew a small picture here in the text to show the shape of a typical one of these houses.

64. The *troika* is the familiar Russian sleigh drawn by three horses abreast.

Russian money. Marks, zlotty, dollars—yes.[65] *But no roubles. We arrive at*
L⌐   ⌐. *The border. A fine Polish station. Many police & soldiers.*
Another hour lost here. Then accross the line into Russia Negoreljove. It is
night now. More soldiers & passport agents. One senses a change at once.
Something softer—more emotional, less iron. It is made clear to me that I
change cars here. The "dear comrade". My bags are passed. I am taken
into what appears to be a depot reception hall as a delegate. The band. The
speeches. The replies. We are given food. Mr. Gee of Chicago—a Chi-
nese delegate from Chicago—who knows of me. Mr. Leo of San Francisco
(Leland Stanford) who also knows of me). Both speak German. Afterwards
we are escorted to the train by the band & I am put in the same compart-
ment with Mr. "Gee". He says: "I did not expect so much as this on this
earth". More speeches—this time by delegates—including Mr. Leo—from
the train, but in German. Also against Das Kapitalisms. I leave my bags.
A telegram from Moscow transfers me to a private compartment. 12 PM.
before my bed is made The filthy french comrade next door.

65. Zlotty (zloty): the basic monetary unit of Poland.

MOSCOW

Friday. Nov 4–1927 In Russia

6 AM It is snowing out. The north seems addicted to a small gut-tered or shallow wagon and a single horse. As in Norway they protect the railroad tracks from snow in winter by growing hedges or placing fences on either side. In so far as I can see, these are the true people of Russias great writers—Tolstoy, Gogol, Turgeniev, Dostoievsky & Salty-kov.[1] One sees their types everywhere—the heavy & yet shrewd peasents; the self-concerned and even now, under communism, rather authoritative petty officials (Railroad conductors, station masters, etc.) I see a peasent in a ragged coat & cap go by & he lifts his cap to a depot official. I see them—working classes deliberately & rather stodgily doing this or that. That quick, nervous energy which one often sees even in the commonest of American laborers is wanting here.

It is 2³⁰ and we are to arrive at 3. Some French communists in the next compartment are obviously preparing an address to the fellow-internationals in Moscow and have borrowed my fountain pen where with to do it. I hear "confreres" with the peculiarly French intonation. Also "Vive la Commune"—and "<u>capital</u>" accented in a purely French way. They are going to have a grand time when they get there. And then Mos-cow itself. Not very impressive. On a distant road—as seen from the train—a bus. And outside the town some small new dwellings. As the train stops, a band playing what I learn is the red—or international song.[2] And a most uninspired thing it is. Next addresses—perhaps among them—the one I heard being composed. But special agents (two jews by the way) find me & lead me off to an automobile and the Grand Hotel near the Red Square.[3] But the wretched collection of autos in front of this station. The shabbiest Georgia or Wyoming town would outclass them. And the people! This mixture of Europeans & Asiatics! International Asiatic life mixed with some Europeans. One gets a sense of strangeness and delapidation,—old—and not so pleasingly constructed stores mingled with exotic theatres, halls & most of all churches. An aged Luna Park.[4]

1. Mikhail Yevgrafovich Saltykov (1826–89), poet and satirist who wrote under the pen name N. Shchedrin. Saltykov was a member with Dostoevsky of the Petrashevsky circle and was exiled to Vyatka in eastern Russia for his early writings. His best-known work is the multivolume novel *Gospoda* (1872–76).

2. The *Internationale* was a revolutionary song first sung in France in 1871 and after-ward popular as an anthem for communist workers and sympathizers.

3. The Grand Hotel de Paris, an establishment in Moscow frequented by western visi-tors.

4. Lluna Park, in the Grünwald area outside Berlin, was a popular location for public amusements.

I settle in room 112—on the second floor: rococo and shabby grand. But said to be high in price. Almost instantly Mr. Dinamov of the government publishing house & what I take to be his young mistress arrive.[5] They are over alive with a sense of obligation. I am exotically important in their eyes. Ah, will I have this and will I have that. Whom will I see? Whom meet? And I am wondering who will meet me. But a list is made. As we talk the representative of the Chicago Daily News arrives. He comes to offer the use of his stenographer, his papers & books. He has a room in the same hotel. Some ten minutes later Scott Nearing, who has crossed Asia & the Pacific, walks in.[6] He wishes to be of service—to "wise me up" on Russia & promises to be on my right hand. And then Messrs Biedenkapp and Kreat—the one the representative of the International Workers Aid of America—the other the same of France. They wish to be of service in laying out a plan for me. And after them <u>the representative of the Associated Press. He wishes to send off a cable and invite me to a party. I decide to accept for this coming week.</u> At 10—roughly I am done—call for food & eat while the telephone bell rings in vain. Later I frame questions which might be asked of Stalin. Write three letters, among them one to Helen—and turn in. I have seen nothing resembling red slippers in Moscow as yet.

<u>Saturday, Nov. 5–1927 – Hotel Grand, Moscow</u>

Positively the Russians are a strange and wonderful people. I have spent a half day in their principal and severest prison. It was Biendenkapp who arranged this for me—a small, aggressive, self-opinionated & almost pushing person—but well meaning (I think) and rather pro-communist, or imagines that he is. He comes at 9<u>15</u> AM. to tell me that I must not miss this. It will illustrate the communistic idea of crime, punishment and reformation. And truly it did . . . . In a taxi with three others and an interpreter I rode to the ⌊   ⌋ prison.[7] Laid out like the letter K with five tiers of cells— one above the other. The smell. The cells. Yet all a great improvement on what was in the days of the Czar. All underground cells abandoned

---

5. Sergei Dinamov (1901–39), Dreiser's chief advocate in Soviet literary circles and the editor of the first Soviet edition of Dreiser's collected works. Dinamov, a Bolshevik, served in the Red Army during the Revolution. Before his early death, he had become Director of the Institute of Red Professors.

6. Scott Nearing (1883–1983), American socialist and radical activist. He was fired from teaching positions at both the University of Pennsylvania and the University of Toledo for his political views and his pacifism. His best-known book is *The Making of a Radical* (1972).

7. Probably the Butyrka Prison, built in 1879 near Butyrka Gate in Moscow.

& turned into work rooms with textile machinery. The old central chapel with sealed booths, through a small slot in which a prisoner could only peek at the priest & the services, turned into a public hall for prisoners where cinema and other entertainments are given. No more solitary comfinement in the old sense. Only five grades of punishment—as follows:

L   ⌐—The barber was a murderer here for ten years. The head chef—also a murderer. One of the interesting prisoners was an old & rather simple looking and yet perhaps crafty Russian who in the Czars day had been an "Agent Provacture". On the one hand he had joined the Nihilists and helped on a plot to blow up the Czars train which failed—but in which attempt he took part—or was supposed to. On the other hand after the Czar was slain & the secret records of the police opened by the Reds, it appeared that this man had been in the pay of the police and had helped to egg on the Nihilists for cash. All this he told in answer to questions put by our guide at the prompting of various sightseers. And he told it all quite simply and directly. Was he sorry? he was asked. Yes. He had been mistaken. Had the Soviet treated him fairly, since the discovery of his crime? Yes. Was the prison life here fair—humane? Very. When would he be free? In six years. "They should have shot the bloody bastard" said an Englishman behind me.

There was another interesting prisoner, a Russian small village priest. With another man he plotted the murder of a man and carried it out. He was sentenced to 10 years—the maximum sentence under the new law. But him! A character out of Opera Bouffé. A Cambodian! A Korean with a high straw hat—the size & shape of a silk dicer—& this set on top of some kind of a yellow silk head band. And a long, dirty ragged & yet swathing coat—but on the order of a linen duster. And the pale, weak eyes. A strangely Chinese-like face & figure. —and yet what—lunatic, zealot, neurotic dreamer? Possibly & possibly not. Russian jurists today are extremely careful students of neuroses of all kinds & their relations to crime . . . . . . Through the interpreter I talk to him. His voice & gestures indicated a chemical cosmos so remote from my own that it was as though I were talking to a being from another. Dostoievsky in his most erratic psychologic divagations never evolved a more unbelievable figure or temperament than this. Yes—he had been a priest in a village 300 miles away. It was true he was accused of murder—he and another citizen. But his accusers were mistaken. And for how long had he been sentenced? Ten years. And would be shortened by labor or good behavior? Yes—to six years. And was he, too, permitted to leave the prison annually on a vacation? Yes. And would he, after he was released, return to the region from which he was convicted? Yes. Why? It was where he was born! And would he be able to resume a normal life? He hoped so. . . . . . . I left him strangely dreaming in one of the halls of the prison—leaning one of his thin, almost emaciated shoulders against the stone wall.

One of the oddities of this prison was that in this prison kitchen—and on account of the 10th anniversary of the October Revolution of 1917, they were baking each of the prisoners a one pound loaf of white bread—their ordinary bread year in & year out being a very dark brown, soggy & sour loaf—the taste of which I could not endure.

The guards carry no guns. Are not allowed to kill in case of attempted escape. A basket ball net in the main court. . . . . We return to the hotel and find Dinamov. We take dinner in the hotel and he has a plan for a walk, after which I am to visit Bill Heywood.[8] After dinner Biedenkapp comes & suggests that I take a front room viewing the gate to the Red Square. I decide to move—but sleep first. Dorothy Thompson calls but I pretend to be asleep. At five we move to the new room (302) and order supper. I write letters and afterwards we start walking but it is raining & instead we take a taxi to the Hotel Lux.[9] I am called upon to show my passport—(all visitors to this building are) and afterwards go with Dinamov to Ruth Cornells room.[10] I see plainly that they have a sex relation of some kind; after a talk we visit Heywood in his room below. It is crowded with dubious radicals. He himself has aged dreadfully. I would not have believed

8. William D. "Big Bill" Haywood (1869–1928), a famous union organizer for the International Workers of the World (IWW). Haywood was known for his ability to unite workers of different ethnic and religious groups in common cause. Dreiser had known him earlier in Chicago and had used the 1913 Paterson Silk Strike, in which Haywood was active, as the background for his one-act play "The Girl in the Coffin" (1917). See Keith Newlin, "Dreiser's 'The Girl in the Coffin' in the Little Theatre," Dreiser Studies 25 (Spring 1994):31–50. Imprisoned for his labor activities, Haywood jumped bail in 1920 and escaped to the Soviet Union, where he became the first manager of the American Autonomous Industrial Colony Kuzbas, a coal-mining operation. Forced to retire because of diabetes, he became a pensioner of the Soviet government and lived in a room on the second floor of the Lux Hotel. He died on 18 May 1928; his ashes were divided and interred partly in the Kremlin Wall and partly in the Waldheim Cemetery in Chicago.

9. The Hotel Lux, renamed the Tsentralnaya in 1953, was completed in 1911. When the Bolshevik government moved to Moscow from Petrograd, it reserved the hotel for party functionaries. In 1920 it was closed to the public and used exclusively thereafter by the Comintern. Foreign guests and European communists were put up here by the Soviets, and security was very tight, as Dreiser's need to show a passport for entry indicates. Its restaurant, shops, and even an outpatient clinic made it similar to a small city within a city.

10. Dreiser means Ruth Kennell.

Big Bill Haywood, International Workers of the World labor
leader. (From Joseph R. Conlin, *Big Bill Haywood and the Radical Union Movement* [Syracuse, N.Y.: Syracuse University Press,
1969])

that one so forceful could have sagged & become so flaccid and buttery.
But life has beaten him as it beats us all. He said he had been sick—very,
two years before. Also that he had married a Russian woman 1 year be-
fore. She came in later—a kind of Slav slave. Also he had been writing his
memoirs & now exhibited a childish pride in what he had achieved.[11] *But he*

11. Haywood's memoirs were published as *Bill Haywood's Book: The Autobiography of*
William D. Haywood (New York: International Publishers, 1929).

Ruth Kennell in Red Square during Dreiser's visit. (From
Ruth Epperson Kennell, *Theodore Dreiser and the Soviet Union*
[New York: International Publishers, 1969], p. 208)

admitted that he was through—this was his last shot—(He of the Colorado Mine Strike—of Lawrence, Lowell, Patterson, of the I.W.W. & the Chicago Trial). I could not believe it. Would I not come & read a few chapters of his book & tell him what I thought. I told him that I would. . . . . . . Then up with Ruth Cornell & Dinamov—and I leave. But she follows out into the hall & I announce that I am going to walk back. She suggests walking herself—and we do—viewing the decorations for the Red celebration as we go. When we get to the hotel she suggests a walk into the Red Square and I agree—whereupon Dinamov leaves—whether peeved or not I cannot say. And we view the Soviet General Store,[12] Lenins tomb, and she tells me that already to the superstitious Russian temperament Lenin has become a saint. Actually—as yet—the Central Soviet does not dare to bury or burn the body. It has become a shrine. And with it, in the Russian mind—has risen the idea that so long as it is there—and maybe no longer—that communistic principles will prevail in Russia! And then I see Jack Reeds grave and so to the hotel.[13] I complain of loneliness & she comes up. We finally reach an understanding and she stays until two. Before going she fusses with me for not protecting her. But she promises to come again tomorrow or Monday.

Sunday. Nov. 6 - 1927- Moscow- Hotel Grand

Still grey & rainy. I write most of the day. In the morning Vox⌞   ⌟, that takes care of such visitors as myself here, sends a guide and interpreter who is to be with me all day.[14] But I send him away, telling him to return at one. Meanwhile various visitors,—Prof. H. W. L. Dana of the New School for Social Research in N.Y.,[15] Scott Nearing, the representa-

---

12. Dreiser is referring to the GUM Department Store, the facade of which stretches for more than 800 feet and bounds the east side of Red Square. Completed in 1893, it was called the Upper Trading Arcade, and its numerous shops were rented to merchants by the czar. After the revolution, it was taken over by the government and became famous as the largest store in the Soviet Union. GUM stands for *Gosudarstvenny Universalny Magazin*, or "Universal State Department Store."

13. John Reed (1887–1920), American labor leader, author, and publicist. Reed came to Russia in August 1917 to cover the Revolution, during which he sided enthusiastically with the Bolsheviks. Back in the United States in 1918 he helped to organize various socialist and communist groups and lectured and wrote extensively. His best-known work is *Ten Days That Shook the World* (1919). Reed returned to Russia shortly after publication of the book and became an associate of Lenin and a member of the executive committee of the Communist International. He died of typhus the following year and is buried in Red Square at the Kremlin Wall. John Reed Clubs, for writers of leftist tendencies, were founded in the United States beginning in 1929.

14. VOX (the Society for Cultural Relations with Foreigners) functioned as, among other things, the government's official tourist agency.

15. Henry Wadsworth Longfellow Dana, teacher at the New School and author of *Handbook on Soviet Drama* (1938) and *Drama in Wartime Russia* (1943).

tive of the Chicago Daily News, the head of ⌊   ⌋ and others who tell me different things about Russia & what is in store for me. After the celebration I am to be permitted to see some of leaders & directors of the Communist Party—who rule in Russia, and after that given a guide & my transportation to and lodging in such points in Russia as I wish to visit. Nearing suggests Ruth Cornell, since she talks both Russian & English— and since we are already so close it strikes me as almost an ideal choice. At 4$\frac{30}{}$ in the afternoon is to be the opening—of the ten days celebration as well as the welcoming of foreign communists & visitors. I am brought a box ticket and go—for the opening at least . . . . . Very impressive— especially the memorial song for the dead played by a competent orchestra & listened to, standing, by the huge assembly. This opera house within & without is more impressive than quite any in Europe[16] . . . . At five thirty I leave & return to find Ruth Cornell & Dinamov here. She is to take me to see a Russian folk play at one of the little theatre art schools which proves to a fascinating picture of village life at the time of the over-throw of the Tzar and the inauguration of the Soviet. It is too long, but if cut would prove successful in America. I am sure. After the show I leave her at box & return to write . . . .

The Russians are surely an easy going people—practical in some things, indifferent or impractical in others. This hotel for instance. Archi-tecturally in the inside all its features are semi-palatial—great halls, great chambers—extravagant, Grand Louis furniture, and yet here & there with torn rugs, indifferent bedding, the plumbing out of order, two minute eleva-tors carrying only two persons at a time, locks that dont work; often no hot water after 9 at night, indifferent room service at night. Yet such service as you get always courteous—except in the main office where one can stand for hours unless one can make oneself understood in the language of the particular clerk on guard. And it is assumed to be an international hotel under direct charge of the Soviet Central Government. . . . .

Again the theatre we visited tonight had but one entrance and no exit for as many as 800 or 900 people. And because all wraps & over shoes must be left at the door an almost disgraceful crush or fight to get in and again to get out! The theatre itself—the building, was formerly a really gorgeous private residence taken from one of the rich bourgeois families by the Soviet. "And where are its members", I asked. "Does anyone know?" "Dead or working in New York or Paris as waiters".

16. Dreiser is referring to the famous Bolshoi Theater, which dates in its present form from the remodeling by the architect Cavos after a fire in 1853 destroyed the interior.

Monday. Nov. 7–1927– Grand Hotel. Moscow

I am awakened by the music of a band and the tramp, tramp, tramp of soldiers entering the Red Square. It is the beginning of the 10 days celebration of the 10ᵗʰ anniversary. And although it is only 8³⁰, here they come—long lines of marching troops—The Red Guard—Kurds from Kurdistan. The Den Cossacks in long flying coats, boots, spurs & fur caps and riding small but apparently strong & swift horses. And a few companies of Siberian rifles. And now the railroad gaurds in long great over coats and some special design of caps—and all shoulders slung with rifles: and so the frontier gaurds; and a troop of revolutionists from far Georgia with grey beards & heavy furs & riding smart black horses. It is said that they fought bitterly against the white imperialists and are all that are left of a large division of fighting men: And now Caucasus Mountain artillery with light mountain wagons fitted with small cannon & machine guns. And so on—file after file until 11 AM. And the workers appear—first arrived trades unionists—machinists, wood carvers, glass makers, shoe machine men, furniture men, stone cutters—a hundred lines—and all armed. And after them the great parade of communist sympathizers—thousands & thousands of men & women, boys & girls in all lines of work—some in white; some in blue—some wearing white caps, some red—and after the Russian temperament all rather vivid & gay. They approach the entrances to the Red Square—which is directly in front of my room in four converging lines— twelve abreast. And the marching continuous from 11 until night. They are marching to show the world how great is their faith in red Russia. And here, where so recently was only poverty, ignorance & blind faith are now more or less educated & trained men & women, boys & girls. One sees all sorts of intelligent, illustrative floats, visually demonstrating what Russia is now achieving commercially—reapers, binders, tractors, hay balers, engines, cars, steel building bars—commercial wares of all kinds and the whole interspersed with banners, banners, banners telling the world, I suppose, that Soviet Russia will never again endure capitalist tyranny—or words to that effect. And these bands and hurrahs. One gathers that at last Mother Asia—which is mostly Russia today, is at last awake & alive to modern conditions. This enormous giant is at last rousing itself from the sleep of centuries—equipping itself—entering (for it) upon a strange new day and mission. I never expected to see so strange a thing—the marching asiatics of all casts of countenance—from Chinese to European, and singing hymns of brotherhood—and saluting reverently as they pass the mausoleum of the master of them all—Lenin. No Priests, no banners; just symbols of human determination to make life more bearable for all. I think—if only human

Sunday. Nov. 7-1927- Grand Hotel. Moscow
I am awakened by the music of a band
and the tramp, tramp tramp of soldiers
entering the Red Square. It is the beginning of the 10 days celebration of the
10th anniversary. And although it is only
8:30 here there come - long lines of marching
troops - The Red Guard - Kurds from Kurdistan
The Don Cossacks in long flowing coats, boots
spurs & fur caps and riding small but
efficiently strong & swift horses. And
a few companies of Siberian rifles. And
here the railroad guards in long great
overcoats and some special design of
caps - and all shoulder slung with rifles.
And so the frontier guards; and the
a troop of revolutionist from far Georgia
with grey beards & heavy furs & riding
small black horses. It was is said that
they fought bitterly against the white
imperialists and are all that are left
of a large division of fighting men. And
now Caucasus mountain artillery
with light mountain wagons fitted
with small cannon & machine guns

Diary leaf 110, an entry handwritten by Dreiser. (From the Theodore Dreiser Collection, Special Collections Department, Van Pelt–Dietrich Library Center, University of Pennsylvania, Philadelphia)

Marchers in Red Square during the tenth anniversary of the Russian Revolution. (From the Russian State Archives of Film and Photo Documents, Moscow)

nature can rise to the opourtunity—here is one for the genuine betterment of man. But, mayhap, the program is too beautiful to succeed;—an ideal of existence to which frail & selfish humanity can never rise. Yet I earnestly hope that this is not true—that this is truly the beginning of a better—or brighter, day for all. . . . .

9³⁰ A.M. I go to Red Square and witness the parade from the grand stand. Meet Scott Nearing & some fellow collectivist who has just returned from 9 years of life in Peking. He tells how the economic & social advance of the last ten or twenty years has been almost completely checked by the fighting between the Communists & the non-communists. England & Japan—aided—as usual by American high finance—have joined to check the communistic advance of South China. In the melee, hospitals, laboratories, universities, business and social enterprises of all kinds have gone by the board—the work of years undone. And the outlook, according to him, even worse. Like Nearing he also had crossed Siberia to Moscow. Saw the country & cities enroute. The poor clothes of all the population—and especially the peasents, had depressed him—but physically—he thought—

View of the Trade Union Building during the celebration of the tenth anniversary of the Russian Revolution. (From the Russian State Archives of Film and Photo Documents, Moscow)

they looked hale enough. But there would have to come much in clothing & building & supplies in stores, before the nation would look anything but strained . . . .

At 11ᵘ⁰ I leave here and watch the files still parading before my windows. The big engine (life size) and the thrasher & reaper. They stand in front of the hotel for hours before they join a procession of floats. Later after writing letters I follow one of the approaching lines to its end. Studying thousands of Russians so, I conclude that as yet the women—and many of the men, are physically too heavy & stodgy to be attractive. And just now their clothes are too sombre. But here & there one sees a boy or a girl—or a man or woman, who is attractive and semi-smart. But the semi-orientalism of it all weighs on me. So much is needed to modernize the city. . . . . At the end of the line—and as I turn off to go back by another, I encounter Ruth (Kennell). She has done her bit in the procession & dropped out. We walk back to the hotel together, visiting a church or two. At the hotel she comes & we play about until dinner which I order in the room. Then Dorothy Thomp-

son and ∟   ⌐ arrive—and also stay, and there is a long discussion of communism as opposed to capitalism. Miss Thompson makes some severe comments on the general communistic assumption that capitalism, particularly in America, has no advantages. She is not wholly for individualism but feels that communism—as expressed thus far in Russia, is a drab affair—more a matter of mental or idealistic enthusiasm on the part of its members than of actual material improvement. The Moscow decorations. I say they remind me of a 14$\underline{\text{th}}$ St. Fire Sale. At 7$\underline{30}$ Scott Nearing & Prof. Dana arrive. We are supposed to go and see the young dancers of the Irina Duncan School dance.[17] We walk there—but the dancers having marched all day are too tired to dance & the invitation is put over until Thursday. Then—with Dorothy Thompson, Nearing & Dana I visit the Cathedral of Our Savior—on the Moscow River—said to be the largest in Russia.[18] It is fascinating in the moonlight outside & the gloom—broken by a few candles on the inside. I gather en route that D. T____ is making overtures to me. Afterwards Nearing leads us to the Chinese Eastern "University"—really a Red School for Chinese Communists, 200 of whom are sent here annually by the Koumintang—the Communist Central Organization in China.[19] I hear—from young Chinese—and in English—the state of Communism in China. It is shot through with proletarian unrest, fired by Russia. 20,000 Communists have been killed by conservatives. A northern white or capitalistic army—engineered & backed by England, Japan & the United States is fighting & killing communists but not seriously affecting the Red Revolution. To be caught reading communistic literature or venture the Soviet idea in any form means death. And the Communists are replying with death to those who kill their comrades. The 200 students of this class—the entire 400 in the school (the total "university" course is for two years!) expect to return in China & fight—and also to die inside of 3½ years. Their young minds have been set on fire by Communist leaders in Russia . . . . . The Chinese <u>Wall</u> newspaper! The poems translated & then beautifully recited in Chinese. The young movie queen—Chinese girl student. Hollywood would prize her. And it is obvious from what source her beauty technique has been derived—the American movies in China. . . . .

17. Dreiser means the dance school begun by Isadora Duncan in Moscow in 1921. Irina Duncan was her sister; see entry for 10 November.

18. Dreiser is mistaken here. The cathedral lies on the Yauza River, a large tributary of the Moscow. Built between 1410 and 1427 of white stone, it lies within the Spasso-Andronikovsky Monestary, a famous Russian center of culture.

19. For references to this university, see Dorothy Thompson, The New Russia (New York: Henry Holt, 1928), 173, 237, 254.

*We go to Scott Nearings room in the Hotel Passage. D___ T___ & I
continue our flirtation. After a supper with the American delegation she
comes to my room with me to discuss communism & we find we agree on
many of its present lacks as well as its hopeful possibilities. I ask her to
stay but she will not—tonight.*

Tuesday Nov. 8–1927– Moscow. Hotel Grand
*Very bright & fairly warm—like an April day in America. I decide—since
it is a holiday, to do the churches. Ruth Kennell—who is now my secretary, arrives & we hire a Droschy[20] for 2 roubles an hour (7[00]). Then we
set forth and visit the following churches.*

*But after visiting Vassile Blagenoi[21] we cross the stone or ⌐   ⌐
bridge of the Moscow River & I get out to look at the Kremlin (Kreml)—
quite the loveliest imperial enclosure I have ever seen. The towers! The
spires! The pinapple domes. And so gloriously colored—red, gold, blue,
green, brown, white. And really sparkling in the sun. Baghdad! The fabled
cities of Aladdins world! and yet real! Here before my eyes. As we stand
here Ruth tells me the story of Tzar Theodore—now being given at the
Bolshoi Theatre, and the scenes of which were laid in this very Kreml.[22]
But I dream of still older days—of fantastic gayeties & delights & splen-
dors that never were—things of my own creating. And all the while the
muddy water of the Moscow River running under my feet—this quaint—
the oriental droschy is clattering here & there; the suns rays being refracted
by the glorious pinnacles before me. . . . . And then once more the Church
of Our Savior—by day. And Ruth tells me how she—born a Lutheran,
married a Methodist Minister and really wrecked his life. It would make
a novel. And she describes how, on Easter night, this Cathedral is lighted
with 10,000 candles, how the faithful gather by thousands in the square
outside, each bearing a lighted candle. And to be fortunate—or blessed—
one must take ones candle home with the light unextinguished. How the
priests go in procession about the church praying before each tower, and*

20. A *droshka* is typically a one-horse peasant wagon with small wheels.
21. Vasili Blazhenni Cathedral, or the Cathedral of St. Basil, is one of the most singular
structures in Moscow. Begun by Ivan the Terrible in 1554 and completed in 1679, it consists
of eleven small chapels arranged in two stories and is surmounted by variously shaped domes
and spires painted in many colors.
22. Dreiser might be referring to Moussorgsky's opera *Boris Godunov*, in which Czar
Boris's son, the Czarevitch Feodor (Theodore), is a character.

how—as they pray—red fire bursts from the belfry of each. And then the bells of the city—thousands; the admixture of reverence—holiday. I see it all as she tells it. . . . . And then

We buy candy—and I dream over little churches & big—the brass work—the altars, ikons, vestments, lettering, prayers—architecture,—the world of handicraft and devotion that has gone to make these 484 treasure troves of the city. I do not [unreadable word]. I cannot. None of the refined Russians in successful neighborhoods or the grosser or duller ones in poorer neighborhoods. The church takes in whose single room no more than 10 × 12—lived 7 people. And the Russian cats on fences & in doors, the charming grass grown courtyards here & there. The exotic looking Russian priests with their long silky hair & beards, their strange caps & long girdled velvet coats. I am never weary of looking.—It is all so new to me & so different. Asia—and the west . . . . . . At 4$\frac{30}{}$ *we go for chocolate. These Russian shops are so poor. Shabby really. And then to the hotel. There are calls. I am to do this & that. Come to see such & such. We decide to dine in the hotel. At dinner I am told by one Schwarz, the correspondent of the New York World, that because I asked the American Embassy at Berlin what to do about my passport a rumor was abroad that I was being detained against my will by the Soviet and that a cable had come from London, asking about it. I immediately wire Berlin that my passport has been found. Next one ⌊   ⌋ Durante of the London Post calls to ask me.[23] On his invitation Ruth, Schwarz & myself go to his rooms—the best I have seen here, for tea & to sit before an open fire—the only one I have seen here. More discussion of Russia. How does one pay ones rent! How does one hire a servant? How buy food, clothing & the like.*

*Moscow, Tuesday, Nov. 8th, 1927.

We hired a very seedy looking izvozchik[24] at two roubles an hour and set off through the Red Square to the section which lies on the other side of the Moscow River. We stopped at the church facing the Red Square, the many-domed 'Pamyat Vasiliya Blazhenova.' The

23. Walter Duranty was associated with both the *New York Times* and the *London Post*; he was regarded as the dean of American correspondents in Moscow. See *Duranty Reports Russia* (New York: Viking, 1934).

24. An *izvozchik* is a cabman or drayman, typically a peasant in a heavy sheepskin coat.

*Here begins Ruth Kennell's typescript. Her typographical errors, like Dreiser's slips of the pen, are left uncorrected.

upper part of the building, now a museum, was closed but the small chapel below where services were still held was open and we looked into the dim, chill place, lighted by tapers.

On the Moscow River bridge, we stood looking at the wonderful view of the Kremlin, which opens out across the river. Crossing the bridge, we drove along the bank to the next bridge, crossed over on the other side again and went up to the great cathedral of the five enormous golden domes, 'Krama Christa Spacitelya', (Church of the Saviour). There was no service today but admission was being charged to go inside. This magnificent edifice was built only about 25 years ago and is the richest of the Moscow churches.

Re-crossing the bridge we went along a street leading across the canal to the very old section of the city. Enroute on Bolshaya Polyanka Street we stopped at a chapel, a kind of hole in the wall set among shabby shops and factories. Further was a very interesting looking brick colored church whose blue domes were studded with golden stars.

Circling the *Konydeum* Square we struck off into a side street and stopped at a very large church with a courtyard. It was closed but the watch-woman offered to open it for us; but it threatened to be a long performance and we contented ourselves with looking into her dwelling by the gate, a one-room hut with an entry and woodshed. She told us that she and her mother, her husband, two sisters and two children all live in this very small room. It had a brick stove and one bed, a table, chairs and an alter. Our isvozchik, jealously noting our interest in these living conditions, volunteered the information that he lives much worse. At the next church, when D. jumped out and started into the courtyard, he admiringly exclaimed: 'Molodetz, vash barin!' 'A good sport, your lord!'

On the Bolshaya Ordinka we found the most beautiful church. Built about 15 years ago the Pokrova Boshey Materi is graceful and harmonious in every detail. It is of gray stone, with very full rounded domes of black metal, and black metal porticoes hang over the heavy carved doors and the white glass windows. Even the rain pipes are harmoniously constructed of a greenish metal. Inside, the mural decorations are quite perfect in form and color, much more modern in style than in any other Moscow church. The artist is Nesterov, a well known painter. Rich blues predominate against light gray walls and low rounded ceilings.

Returning by side streets to the river, we passed any number of interesting churches, white with blue domes, yellow with white domes, each entirely different from all the others. Keeping to the bank of the canal, we rode some distance in the opposite direction from the Kremlin. We came upon a very extensive monastery, with walls and a tower falling into decay and a beautiful ruined church and graveyard. It seemed that here was a factory, a box factory which occupied one of the stone buildings in the court. Receiving permission from the gateman to enter, we were shown about by a militia man after I had explained that the visitor was an American delegate. The factory was closed, as it was a holiday, but he insisted on showing us the factory school for the liquidation of illiteracy and the club and library. About 500 workers are employed here and live in the low building, which no doubt was the dwelling of the monks formerly. In the basement of the church, construction work was in full swing, as living quarters are being made there. The great old church itself was locked, the keys being in the hands of the Chief Scientific Department. The tombstones were broken and lying about, and it seemed on the whole a very depressing atmosphere for workers to work and live in.

We turned toward the center of town again and passing through the Chinese Wall into the old street Nikolskaya, we passed at the gates to Lubyanskaya Ploschad (Square) a little church with blue domes whose spikes were painted with gold; this quaint church is 500 years old.

Moscow, Nov. 8th, Evening.

Decided to go to Prince Igor at the Bolshoi Opera House, but found that all tickets for theaters had been distributed to trade unions free of charge for these performances.[25] Hearing from Louis Fischer that there was a rumour that D. was being held virtually a prisoner by the Soviet Government, we went with Fischer to see Duranti of the Associated Press. Duranti lives in quite palatial quarters for Moscow, three or four large rooms, one room with a small fireplace in which a wood fire was burning, the first grate I have ever seen in Moscow. The discussion turned to the Housing Department.

25. *Prince Igor* is the only opera of the composer Aleksandr Borodin; it tells the story of the defeat of Prince Igor Sviatoslavich at the hands of the Polovtsky tribe in 1185.

Duranti explained that each dwelling house has its House Committee, which is responsible to the Central Housing Dept. of the city. In 1921 Duranti was given a three years' lease on the place on condition that he would repair it. He made extensive repairs but at the end of the three years the apartment reverted to the Housing Dept. to which through the House Comm. he pays 125 dollars a month rent. The tenants elect the House Committee and two or three times a year meetings are held to hear the committee's report and check accounts. This makes grafting difficult. Besides, there is the Workers and Peasants Inspection which can at any moment drop in and look at the books. This Inspection is a check on every department of the government, and can clean out a whole office force if it finds graft or inefficiency and has full powers at all times.

Duranti claimed that the graft system in America makes for cheaper production, citing the price of canned meat in America, 10 cents, as compared with 30 cents in Russia. Fischer maintained that this was due to rationalisation of industry and not to the graft system.

On the subject of bureaucracy, it was shown that although still very much in evidence in Russian institutions, it is being very rapidly decreased. In 1922 it took 45 minutes to get money from the bank, now 3 minutes. While in Germany there are 3 paper records in railroad reports, in Russia there were 48, but this number has been reduced considerably. The fact that there is so much unemployment makes it difficult to decrease office forces which make for greater bureaucratic methods.

In regard to unemployment, it was said that in fact more people are now comparatively speaking being employed, but that more peasants are coming to the cities. The people are land hungry because there is no money to develop the land and build roads.

The Soviet experiment will be a success if 1) there will not be a civil war or 2) a foreign war and 3) get American help.

As to foreign debts, Russia says she is ready to pay but does not recognise the debts. Russia cannot get loans because while she has never failed to meet an obligation, she cannot give security, and this record of her reliability is the only guarantee she can offer. She does not want to pay debts but aspires to renew them. Although the International Harvester Co. lost through the revolution on account of being nationalised, nevertheless, it is giving more credits to Soviet Russia than any other country.

Earlier in the evening, the servant problem was touched on. Servants are hired through the trade unions, an agreement is drawn up, eight hour day, special clothing, holidays, and month's notice of discharge, and social insurance must be paid monthly.

Moscow, Nov. 9th–1927 – (Wednesday) Grand Hotel
Nothing much. I write in the morning. In the afternoon visit the peasent museum & buy a green silk muffler. Afterwards to a vegetarian restau-rant. These restaurants in Russia (Moscow I mean) are very poor. There is nothing smart—no night life—unless it is private. The reason for this is— I am told—that officials, tradesman and even workers, if they have any spare cash, are afraid to be seen spending it any where because if they are it means that their incomes will be looked into and their taxes increased. So about all that is left of night life is family visiting, the theatres, movies, opera and private relations with women. At Kennells I have dessert—and a long discussion of the import of this Soviet movement. It results in a head-ache for her. At $8\frac{30}{}$ I return here, clip items about Russia, post the notes. To bed at about midnight.

Moscow – Thursday. Nov 10–1927 – Grand Hotel
THE CENTRAL GUEST HOUSE OF THE PEASANTS. This is a five story brick building covering half a block and located in the center of Moscow. It is one of 380 peasant guest houses in Russia. The director, Grinuk, explained the purpose of these houses. Before the Revolution, the peasant coming to the city, was always a victim of all sorts of exploitation and plundering, he got drunk, lost his money, etc. Now the Government operates these guest houses for the general comfort and education of the peasant visiting the city. The director himself was a teacher in a village before the revolution; being a Communist he became local Commissar of Production after the Revolution, then manager of a large Government Grain Trust. Then the Party said to him: 'We have more important work for you to do, and turned over to him the management of the Central Guest House of the Peasants.

Any peasant has a right to come to a guest house and live dur-ing his stay in the city. The average length of time is ten days, but if his business keeps him longer, he can stay longer in the guest house. There are three to six beds in a room and his bed costs him 25 kopecks a day, breakfast 25 k. and dinner 30 k. If a peasant is very poor, he can either stay free of charge or at reduced rates. The rooms are large, light and clean, the beds have clean linen and blankets and look comfortable. The guests can also have tea in their rooms. At one o'clock all guests must be in bed and lights out. The peasants can receive court service free of charge. A staff of expert attorneys are at the service of the peasants and a long line of peasants was waiting for consultation with attorneys. There are also free clinics with 84 doctors in attendance. There are exhibits in charge of agronomes, lectures, moving pictures and plays in the large auditorium, excursions to museums, etc. *The peasent—and rightly—is requested to take a bath in the "banya" or steam bath house on his arrival.*[26] *If only he could be persuaded daily to do the same.*

There is a reading room and a 'Lenin Corner' with many posters propagandizing the peasant in the meaning and organisation of his government, union of peasants and workers, the Communist party, anti-religion, etc. The library has 12,000 books and 80 visitors daily. There is also a large museum containing posters and diagrams about agricultural methods and statistics, exhibits of products, the latest agricultural machinery, especially electric motors and power machinery, sanitation and hygiene for stock and people, diseases of live stock, etc. etc.

The Central Guest House accomodates 400 peasants.

In the interview with Grinuk, the following questions were answered:

About the size of *the land* holdings of peasants? The average size is 40 to 60 acres.

About the rich peasant, a 'kulak'?[27] The maximum size of his land is 1000 acres. His income is not more than 5,000 roubles *a year* and there is a progressive tax on this income running from 2 k. on the first 20 roubles to 22 k. on 60 roubles.

Why does the Government fear the rich peasant? Before the Revolution the "<u>kulak</u>" was practically ruler of the villages. The

---

26. A *banya* is a bath, typically a steam bath in a separate building.
27. The term *kulak* was applied before 1917 to miserly tradesmen or to village usurers. After the Revolution it was used to designate prosperous peasants, many of whom were disfranchised and taxed heavily. Some were deported to corrective labor camps.

poor and middle peasants usually needed money in the winter and had to work for the rich peasant and thus come into his power. But now, although his income is sometimes much higher than the other peasants, he is not only heavily taxed but if he hires labor he is disfranchised. There are three forms of power which his wealth takes, machinery, labor and speculation. The Government encourages the first because this lessens the need for hiring labor and increases the general production and standard of agriculture, and machines are not taxed; the second is discouraged and regulated; the third is an evil—for instance, in the fall when grain is cheap the rich peasant will buy it up and then sell it at a high price in the spring.

What is the difference in the standard of living between rich peasants and other peasants? The middle peasant has an income of on the average 500 roubles, the poor peasant, 200 roubles a year as compared with 2000 to 5000 for the "kulak." The difference in standard of living is a difference only of more comfortable home and better food and clothing, and the contrast is not excessive. The children of rich peasants of course can be better fed and clothed than the other children, but must go to the same schools and have the same social advantages as the rest, since there are not private schools in the villages. The Government encourages collectives of peasants as much as possible, perhaps only in the ownership of a tractor, or further in cultivation of the land or in a pure commune where all labor and social life are shared. *From a long conversation in and investigation of the first peasents guest house we went to a second.*
THE MOSCOW GUBERNIA HOUSE OF THE PEASANTS. This was formerly the beautiful Hermitage Hotel and restaurant. It is now a guest house for the peasants of the Moscow Gubernia, *or state* which is about the size of the state of Ohio. Here also is a beautiful auditorium, museum, posters and maps, etc., reading room, Lenin Corner, and the sleeping rooms are very elegantly decorated and furnished. The same rates are charged and the same free services given.

At the door as we went out we saw a remarkable group of guests arriving from Izbekistan, or Turkestan. They wore enormous shaggy fur hats and bright colored robes tied at the waist with sashes. They were busy piling their baggage, which consisted of numerous bags made of Turkish rugs and rolls of blankets, on the sidewalk in front of the door, and they were talking in a strange tongue. *From here we*

went to a Moscow department store. It—like many others, is run directly
by the Government and I question Ruth as to whether the spirit of indiffer-
ence which characterizes it is not due to government control—officialdom.
She thinks not. The Russian temperament is slow. Patient, lackadaiscal.
It wants to buy but it can take its time. Here—as yet—there is no least
smartness in the new controlling classes and no money. Later when they
have money as well as leisure from the seven hour day we shall see.

Next we visit the Novo Denechi Monastery built in 1594 and where the
wife of Tzar Theodore became Prioress after his death, or when she was
divorced rather.[28] *We took an izvoszschik—The evening was cloudy &*
chilly. "The melancholy days have come—the saddest of the year". And
how I felt that mood here. It is an old white and gray affair with a church
or two topped with gold domes of course and is strongly fortified with a
high wall and embattled towers running around it. Napoleon in his
march on Moscow tried to seize the monastery but failed. He placed
a mine in the basement of the main church, but one of the nuns
discovered it in time. There is one very beautiful main church, of a
light gray with five round golden domes, and another old red church.
These are now museums but services are still held in a smaller building where many beautiful ikons and paintings, etc. are still kept.
There is a large grave yard with many elaborate tomb stones.[29] One
is in the form of a lovely little white temple with golden roof, and
was built in memory of a rich merchant before the 1917 Revolution. Chekov's gravestone is one of the most artistic, but is crowded
in among many other long forgotten graves. Someone had lit thĕ
candle in a lantern over one of the graves, and we wondered if the
dead would still be so remembered in five years. It was a new grave,
only a year old.

28. The Novodevichy Monastery (New Maiden's Convent) was one of a ring of fortified
monasteries, which from the sixteenth century onward were constructed outside the center
of Moscow. Novodevichy was built to celebrate the liberation of the city of Smolensk from
Polish-Lithuanian occupation in 1524. Dreiser's reference is to Czar Theodore I's widow, who
was the sister of Boris Godunov. In 1598, Godunov sought sanctuary at the convent with his
sister and waited there for the nobles and boyars to ask him to become the czar.

29. The Novodevichy Cemetery lies next to the southern wall of the convent. This is
the cemetery that in the nineteenth century became the burial ground for Russia's famous
men and women. Philosophers, artists, writers, musicians, scientists, politicians, and others
who had gained a place in Russian history were the only persons allowed space here. Dreiser's
reference in the next entry to Chekhov's gravestone is his way of describing a white stone
with a metal roof that looks like a simple village house. Dreiser seems not to have understood
the character of the cemetery, believing that the Russian writer was laid to rest among "long
forgotten graves."

At six in the evening we attended the opening session of the Congress of the Friends of Soviet Russia, or rather for the organisation of such a body. Krupskaya, the wife of Lenin, Clara Zetkin, the German Communist, Rykov and Henri Barbusse participated in the meeting.[30]

After this was over—or in spite of it I was supposed to attend an exhibition of the dancers of Irina Duncan, the sister of Isadora—who has a school here. Russian fashion those who were supposed to get and conduct me failed to appear—and since I did not know how to make my way about here I stuck, writing notes, reading up on the Soviet and its achievements in the past ten years and brooding on America. At midnight some one taps on the door. I fear it is some girl & since I do not feel up to more excitement do not open it. But I guess who.

Friday, Nov. 11 -1927-Moscow-Grand Hotel
Rainy in the morning; cold and dry at night. My bronchitis seems to be reducing its grip a little here. Last night I had an odd dream. I have been feeling rather heavy & lethargic of late. The first symtoms of age as I take it. But in my dream I was delightfully vigorous & gay—not changed in years or strength. It seemed as though I were in an enclosed court where were paths & grass—and that along one of the paths I was dancing—quite naked—a double-barrel club in my hand & swinging the same high above my head—the while I threw myself joyfully here & there—now in one leaping or dancing position—and in another. Yet soon I saw coming toward me—or going and by another path, an elderly man in dark clothes—one of the conservative and learned types. And suddenly—I found myself slightly afraid—as though he might be able to do some thing to me. Yet as I felt this I also felt—how can he & what can he really do. And in the same instant I awoke.

Chekov's grave in the Novo Denechi Monastery Yard. I wish they would either creamate all great men & throw their ashes to the winds or bury them apart from there fellows in some singular place where one could go and meditate on each his special significance—(charm or peace). But

---

30. Lenin's wife was Nadezhda Konstantinovna Krupskaya (b. 1869); she married Lenin in 1894 and was sent with him to exile in Siberia in 1896. After the Revolution she devoted her efforts to public education and the fight against illiteracy. Clara Zetkin was a socialist active in women's movements of the time; she organized the first International Woman's Day in 1909. Aleksey Ivanovich Rykov (1881–1938), a Bolshevik leader, was one of Stalin's major opponents at this time; he would be executed in the purges of 1938. Henri Barbusse (1873?–1935) was a French journalist and author.

this way—crowded wretchedly among so many—like Chopin in Pere la Chaise.[31] I do not like it. It would be better the other way. . . . .

Lenin. A new world hero I presume. If the world goes over to the dictatorship of the proletariat, as I assume it will, how great will he not be. Another Washington. Another Cromwell. Already Russia is thick with his fame. His statues & pictures are so numerous as to constitute an atmosphere. In Moscow alone there are so many busts & statues of him that they seem to constitute an addition to the population. Thus: Population of Moscow—without statues of Lenin—2,000,000, with statues of Lenin,— 3,000,000. . . .

After wasting the whole morning in planning what to do, since Smidovich could not receive us, but arranged for us to go to the Central Committee of the Russian Communist Party, we finally at 11:30 a.m. arrived at the headquarters. This is an enormous gray stone building covering a square block. We circled the building to get our propusks,[32] and went to the sixth floor where the Women's Section is located. A stout woman who was sitting at a desk surrounded by exceedingly occupied women, received us. I did not know where to begin in the conversation, so she brought forward two large colored posters addressed to Eastern women which showed the old and the new condition of women in Turkestan, the harem, the ill treatment of the wives, veils, isolation and then today monogamy, economic independence, no veils, and participation in the soviets. In answer to my question, Kachilina (who is assistant director of the Women's Section and a peasant) answered that monogamy is the recognised family relationship in the Soviet Union and polygamy is not recognised. In answer to my question as to the difference between sex regulations in America and in Russia, she answered that before the revolution in Russia as well as now in America, only registered marriages were recognised, whereas now in Soviet Russia if a man and a woman live together, the woman has the same rights as a registered wife, her children are protected by law—the father must be jointly responsible for them—and if either the woman or man should be ill or in need, the other is under obligation to care for her or him. Divorce is very simple. Only the wish of one or the other or of both being sufficient to have the marriage annulled. In case of separa-

31. Chopin is buried in the crowded and much-visited Cemetery of Père-Lachaise in Paris; a monument of a weeping muse with a broken lyre marks his grave.
32. A *propusk* is a pass or an identity card that will admit one to a building.

tion or of death of one parent, the joint property is divided equally among the parent and children; the children are usually given into the custody of the mother but if there is an appeal, the court decides on the grounds of the competency of the parents to care for the children. The other parent must give a certain percentage of his or her income to the support of the children.

What rights have the parents over the children? No right at all beyond the welfare of the child. If it can be proved that a parent is harmful to the child, it can be taken from him by the state. If children are willful and wild, run away from home or otherwise are so unruly with their parents as to be dangerous, they can be taken away by the district section of the Dept. of Education and placed in an institution for defective children.

As to moral education of the child, there is of course no religious instruction whatever. In its place there is the study of science. In the elementary schools nature, political economy and moral instruction is all confined to the children's movement represented by the Young Pioneers, an organisation composed of boys and girls from 7–14 and the Young Communists, from 14–21. In these groups which work in connection with the schools, and in close contact with the teachers, questions of sex hygiene, of the dangers to health of early or promiscuous sex relations, duties as citizens, duties at home, truthfulness, honesty, the evil of smoking and drinking, etc. In the beginning, (1918–21) sex relations were too free but now *this freedom has been modified.*[33]

What difference is there between the unmarried girl today in her position and attitude to life and the former times? Formerly, the girl had no choice whatever in the matter of marriage. Her parents arranged the union without consulting her wishes and she was a wife and mother and nothing else. Now the girl is absolutely free to choose whom she wishes and to live with him only as long as she wishes. There is no social compulsion to remain with a husband, if she does not want to do so.

Furthermore, the married woman is encouraged to maintain economic independence, continue her work, and if there are children, place them in the day nurseries and kindergartens. When the work-

33. The dates and the words "this freedom has been modified" are in Ruth Kennell's hand.

ing woman has a baby, she receives two months before the birth and two months after vacation on pay, a sum of money for milk and clothing, free medical care, and two hours off during her working day to nurse the baby the first year.

The interview came to an abrupt end as we had to hurry off to an interview with Kogan, director of the State Academy of Artistic Science.

My attention was called to the name of this institution *and* as we went in *I* questioned the possibility of art being a science. The discussion began with this question and ended with the question being tabled until another time. Kogan maintained that the Academy was for the purpose of scientific study of art. I maintained that science has nothing to do with art. He explained that art has three phases: 1. the materials of the artist (clay, paints, canvas, stone, etc.), 2. Technique of the artist, and creative ideas, and 3: History and influence on society of the works of artists. I said that the materials and technique could be left to mechanics and the only thing of importance was the creative idea of the artist and science could not study that. There could not be more than research and criticism for the student. Kogan said that in the Academy were not students but scholars making scientific research into art and the interview was cut short with a sort of compromise statement on my part that the Academy could turn out research workers and critics of art, but not scientists. (Note of Sec.: you behaved like a steam roller in a china store.)

From the Academy we walked to the Tolstoy Museum nearby. The Tolstoy Society maintains this museum which contains an enormous collection of photographs of Tolstoy and his family, busts and statues of Tolstoy, editions of his works, relics, illustrations from his works, death mask, etc. One large oil painting appealed to me. Tolstoy, already an old man, is sitting on the rocks contemplating the Black Sea. 'Nothing left', was my comment.

I wanted next to take an izvozchik and ride down to the Moscow River Bridge to see again the beautiful view of the Kremlin from the river. Dinamov made some arrangement with the driver and went on. We rode past the great church, across Kameni Most (the Stone Bridge) and following the river bank on the other side came to the second bridge. Here we alighted and asked the izvozchik, a young fellow, the charge. He said two roubles, we protested and he said we had agreed to pay one and a half to the Stone Bridge. We said we had neglected to make any agreement with him, and would pay no more than one rouble. He demanded one and a half. We gave him a three rouble note and he gave back only one and a half. Both of us demanded 50 kopeks more. A crowd had begun to gather about us and a policeman appeared. He asked what was the matter and the driver explained that we had agreed to pay one and a half to the Stone Bridge, he had taken us to the second bridge and we offered only a rouble. The policeman asked where we had come from and on being told from the Big Church he said a rouble was enough and the crowd echoed his verdict 'Dovolno!', 'Taking advantage of a foreigner' while the driver muttered something about robbing a poor man. The driver with reluctance reached under his long coat and extracted 25 kopeks which he gave me. We demanded the remaining 25 k. 'Give them the rest', the policeman ordered and the driver with greater alacrity again extracted two 15 kopek pieces and handed them over without even asking for the 5 k. change. The crowd after some discussion among themselves and with curious glances at me, dispersed. I stood on the bridge in the cold wind a long time looking at the wonderful little walled city across the river and thought it the most beautiful thing I had ever seen. The crows were circling about the towers and golden domes; historic memory seemed to hang over the scene, a fragment of the long ago, a breath of the East.

xxxxxxxxxxxxxxxxxxxx

I had dinner with my secretary in the Lux, and listened to the story of her life.[34]

Moscow, Sat Nov. 12–1927 – Grand Hotel

In the morning we went to an exhibit of the Department of Mother and Child Protection of the Department of Health. I thought it a beautiful display. The very attractive colored posters, photographs and still life exhibits, charts, etc. simply and clearly set forth all the latest ideas and systems of child care, feeding, sanitation, infection, diseases and general hygiene. From there we went out into a court carrying white aprons on our arms and walked in a little procession of a dozen foreign delegates across endless courts and open spaces to the Institute for Research in Child's Diseases.

---

34. Dreiser later wrote a sketch, "Ernita," based on the story Kennell told him. It was published in *A Gallery of Women* (New York: Horace Liveright, 1929).

Here was space for 300 children, all ill, and kept here free of charge for treatment and observation. If the mother still nurses the child, she also stays, or wet nurses are hired to feed them. The babies are kept in small rooms, and the first few weeks are kept in isolation to prevent contagious diseases. Then we went to a day nursery for children of working mothers. Here was space for 40 children with all the best and latest equipment in playthings, furniture and other equipment. There are many such nurseries in Moscow, and the mother can bring her baby here and leave it for 8 hours. The nurses in charge are especially trained for their work, and certainly the child is much better off here than playing alone in a home not built for him.

We next went to the Soviet Exhibit in the Petrovsky Passage, a very large exhibit covering the whole range of the work of the Soviet Union in innumerable graphic charts, machinery, maps, products, etc. Statistics on every conceivable phase of the life of the country can be found in graphic charts.

In the evening we went to another session of the Congress of the Friends of Russia in the Hall of the Columns. It was inspiring. Different individuals noted in the international movement were given medals of honor by the Red Army officers and kissed on both cheeks, among them Sadoul, BelaKun and Marty (now imprisoned in France). Then followed speeches by several representatives from different countries, including the presentation of a flag to the Russian Trade Unions from the Chinese workers, accompanied by the speech of a spirited Chinese girl who spoke in her own language. Then a husky peasant woman from the village got up and made the most of her opportunity to speak on such an occasion. *The trouble with these people is that they seemed convinced that in changing a form of government they are changing humanity. But right here in Moscow—and among themselves as well as the Russians, I see sufficient to convince me that in no way has humanity changed. It is dreaming a new dream. Yet governments can be improved—and will be.*

At 11 p.m. I put on my evening suit and went to the reception of the Foreign Department to foreign press men. This was held in the magnificent palace of the *former* sugar king, Kereshnikov, facing the Kremlin on the opposite bank of the river. It was a gala affair participated in by the leading lights of official circles and foreign guests. Here I met Doletsky and Umansky of TASS, Madame Kollantay, *author of Red.*[35] Litvinova, Goldschmidt. Among the guests was Lunacharsky, Kogan, and the Mexican artist. We sat in the dining room and partook of an endless succession of dainty food, coffee and wines. I had an interesting talk with Gorkin of Izvestia on the freedom of the press and other topics. He claimed that there is more freedom of the press here because the newspapers openly criticise when they find faults, telling the truth because it is necessary, not to criticise for destructive but for constructive purposes. Madame Kollantay came and sat next to me on the divan and I asked her to tell me something. We began talking about the progress here. She said in answer to my remark that Russia not necessarily will follow the auto development of U.S. but might go straight to aeroplanes. About the penetration of the Soviet idea, Anna Louise Strong gave a long story about the Soviet power in an Arctic village.[35a] Kollantay thought that the most striking thing about the new society here is the change in mentality—the point of view of the people. The new generation thinks and acts socially, cooperatively, and its paramount idea is its social responsibility. In answer to the question of the reaction of the 14-year old to the new environment, she said that the Party is the guiding spirit in his life, not a religion, but in place of religion. Duty to the Soviet idea is paramount. The Party is his spiritual guide. But the other striking thing in the new society is the position of women, their determination not to be parasites, the social stigma on the parasite and even the housewife, the numbers of women who come to her department begging for work, to have a part in the building of the new society.

When we came out of the palace at 2 a.m., a wet snow was falling, the ground was covered with soft snow and a cold wind from the river swept the snow into our faces. When we at last found an izvozchik we accepted his terms without question and gratefully rode the rest of the way home. *At the hotel I found a jazz dance in full swing— and an American jazz tune—A Night of Love. And Russian men in evening dress—and Russian girls, the smartest of course, in short skirts, and bobbed hair dancing the latest steps. But since the costs here are high and each is limited under the laws to a low rate of income I wondered about*

35. Aleksandra Mikhaylovna Kollontay (1872–1952), Russian revolutionary and social reformer who served as Commisar for Public Welfare in the first Bolshevik government. Dreiser refers to her book *Red Love* (1927), which treats free love and sexual emancipation.

35a. Anna Louise Strong, journalist and friend of Sinclair Lewis.

this. After all, the world in Soviet Russia is not so different—and that only 10 years after the street fighting here. Beggars in the streets; and pretentious men & women who know no more of equality or "comrade" than ever the world has known since ever it began.

<u>Moscow, Sunday, Nov. 13–1927. Grand Hotel</u>
Because of last night I slept late and at 11 Ruth arrived with data for the day & Monday. Dinamov was to come at 11 & take us to his home & there to the homes of some workers in new workers apartments in his vicinity—and he kept his word—but rather late—arriving at 12:<u>30</u>. Then we took a street car in order to see a Peoples Sunday market somewhere out in his direction. Every country has its specialties & here were many that I had never seen,—the "gristle" of figs turned into a kind of dried jelly or glue—which is pressed into thin leaves or sheets—pink or white & done up in small bundles, sour cream in great tubs—at 50 kopecks the pound; Sugar in blocks 2 inches square, sunflower seeds at 20 kopecks the pound, and some grains that I never saw sold before. Also black bread & kvas.
After a half hour of this we continued our trip on to Dinamovs which is in an old working class, factory district of the city. He has three small rooms in a shabby frame building, and there are four members of his family. He lived in one of the small rooms with his mother 14 years ago when they both worked in a factory (textile), he ten and one half hours at 14 roubles a month. His mother worked 30 years in a textile factory and received 25 roubles a month. Now she would receive 70 roubles and the free services. Serge had invited three workers to come and talk with me.

One worker was a welder in an auto factory and received 18 roubles a week, the second a stoker in a textile factory, the third a clerk in a branch bank. *I talked to them all about their lives, trying to get the new attitude of the young Russian worker brought up under communism. And I gathered that they were thoroughly seized with all the doctrines of Marxism—as much as is any Catholic with the doctrines of Catholicism. Only in the case of communism—I assumed—the doctrines worked out more to their material advantage—or promised to. The worker in the auto factory:* he had a wife and two children, although only 24 years old, and said that he was able to live on this amount. As to money for clothing and extraordinary expenditures, he was able to receive advances from a factory fund and also buy on credit. He lived in one room and was satisfied with his living conditions. The second worker was also only 24, a nice looking brown-eyed fellow, with a nervous twitch to his face. He was a less skilled worker than the first, a stoker in a textile factory, and with overtime one day a week made about 18 roubles per week. He also has two children, and a good room for which he paid a nominal rent of two and one half roubles a month. He *had* joined with another family in taking over a flat, making an agreement for free rent *for* the first three years, and *taking* over responsibility for the upkeep and repairs on the flat, and then the above sum per month after three years. He had, *he said*, a harder struggle to make ends meet because conditions were not so good in his factory. Loan and credit funds *had* not *as yet* been established because most of the workers were highly skilled and *did* not demand *them*. As to the question of recreation, both replied that they *went* to their factory clubs often, to unions meetings, lectures, political circles, moving pictures, entertainments with living newspapers and Blue Blouses, and sometimes received free tickets through the union to the theater and kino.[36] (But the second worker said that for a man with a family, there really wasnt much time for recreation and reading.) They also participated in sports in their clubs, boating in summer or skating and skeeing in winter, equipment being furnished free to members. As to the children, the second worker had no particular plans for them, beyond simple moral instruction, some anti-religious propaganda to counteract the teachings of the grand mother such as singing revolutionary and Pioneer songs instead of religious, elementary school education, and, if they wished, higher, or a trade or profession according to their desires. In answer to the question as to his ambitions for them to occupy a high position in life, like *that of a* government official *for instance*, he replied that it was all the same to him; that they would get what they deserved and as for material compensation, a government official might get 225 roubles or more, and a factory worker, skilled, could also make as much. Besides the income of the children did not concern the father. As to the daughter, no, he had no ambition to see her grow up and be married and be a respectable wife and mother. What she did with her life was her business. If she wanted to marry and live with one *man* all right. If she wanted to divorce him and take another all right; that was all her choice. The important thing was that she

36. A *kino* in Europe and Russia is a motion picture theater.

should be an independent individual, able to make her own living. The first worker made similar answers. The bank clerk was 27, made 130 roubles a month and expected a baby soon. He was a worker 14 years before he became a clerk, first a shepherd boy of ten years and then an unskilled worker. He studied and learned office work and for two years had worked as an 'intellectual worker.' No, his new job did not give him a superior social position and he felt much nearer to the workers than to the 'sluzhishchi'.[37] In reply to a general question as to the difficulties of living on a small income, the second worker smiled and replied: "If we have less we spend less and if we have more we spend more, and always we manage to live somehow."

Some questions were asked about conditions in America, and I described the high standard of living there, the high state of industrialisation and the debt the world owes to the capitalists who developed the industrial power of the country.

The quarters of Dinamov are very simple, there is no sanitary toilet and no bath in the house. We went to visit the new workers flats in the neighbourhood.

About this time Dinamov suggested that we visit a group of new workers tenements or apartments—model tenements, as we would call them, in America. They were only a short walk from his house and consisted of six or seven buildings, each fifty by a hundred and four stories high. They were of red brick, not at all dismal, but set down in an unpaved square or court which, for want of walks or paving of any kind, was muddy & even sloppy—planks being laid here & there to permit one to walk. Inside the walls of halls & rooms were very bare, no particular painting of anything save the iron hand rails of stairs and the wooden baseboards & doors. Each floor contained 8 apartments of 3 rooms each—no bath—one toilet of 1 seat, one hand or wash bowl in the kitchen & one gas stove for all occupants in the same kitchen. Also 1 wash tub. But in each room dwell from two to seven people—making for each apartment (of three rooms) an average of 10 to 15 people. And all of these were supposed— and I presume did use the same toilet in turn, the same wash tubs, hand bowl & single gas stove to cook on. No privacy of any kind. Two married couples with say a child a peice—and others expected living, dressing & undressing & having their various sexual relations in the same room— and with the children present. In another room might be one or two men

---

37. The *sluzhishchi* literally were "service people," that is, officials and bureaucrats.

and one or two women. And the wretched taste of most of them. Despite new walls & floors and a comparatively sanitary arrangement the rooms gave one the mood of a slum—or a Pennsylvania mining village under the rankest tyranny of capitalism. Ah—for taste in furniture, bedding, chairs, knick-knacks. Even a sense of order would have helped. But disorder. And yet with it all geniality and social helpfulness. The will to do cheerfully & well by one another! A strange & interesting people.

Each such group of workers apartments has a club room—this group in a basement of one of the buildings. And the walls, as usual, covered with communist propaganda—a haughty Croesus sitting on a throne—one foot on a chained worker slave! And slogans. "The interest of each is the interest of all." "Comrades remember you are building the state for yourselves." And red flags & banners. And a gun & its workings shown ideographically. As well as instructions in connection with the workers duty to the state; physical and technical preparedness. All are led to believe that Europe is ready to pounce on them. Also that it is their duty, once they are strong, to free the worker the world over. In one sense—from the point of view of aggressive as well as defensive thought, Russia is an armed camp.

About this time we returned to Dynamovs and a young tailor in business for himself dropped in and invited us to a christening at his house. We *also* heard that there was a christening at the neighborhood church at five and took a droshky there first. But we arrived too late. The ceremonies were over. But the magnificent interior of the church, lit dimly by candles which cast a soft light here and there on the gleaming golden altars, ikons and lofty ceilings, *repaid me. Obviously* the Russian people formerly poured all of their wealth into their churches, *while they* themselves lived in wretched poverty. This property still belongs to the religious societies.

From here we went to the tailors house, but since the christening was not to be until 9$\underline{^{30}}$ or 10 and it was then only 6—I gave up. In slush & snow we returned via a droshky—my favorite conveyance, to the hotel and later this same night I went with Dynamov to a Russian movie of the middle class. It was not much—might have been called Red Love—since it concerned a love affair under the fighting between the Whites (Kolchak) and the Reds—sometime during 1919-20-21. An English Gold mining company has a concession (from the Whites of course) for mining in Siberia. The English manager (capitalist) has a lovely English daughter played by a solid, rotund Russian girl. The red army threatens. The English concessionaires have to flee, leaving lovely daughter & a young manager to shift for them-

selves. (They are lost in the escape.) And so in good old Siberian snow they come—accidently—upon the lone camp of a Red Engineer—very handsome—and snowed in for the winter. Result rivalry between the Red Engineer and the capitalistic English employe for the hand of the girl. And who should win in Soviet Russia—but the <u>Red</u> Engineer. But justly. The capitalistic employe—to whom by the way the girl was engaged, was a bounder. He could not trap or hunt or fish. He tried to kill the handsome fair minded red—(and secretly), while at the same time the gallantry of the Red in every way was winning the girls heart. Finally in a fight—a threatened fight, between the two men she shuts her old lover out in the snow to die—and he does die. Meantime spring. And innocent relations all this while—between the Russian-English girl & the Red. She even dreams of marriage with him in a formal English way all winter long. Luxury stuff shown in dreams.

But along come the Whites (Kolchakers).[38] *They have been sent from England to rescue the girl. Only meantime—we learn, the Reds have defeated the whites and are coming—by another route, to inform the Red engineer—who was here hiding from the whites. The girl is found & is told she can come home. She wants to take the Red Engineer. He will not go. She must stay here & join the revolution. They argue. She pleads. Meantime her rescuers learn that her lover is a Red & decide to kill him. He thinks that she has connived with them & flees, seizing the auto boat on which her rescuers come. And with her white friends she is left weeping at the deserted camp at the opening of spring . . . . . Not quite as bad as Hollywood but almost.*

N. B. These Russian movie houses are built on a better plan than the American. Instead of the crowds waiting in the street & blockading traffic as well as suffering in cold or rain, all are permitted to enter & wait in a great enclosed lobby where, during the waiting, an orchestra plays American jazz & sentimental songs. When the first show crowd is out, the second is admitted from this lobby. . . . . I know these words. chi = tea; molokai = milk; Saccha-sugar; Pschallister = please; auchin or ochin = very; Narrasho = good, (as we say "good, good"; Tovarisch = Comrade; Kascha = cat; ⌊   ⌋ *= dog; "wool, wool, wool"—said to a dog or cat means hyuh—or come here.*

---

38. So called after one of their leaders, Aleksandr Vasilyevich Kolchak (1874–1920), a Russian counterrevolutionary and admiral.

Moscow
Monday, Nov. 14th, 1927.

In the morning, I went to the candy factory Krasni Oktyabr (Red October), a very large plant lying on the opposite bank of the river from the Kremlin. We were first taken to the factory committee rooms where I talked with one of the members of the 'Fab-kom'. He explained that as in every factory, there is a committee elected by the workers through their trade union local to look after their interests on the job. This committee consists of 15 members, including eight candidates, and three of these devote all their time to the work and receive salaries from the factory. This committee makes a collective agreement between the workers and the management which is agreed upon point by point at the local trade union meeting. The chief duties of the committee are to see that this agreement is carried out, and in general to look after the interests of the workers individually and collectively. In case of disputes between employer and worker, there is a Conflict Commission on which are equally represented the management and the workers to settle them. The committee also investigates the productive ability of the worker, and if he falls below a certain norm supports the employer in his complaint. The trade union local, 'Mestkom', also elects a representative to the Moscow Soviets and this representative each day during the dinner hour sits in the Fabkom office to interview individual workers. The workers eat their dinner in the dining room of the factory. The union has a club in the factory also. Red October has 2,600 workers and employees.

In reply to the question as to raw materials, the comm. member explained that the Food Dept. of the government supplies all materials to food product factories through its ware houses. As to the possibility of graft here, the workers in the Fabkom who had gathered about us, were unanimous in thinking that it was practically impossible, because of the strict control and the Workers and Peasants Inspection.

This same committee, by the way, is one of the high executive bodys of the government sitting in Moscow. It can, of its own volition or on complaint, enter any factory, office, bureau or what you will, examine the books, question employes, discharge or hire whom it pleases—even abolish the work or department in its entirety and lay indictments against any whom it deems to have offended against the law. It is not responsible to any higher ups. How it really functions I do not know as yet.

In the same rooms with the Fabkom *factory committee of union workers* are the headquarters of the factory nucleus of the Communist Party, which is the directing influence in the whole factory apparatus.

We then went to the nursery of the factory, which is used by 88% of the women workers. Young children and infants can be brought and left here for ten hours of the day. Nursing mothers are given two hours freedom from their working time (on pay) to come to the nursery and nurse their babies. I was *much* impressed by the idea of the day nursery and also by the modern equipment and attractiveness of the nursery. There were rooms for infants with cribs with trained nurses in attendance, play rooms for the older children, and beds in which they take their mid-day sleep, dining rooms where they are fed and a glass enclosed promenade in process of construction. The head nurse said the death rate in these nurseries was very low compared with former times.

We then went through the factory itself, where various kinds of candy, chocolate and sweet biscuits are made. The machinery was fairly up to date, the rooms clean and orderly, the workers in white aprons, but the wrapping of the many assorted candies is done by hand.

Moscow, Tuesday. Nov. 15, 1927– Grand Hotel

We took an izvozchik to the porcelain museum; the air was frosty and exhilarating. The collection is in the fine old mansion of a textile manufacturer. The outside as usual with Russian houses is unimposing and drab, but inside the rooms are rich and harmonious in furnishings and color. In the den *was* a magnificent fireplace and beautiful wood carving. *Three* rooms are given over to Russian porcelains which are by far the loveliest in the collection. The figures in native costumes in bright colors are the most charming articles, but there are many unusual plates and vases. There is a large exhibition from the factory of Popov, and the majority of the porcelain is from the Imperial Factory. The German things are stodgy, the English collection very small and uninteresting, but the French has a few fine pieces. It is the best collection of its kind I have seen anywhere.

From here we hurried over to keep an appointment with Biedenkapp at the Passage at one o'clock. My secretary finally left me in
Gropper's room and went to attend a meeting at VOKS of Americans as my representative. B. telephoned that he would not be able
to come until two. After waiting until almost three I came home.

The meeting at VOKS was to discuss *its branch* organisation in
America and was participated in by most of the American guests
now in Moscow. Madam Kameneva gave a long report on the work
of the central organisation, and suggestions for the work in the U.S.

In the evening I attended the banquet of the Presidium of the
Moscow Soviets, at which perhaps a thousand foreign guests were
present. *(This invitation was extended by the Central Committee of the
Moscow Soviets. Here I met Biedenkapp who was the original mover in
my trip to Russia. Since coming here I had become dissatisfied with the
complete indifference of the Society of Cultural Relations (which extended
the invitation for the Soviet Government) to my presence here. Many affairs had occurred to which I was not invited—and worse—because of
some quarrel between the Society and Madame Kameneva, its head, and
Biendenkapp—and his International Workers Aid—also a Soviet Agency,
I was being ignored. Even the promised tour of Russia—agreed upon between me & Biedenkapp, was in question. And all that had previously
been fully explained to me by my local secretary—Ruth Kennell. And made
angry by this development I had—late Sunday night—stated to Merwich
of the Associated Press, who had dropped into my room, that unless things
were straightened out very quickly I was going to return to New York. This
caused him, on his own initiative, to warn the foreign office that I was about
so to do and that the effect on public sentiment might not be of the best. He
had told me—over the telephone—and just before my coming to this dinner
—that he had so done, and he was satisfied from what he heard there that
the foreign office would take action at once and that Vox (Russian conden-
sation of the words which mean Society for Cultural Relations—Madame
Kameneva, Komissar) would be frightened into immediate action. And so
it proved. For no sooner was I seated in the hall then first a Miss Brannan
—American Secretary of the American or New York office of this Soviet
department came over to my table and inquired if I would be the guest of
Kameneva at some function for foreign writers. I told her I would not &
then proceeded in no uncertain terms to say why. She became so nervous
as I talked that her voice trembled as she talked. But, oh, she was so sorry.
She was so sure that Madame Kameneva had not understood. The mistake*

had been that I had first been invited by Biedenkamp, but she was sure that it all could & would be straightened out if only I would accept Madame Kamenevas attentions from now on. "Listen—I said. "I am under no obligations to anyone here. I was invited by the Soviet Government. Cables exchanged between the Amalgamated Bank of New York and Kameneva & the Soviet Foreign Office prove that. Yet I have been treated vilely. Now Madame Kameneva and the Soviet Government can go to hell. I have employed a secretary of my own, although I was offered one from New York & back, & I have spent my own money for what I have seen. What I desire is the cash return of my expenditures and that is all. Then I shall go". But evidently the foreign office had already spoken, for now came hurrying Madame Kameneva herself. And with an interpreter. There was singing and Caucasian folk dances going on at the time. Ah, she would like to speak with me. There had been a mistake. She had not understood clearly. She had assumed that I was being taken care of. Of course, of course. I had a reason for anger. But tomorrow early her secretary would wait on me. Any trip I planned, any thing I wish to see; and people—Soviet executives or leaders I wished to meet, were at my disposal. All would be arranged— my expenses—my least wishes. I merely looked at her meaningfully & let it go. And although she requested me to wait & meet Rykov, Chairman of the Council of Peoples Commissaries of USSR—I left at 11^{00}.

After in the lobby of the hotel I met Rezkov. (Associated Press). He was waiting to repeat what he had said over the telephone. I said that evidently the foreign office had acted & explained why. He agreed & told me that they had assured him that all my wishes from now on would be respected.

Moscow–Wednesday, Nov. 16– 1927 – Grand Hotel

At 10 a.m. the secretary of VOKS, Mr. Karenets, with an interpreter to go over my plans for a tour of Russia. Everything seems to be moving at last He was effusively polite and apolgetic. There had been a mistake. Now what did I wish. I explained very succinctly. Arrangements at once—tickets, hotels, local advisers for my travels and stops in various parts of Russia—Leningrad, Novgorod, Sverdlovsk, Ansk, Novorechinsk, Saratov, The Caucasus, Tiflis, Baku, Batumi, The Crimea, Odessa, Kiev, Kharkoff & Vicu. Either Odessa—or Moscow—with full passage—first class—to New York. He agreed. Why of course, of course.

And now as to things here in Moscow. Whom did I wish to meet. I gave him a list—Stalin.

Done. And now sights, museums. The Kremlin. Yes, the Kremlin. He left saying all would begin tomorrow. Oh yes. And my 550 expenses so far. Yes yes. These too.

Afterwards a visit *to* an elementary school which Nearing had recommended. I met him there. The art instructor in the school L ⌐ ⌐ ⌐ ⌐ ⌐ ⌐ ⌐ ⌐ ⌐ ⌐ has his studio in the building and showed us some of his paintings, one of which (a peasant religious procession in the woods) I purchased for 50 roubles. There is a large art class of boys and girls from ten to 15 all working industriously in a small room, drawing pictures of the October celebrations. We looked into a class room where boys and girls of 8 and 9 yrs (2nd grade) were busy at their work. I noticed at once a difference in this classroom. There *was* a loud buzz of noise, the children moving about and talking freely and the teacher here and there helping them. They were weaving baskets out of straw twine.

At the same time, as I learned then, they were discussing the chemical & physical basis of such a product—texture, methods of growth and existence—and its economic & cultural uses in life—in so far as such things could be even touched on by children of that age. At the same time I learned that there are no courses of study in the old sense of the word. The children learn through daily observation and experience. They have four themes in the year; life in spring, life in summer, life in fall and in winter. The teacher's textbook directs *their* observations with questions and problems, for instance, the birds of spring, to be answered after excursions and examination of the birds. The daily routine is first general conversation on the theme of the period, then letter writing on this theme, then physical culture, reading and discussion. This school has self-management, a school committee of five students with various departments such as cultural, sanitation, etc. with other committee members. Always one member is on duty to attend to the carrying out of the routine, discipline, etc. As in every Soviet organisation, whether factory, office or school, the Communist Party exercises a directing influence. Here the Young Pioneers have their club and organisation which because of its united numbers can elect its representative on the Managing Committee. It in turn is directed by the older Party members in the

Young Communist organisation into which the Pioneers eventually graduate.

The general impression *I took was* that the children *were being* kept tremendously busy with interesting and responsible work and had little time for mischief.

Nevertheless I was dubious as to the sexual effect of this early contact. In some of these rooms these boys and girls—9 and 10—or 13 & 14 years of age were alone. And most of them attractive. In two places I saw a boy and a girl flirting—the usual tense approach of youth to youth. And without supervision. I tried to learn by inquiry the general moral condition in these schools but gathered none-too-informed opinions from people not intimately connected with the work. I have yet to learn.

From here to one of the general museums but it was just closing.

Before returning to the hotel, I looked in at the altar on the Red Square, 'The Mother of God' chapel, formerly the 'holiest spot in Russia.'[39] On the wall above have been written the words 'Religion is the Opiate of the People'. The people were taking their opiate in great numbers, picturesque beggars stood in two lines before the door. Inside the tiny place the candles were lighted, and innumerable golden pictures and ikons gleamed. A priest with a long black beard was reading the service and an assistant, *dirty & long bearded,* moved through the crowd contributing to the service at regular intervals with a 'Lord have mercy!' but like an automaton. The worshippers entered, paid for tapers, lighted and placed them on the central altar. The priest took the Bible and, touching the bowed head of each person, repeated phrases such as 'God bless you', 'Love one another', etc. *And possibly such an opiate is worth some thing although for me the soviet idea is better.*

At 6 p.m. I went to keep an appointment with Sergei Eisenstein, *one* of the *Sovekino* movie directors, *also the* author and director of 'Potemkin'.[40] His room, one of a flat of six rooms occupied by six

39. Dreiser is referring to the chapel of the famous Icon of Kazan in Kazan Cathedral. Considered a holy place, it was the object of religious pilgrimages and therefore a special target of the new government. It was destroyed by Stalin in the 1930s; a new cathedral was built in its place in the early 1990s.

40. Sergei Mikhailovich Eisenstein (1898–1948), the most famous Russian movie director of his time. His films include *Strike* (1925), *Battleship Potemkin* (1925), and *October* (1927). His relations with the Soviet government were troubled, especially regarding the two-part film *Ivan the Terrible* (1944–45), an allegory of Stalin. In 1930 Eisenstein, then in Hollywood, collaborated with Ivor Montagu on a script for *An American Tragedy*. Clyde Griffiths was absolved of guilt in this script (the blame was placed on society); Paramount declined to pro-

kept tremendously busy with interesting and responsible work and had little time for mischief.

Nevertheless I was dubious as to the sexual effect of this early control. In some of these rooms these boys and girls - 9 and 10 - or 13 + 14 years of age were alone. And most of them attractive. In two places I saw a boy and a girl flirting - the usual tense approach of youth to youth. And without supervision. I tried to learn by inquiry the general moral condition in these schools but gathered none - too informed opinions from people not intimately connected with the work. I have yet to learn.

From here to one of the general museums but it was just closing

Before returning to the hotel, I looked in at the altar on the Red Square 'The Mother of God' chapel, formerly the 'holiest spot in Russia. On the wall above have been written the words 'Religion is the Opiate of the People'. The people were taking their opiate in great numbers, picturesque beggars stood in two lines before the door. Inside the tiny place the candles were lighted, and innumerable golden pictures and ikons gleamed. A priest with a long black beard was reading the service and an assistant moved through the crowd contributing to the service at regular intervals with a 'Lord have mercy!' Like an automaton The worshippers entered, paid for tapers, lighted and placed them on the central altar. The priest took the Bible and touching the bowed head of each person repeated phrases such as 'God bless you', 'Love one another', etc. And possibly such an opiate is worth something although for me the soviet idea is better.

Diary leaf 164, with Dreiser's autograph insert. (From the Theodore Dreiser Collection, Special Collections Department, Van Pelt–Dietrich Library Center, University of Pennsylvania, Philadelphia)

Sergei Eisenstein around 1927. (From the Russian State Archives of Film and Photo Documents, Moscow)

families, was very *small for New York but* spacious for Moscow. He
had decorated the walls himself with a fantastic bulls eye in a series
of convolutions in color on the ceiling, a placard advertising a new
cream separator above his desk, and kino photos on the walls. He
has a very wide bed, *the largest I have seen in Russia,* and when I remarked that I had seen only very narrow beds thus far, he replied

---

duce the film. See Richard Lingeman, *Theodore Dreiser: An American Journey, 1908–1945* (New
York: G. P. Putnam's Sons, 1990), 340–43; also Keith Cohen, "Eisenstein's Subversive Adap-
tation." In *The Classic American Novel and the Movies,* ed. Gerald Peary and Roger Shatzkin
(New York: Ungar, 1977).

that he had bought this magnificent bed from an American farming commune near Moscow where he was taking pictures. He is a young fellow of 29 years, short, a little stout, with a fair, boyish face and blue eyes, and a mass of thick, curly hair.

I began with a question about the general organisation of the movie industry in Russia. He said that it is all government and comes under the Department of Education (Lunacharsky), as a separate branch with manager, etc. There is strict control as in America, only here it is political whereas in the U.S. it is moral. About kino production, he said that there had been only three or four great pictures produced during the past three years: Potemkin, *his own by the way*, Pudovkin's Mother (from Gorki).[41] The Soviet picture follows three general lines: *His own—or the naturalistic—as he modestly announced; the Western type—meaning those which imitate the American product in all its ramifications and the out and out chronicle of some life or movement. (His own, by the way are not much more than that.) Also, of course—the educational or scientific—and intended for educational and scientific purposes. The theory of Eisenstein as to what is best & greatest in the movies—and as outlined by himself, is first, no plot*, no dramatic stories, but pictures which are more nearly poems; second, no actors, but people direct from the streets or places where the pictures are taken; this is possible because he has no big dramatic scenes, but makes of daily life itself a drama, a natural drama. For instance, his new picture, not yet shown, 'The General Line', is *as he sees it* a demonstration of how a poor village is through cooperation developed.[42]

He considers the Cabinet of Dr. Caligari the wrong method in moving pictures, that expressionism is not adaptable to the kino art![43] He is interested in individual stories only if they are on very broad lines, illustrating general human principles. He is now working on the idea of filming Marx's Capital, like a speech.

I remarked that he was another propagater of the Soviet system, and asked him what he would do with his ideas in South Africa, for instance. He said he would adapt them to suit local conditions, perhaps concentrate on the colonial question. If in America, he would

41. *Mother* (*Mat*), directed by V. I. Pudovkin (1926), from the novel by Maxim Gorky.
42. *The General Line*, Eisenstein's movie project treating agricultural collectives, had been suspended on government orders in 1926. It was remade as *Old and New* (1929).
43. *The Cabinet of Dr. Caligari*, famous German expressionist film directed by Robert Wiene (1919).

try to do only liberal things, perhaps in the negro question. I told him then that he is an 'uplifter'.

About the financial cost of production, October cost 500,000 roubles; Eisenstein received 600 roubles for his scenario 'The General Line', which will cost about 75,000 to produce. Potemkin cost 54,000. The heroine of The General Line received a salary of 150 roubles a month. Of course an old artist of the Art Theater like Leonidov receives 100 roubles a day. He says he has a very bad, little studio, but a new modern studio is under construction.

I remarked in general about Russia that the Russian temperament is such that in 30 yrs. Russia will lead the world. As in America the wilderness *is a great impetus,—also the vast and as yet unpopulated spaces. As yet here is a federation of 167 separate races or nationalities, many of them as yet not speaking the same language or indulging in the same customs, yet all fired & joined by the Soviet idea—and what might not come out of that. Also because of the enormous favor with which the Soviet program is viewed—i.e.—the making over of Russia into a modern economic state, all—apparently without exception, were working for Russia and the achievement of this ideal. Hence it was but natural that writers, artists, poets, playwrights, kino-directors and what you will should be swept into the movie and should see only the uplift as the proper field of drama, poetry, literature, art. As for myself I still considered that the drama of the individual came first, his private trials, terrors & delights, since only through the individual could the mass & its dreams be served and interpreted. He would not agree. Nor was he aware apparently that pictures as good as Potemkin—and in the same field, had been done in America. Dimly he thought he had heard of "Grass"—but not of "Nanook", not of "Chang"; not of "The Iron Horse" or "The Covered Wagon'—yet to me (I did not say so to him) they are just as good.*[44] We had tea & cakes (as usual) and I left. And Ruth Kennell and myself had dinner at the hotel. About nine oclock Karl Rodek, a Polish Jew and an international communist who, at the beginning of the Russian revolution, espoused the cause of Lenin and Trotsky, and during the last three years of his life was very close*

44. Dreiser mentions five American films here: *Grass: A Nation's Battle for Life*, a documentary film about a tribe of nomads in Iran, produced and directed by Merian Cooper, Ernest B. Schoedsack, and Marguerite Harrison (1925); *Nanook of the North*, a film about Eskimos, directed by Robert J. Flaherty (1922); *Chang*, a documentary shot in Magnascope in the jungles of northern Siam, directed by Ernest B. Schoedsack (1927); *The Iron Horse*, John Ford's first major Western (1924); *The Covered Wagon*, one of the earliest and most influential Westerns, directed by James Cruze (1923).

to Lenin—(a personal friend and private as well as official adviser) came to see me. He reminded me in size and tempo of Peter McCord—quite all of the same intellectual fire and much of the same genial human response.[45] He told me much of the Russians, the Revolution and Trotzkys personal life & predilections—a most intimate and fascinating picture. Among other things that he said of Lenin was that he was a tireless worker, fearless, unselfish and generous to a fault. He knew nothing thoroughly of the details of any science or philosophy and yet was thoroughly capable of sensing the drift and meaning of every science and theory and most brilliant in seizing upon any idea in any field which might be of any advantage to Russia. One of the things he said that Lenin said was that electricity and and education should go hand in hand in Russia. Another that Russia, because of its generous and almost sacrificial spirit, was the best country in the world in which to try communism. He described him as short and homely—and unbelievably fascinating—the Socratic temperament. Also he stated that no bust or picture of Lenin as yet resembled him—that there was some thing in his temperament; the mental and emotional feel of him that transcended characterization. He did not read much—only practical books on electricity, economics and industrialization. All other matters including newspapers & magazines had to be read by others & reported to him in a condensed form. When he was very tired physically & mentally he loved to relax and read Conan Doyle—(The Adventures of Sherlock Holmes . . . . . After an hour or so of this, the conversation veered to literature and art—the new communistic literature and art of which he did not think so much; although he believed it might develop. Next we took up the quarrel between Trotzky & Stalin and he explained that—the temperament of the Peasent, the leaning of Stalin toward the Peasent & the faith of Trotzky in the mechanic or industrial worker—who was more malleable, more enthusiastic more receptive to communistic ideals and would be trusted to support the new rule, whereas the peasant could not. At midnight he left & I went to bed.

Because of an introduction to him I had tried to call on him in the Kremlin at four, but the guard at the propusk office said he did not answer the telephone. On arriving home, I telephoned at once to his apartment in the Kremlin and he answered, explaining that no individual foreigners are now being admitted to the Kremlin and that he would come to me. When he did come he explained to me that the rea-

45. Peter McCord, illustrator and friend of Dreiser's during his early days as a journalist. McCord is the "Peter" of Twelve Men.

son no messages were conveyed to him in the Kremlin was that, since the quarrel between Trotzky & Stalin, all friends of Trotzky & especially those living in the Kremlin were being watched, the suspicion being that Trotzky & his followers might attempt to organize a new party. As for himself he said he had lived through the most glorious page in Russian history & was now going to retire and write a history of Lenin. He left at midnight.

Moscow, Thursday, Nov. 17th, 1927.

In the morning, I went in response to Eisenstein's invitation to a special showing of parts of his pictures 'October' and 'The General Line'.

October is a series of scenes from the October Revolution in Petrograd, the storming of the Winter Palace, etc. It moves swiftly and is exciting *but not so moving, to me.*

The General Line is a series of realistic village scenes, for instance, a *peasent* religious procession taken from life, a model government dairy, an incident showing a poor peasant woman coming to a rich peasant and asking for the loan of a horse to help harvest a crop. The rich peasant and his wife are simply rolling in fat, and so are their live stock, but their luxury reminds one of the feudal barons in its primitiveness. Following the appearance of the fat wife on the screen, there is shown a wax figure of a pig whirling coquettishly, and the resemblance to the woman is comical.

At one I had an appointment with the manager of Gossizdat, *the State publishing house of Russia & the one that is about to bring out all my books,* and in the course of fifty minutes we managed to conclude an agreement. *The chief Executive of this concern* offered me 750 roubles for the two books already published, 'Color of a Great City' and three stories from 'Twelve Men'. I refused to accept it and said they could have it as a gift. The manager said he did not wish to accept a gift from me, but wished to make a satisfactory agreement, to clear up past debts in order to have—good relations in the future. After some explanations why the books were cut (to make them accessible to the workers) and why they offered so little, they asked what I would take; I said 1000 dollars, and we made an agreement on this basis, that I should further agree to give them exclusive publishing rights in Russia and send manuscripts to be published not earlier than one month after American and English pub. to be paid for at the rate of 600 dollars to 1000 for each book (Gallery of

Moscow, Thursday, Nov.17th,1927.

In the morning, I went in response to
Eisenstein's invitation to a special showing of
parts of his pictures 'October' and 'The General
Line'.

October is a series of scenes from the
October Revolution in Petrograd, the storming
of the Winter Palace, etc. It moves swiftly
and is ~~deeply~~ exciting *but not so moving. too ~~me~~*
The General Line is a series of realistic
village scenes, for instance, a *reveuy* religious procession taken from life, a model government dairy,
an incident showing a poor peasant woman coming
to a rich peasant and asking for the loan of a
horse to help harvest a crop. The rich peasant
and his wife are simply rolling in fat, and so
are their live stock, but their luxury reminds
one of the feudal barons in its primitiveness.
Following the appearance of the fat wife on the
screen, there is shown a wax figure of a pig
whirling coquettishly, and the resemblance to
the woman is comical.

(The chief executive of this concern) / *the State publishing house of Russia + the one that is about to bring out all my books*

At one I had an appointment with the
manager of Gossizdat, and in the course of fifty
minutes we managed to conclude an agreement.
He offered me £ 750 roubles for the two books
already published 'Color of a Great City' and
three stories from 'Twelve Men'. I refused to
accept it and said they could have it as a gift.
The manager said he did not wish to accept a gift
from me, but wished to make a satisfactory agreement, to clear up past debts in order to have a
good relations in the future. After some explanations why the books were cut (to make them
accessible to the workers) and why they offered
so little, they asked what I would take; I said
1000 dollars, and we made an agreement thatxxI on
this basis, that I should further agree to give
them exclusive publishing rights in Russia and send
manuscripts to be published not earlier than one
month after American and English pub. to be paid
for at the rate of 600 dollars to 1000 for each
book (Gallery of Women, 1000) and advertising campaign for the books and for the ethical publishing
rights *between America and Russia. We then*

Diary leaf 171, with Dreiser's additions. (From the Theodore Dreiser Collection,
Special Collections Department, Van Pelt–Dietrich Library Center, University
of Pennsylvania, Philadelphia)

Women, 1000) and advertising campaign for the books and for ethical publishing rights *between America and Russia.*[46] *We then returned to the hotel, and because I was tired I went to bed and rested until evening.* At six oclock Harold Ware, director of the Government Farm in the Ukraine Sovhoz No. 4, had dinner with me and told me about the work of the American group in introducing American machinery and methods into Russian agriculture. *He and some other American enthusiasts came here some few years ago and secured from the Russian Government a tract of about 70,000 acres in the Caucasus onto which they introduced the very latest American farming machinery—tractors, combination reaper-threshers, 22 blade plows and the like. With this and a permit to work laborers twelve hours at a stretch instead of six (with the next day off) they managed to use the machinery to the limit—and so opened the eyes of the natives and even the Russian Government that representatives of other Russian Agricultural stations came from long distances to see what they were doing. And all this with peasents in the adjoining fields ploughing with single bladed plows—the same hauled by oxen or camels— and the tradition of of hundreds of years. He also told how one day a peasent who had broken his small scythe came to borrow one. They had none to lend him and were about to turn him away when one of the men suggested that, since they had a welding plant, they could fix it. Accordingly they took it & joined it quite as good as new. But when they returned it the peasent would not believe it was his. How could a broken scythe be made whole. He seemed to suspect a miracle, but, since the handle was the same, took it. Soon thereafter a long procession of peasents with broken or injured tools, most of which could be fixed—and which in order to establish cultural relations with them they did fix, finally enlightening and improving technically most of the district in which the great farm lay.*

Another interesting point was this. I asked about the proverbial laziness & slowness of the peasent. Would not this interfere with the proper industrialization of Russia—its dream of keeping step with the world? He seemed to think not. In the first place he said that he was sure that their slowness & laziness was in most part due to undernourishment—due to a not sufficiently varied diet. Mostly their diet was a soup, black bread and potatoes—never meat. And because of this lack of meat they were weak

46. N'iu Iork [*The Color of a Great City*], trans. P. Okhrimenko (Moscow: Gosudarstvennoe Izdate'stvo, 1927); *Gallereia Zhenshchin* [*A Gallery of Women*], trans. V. Stanevich and V. Barbashovaia; intro. S. S. Dinamov (Moscow: Gosudar stvennoe Izdatel'stvo Khudozhestvennaia Literatura, 1933).

and had to rest a great deal. In the case of this experiment station, and to overcome this, he gave orders—without word to any peasent, to put meat in all soups twice a day. The result was a highly increased working capacity, less sleep—or lying about, and much more vivacity. Also he thought that the Russians' present leisurely temperament might & no doubt would be affected & speeded by the machine, which must be worked at its own speed—not at that of the operative.

I was especially interested in his account of the locust plagues which were such a terrible thing in Russia formerly. Two years ago, there was a terrible plague, they swept down from the sandy lowlands where they had hatched in great armies several miles long and wide, and not only laid waste the fields but laid their eggs which hatched out this summer. The local government quickly organised a chemical warfare which was remarkably successful. Every peasant was compelled to serve three days on pay in the work of spraying the fields and was fined if he did not report, and was paid 1.50 a day if he did. In a few days the whole area was completely sprayed and the hatching locusts and their eggs killed. The plague was completely stopped in its beginnings, and it was a wonderful demonstration of united effort.

Another phase of this was as follows: In a certain district twenty or thirty miles wide and forty miles long an enormous cloud of locusts appeared. The sun was darkened. They were flying some where to lay their eggs and eating as they went. An appeal was at once sent to the central Soviet of the region. This in turn, by wire, applied to the Central Soviet Agricultural bureau for advice. The reply was aero-planes with distructive gases. These descended on the cloud from various directions and spraying them distroyed them all. Their eggs were never laid & they did not eat.

In the evening I went to the opera <u>Prince Igor</u>, at the Bolshoi Opera House, with Anna Louise Strong. This is an opera of no particular dramatic value but much local color. Scenically & musically it was beautifully presented. During the intervals Anna & I talked of Russia. Like so many American intellectuals she is enormously fascinated by the Russian temperament. She had traveled from China to Leningrad—spent several years, in fact, wandering here & there. Like so many others, her conclusions are that the Russians are strong, practical, artistic, sensitive, idealistic, brotherly and need only the persistence of such a government as they now have to develop one of the leading governments. True, in Moscow their tends to develop a bureaucratic group which is likely to develop auto-cratic and self-sustaining notions—but so far the check exercised by the workers & peasents is too strong. She told also of rivalries & bitternesses, as in other forms of goverment, but in the main the development of the mass is rapidly being forwarded

Moscow, Friday, Nov. 18– 1927–Grand

The feel of Russia is peculiar—restful to me—and is, I gather, to many. For instance Madame Litvinov, the wife of the foreign minister, told me that when she was out of Russia she was always restless & running here & there, competing with whosoever was competing for anything—clothes, contacts, what not. But once here, all these things seemed to fall away; nothing mattered much. Clothes were poor; social advance all but impossible; wealth impossible—only agreeable personal contacts available, where one could find them. "And yet I am happier" she said. "I dont care. Like everybody else I work—part time for my husband as a typist & translator; part time for one of the government bureaus as a translator. I get 200 roubles a month. You see how I dress. And I have no social life. There is no such thing here—no social doings among the bureaucrats. Once a month my husband and I give a reception to 150. It is dull—official. Yet I am happy here—happier than anywhere I think (and I am English) and often wonder why?" I could not answer her at the time—but now—10 days later, I think I can. It is due to the absence of national worry over ones future,—or the means of subsistence. Here ones future and ones subsistence is really bound up with that of the nation itself. If it prospers you are certain to prosper; if it fails you fail. But so long as it has any prosperity or even a bare living, you have. Each one is allotted so much for what he can do—but no more than 250 roubles a month—and a room or a part of one. There is no graft. His old age, his passing illnesses, his need of rest & fair share of pleasure are all looked after by the state. If he cannot find work at least he gets fifteen roubles a month, treatment when he is ill. Medicine—at last, if necessary, care for himself in a home for the defeated or the incompetent. There are no longer any sly religionists to bedevil him; no preying upon him by police or officials. If he cannot afford fine raiment, neither can anyone else. If his quarters are small or poor, so are those of quite all others. His true station—as yet, is fixed by his mind or his skill or both—and such pleasures as there are are open to all on the same terms. The restaurants and hotels are poor, but there are no better ones to which any can slyly run. And as you walk the streets, at least, you are not made miserable by extremes of poverty and wealth. If there are beggars you know that more or less they are grafters. If their are distinguished people, it is because of their very real present or past achievements and their mental qualities. Family, wealth, titles, even security—other than state security, are all gone.

Another thought which has come to me in connection with the operation of this form of government is this. Considering all the checks and balances—and the apparently graftless phase of all administrative functions, it looks to me as though the destructive evil of adulteration had been cured. Why adulteration of foods, drugs, clothing, "jerry" built houses, machinery, furniture, articles of virtue if there is no private concern competing with another private concern for success in a given field—or for money or position as between individuals? All goods appear to be, and I think they are, real—and well worth—(much more so as capitalistic standards go) all that is asked for them and more. The thought, when it first comes to one, as I went in a land in which graft and fraud and adulteration on every hand is rampant, is thrilling. It gives one an idea of a possible fairness in nature, which judging of life as it has been—seems impossible—as though at last—and first time, the sun of mind has fenestrated and dissolved a miasma of not-mind. So it is that in Russia now, life takes on not only a more secure but even friendly look. It is easier to live because all are agreed apparently to let live—and to work & so help make that possible.

+   +   +   +   +   +   +   +

At 10:30 this morning, by pre-arrangement of course I had an interview with Novokshonov, president of the local trade union of writers and also of the All-Russian Federation of Writers. I was interested to know what a trade union of writers might be like. It was in a charming old building in the ∟   ⌐ part of Moscow, which I very much like. When I entered, Barbusse was sitting in his office signing papers, it seems for membership in the Federation of Writers. These different organisations of writers, including one called 'Proletarian Writers', have their headquarters in this large building set back in a courtyard, formerly the home of Gertzen, the Russian writer.[47]

In answer to my questions regarding the trade union of writers, he explained that the chief function of the union is to protect the interests of their members, for instance in concluding agreements

47. More recently Gertzen's name has been rendered as Alexander Ivanovich Herzen (1812–70), novelist, writer, philosopher, and after 1847 a revolutionary exile in Western Europe; his theory of socialism, influential in Soviet thinking, was based on the peasant commune. In London he began the Russian Press and published the journal *Kolokol* (*The Bell*) from 1857 to 1861.

with publishers, in the carrying out of the agreements, fixing of norms of payment for work. Payment is fixed as follows:

125 roubles min. for 40,000 typographical signs, or 10 pages.

1,500 roubles for the first edition (5,000) and 50% of the original sum for all editions thereafter. An agreement can be entered into for only three years, after which a new agreement must be drawn up.

In connection with the union, is a consultation of attorneys who protect, free of charge, and give advice to the members. The union sends a representative to the Moscow Soviet and to the People's Court, which consists of three members, for instance, 1 a worker, 1 a writer, and the third a permanent member. As an example of the work of the union in defending members, I was given a copy of the case of a libretto writer who wrote the Russian text for Madame Butterfly, against the Bolshoi Opera House, which did not pay him 750 roubles for it. This was an old debt contracted before the revolution. Nevertheless, the decision was to pay the money.

In Moscow there are 1,100 writers, including newspaper men but not workers correspondents, and in all of the Soviet Union, 9,500 writers, all members of the trade union. Asked if there were any writers who did not wish to belong to the union, Novokshonov replied that of course not, as they have everything to gain and nothing to lose by membership. They paid 2 1/2% union dues and received all the usual benefits of members of trade unions in Soviet Russia: free medical treatment, vacations in rest homes in the south, social life in the union clubs, etc.

We then discussed the possibility of my joining the Federation of Russian Writers, which I have decided to do.

I was shown an exhibit of Russian literature in the rooms below, rooms devoted to Pushkin, Tolstoy, Dosteovsky, revolutionary writers, new writers, etc. Everywhere you go you see charts and diagrams giving information in every conceivable form, and here such charts were not missing: analysis of the books about Tolstoy in colors, book production. It was also to be remarked that there were more books being published about authors than by them. There is also a dining room where the writers and dramatists dine very cheaply (40 kopeks for dinner for members), a jolly looking place, no doubt very lively and picturesque when full of literary people.

I went over to VOKS and had a session with Kameneva, Karenets, Trivas and secretary about my programme while in Moscow and about my trip about Russia. *There it was agreed that VOKS (the Government Society For Cultural relations) would undertake to introduce me to principal ministers and members of the Communist party here, also to provide me with two secretaries and all of my needs & introductions for my trip around Russia. A list of all the persons I wished to meet was made. Also I was repaid in cash the $550 expended by me between New York & Moscow (my expenses) and promised every facility for inquiry on the long trip.*

At 5 p.m. I went to have dinner with Miyakovsky, Russia's strongest writer, who belong to the group 'Left'—a young giant, the image of an American prize fighter. Breek, a literary critic and his charming wife, 'Lilichka', Tretyakov, author of the play produced at the Mierhold Theater 'Roar, China', and his wife, Tretyakova, also an editor, were there.[48] These are the center of the Left group and direct its policies. There was also a very friendly bull terrier. We began eating a variety of things, caviar in a huge bowl, several kinds of fish, Russian meat rolls, vodka, wine, and making light jokes which became merrier as time went on. I had already satisfied myself on the first course when the actual dinner, soup, goose with apples, and many other dishes, appeared. Then there were prunes with whipped cream—I added vodka to the cream and made a wonderful discovery, which they said would be known after my departure as 'Dreiser's cream'. Miyakovsky gave me one of his books of—poetry.

They went along on the street car with us, and we parted with them to keep an appointment with Tairov, director of the Kamerni (chamber) theater. Tairov outlined the policies of the theater, which is well known in Europe as well as in Russia.

The theater conducts a theatrical school for actors, *70 students*, not a usual school, *either*, for the student must learn a mixture of arts: opera, drama, comedy, pantomime, tragedy, for the repertoire is thus varied. The stage settings play an important role and follow special principles, rhythmic, dynamic, plastic, architectural. There is no naturalism, and so the player can to the maximum show his art.

---

48. Vladimir Vladimirovich Mayakovsky (1893–1930), Russian futurist poet, whose best-known revolutionary poems are *Vladimir Ilyich Lenin* (1924) and *Khorosho!* (1927). Sergey Mikhaylovich Tret'yakov (1892–1939), Russian futurist poet and playwright, whose works include the collection *Itog* (1923) and the play *Rychi, Kitay* (Roar, China), which is mentioned here. Both men were associated with the "LEF" literary group, named after its journal *Levvy Front*.

The settings must serve the actor, and be as an instrument for the actors to play on.

In the answer to my inquiry as to their treatment of Macbeth, Tairov answered that he would make a large space for the actors and little scenery, one level for the leaders and another for fantasy.

Light plays an important part in production.

The Kamerni makes a specialty of foreign plays. On what principle are they selected? 1. Scenic composition, dynamic possibilities of play, new architecture. 2. Present day problems and spirit.

Why do they present so many foreign plays? They also present many Russian, but modern Russian plays are scarce. The Soviet drama is still young.

In his opinion, the most vital plays today are produced by 1st, America, 2nd, England, and recently France.

We looked in on the second act of the operetta 'Day and Night'. It seemed to be a light piece with a somewhat futuristic setting. At the end of the act, when the chorus came on, they threw little paper aeroplanes into the audience.

From the Kamerni, we went to the House of the Scientists where Gossizdat was giving a banquet to foreign writers. Miyakovsky was sitting in a conspicuous place at the table and made himself heard during the evening. More food: ten kinds of fish and caviar, and roast pigeons, and more vodka and wine. I think the Russians do nothing but eat, and I am getting the habit. There were toasts to the various foreign writers, among the Americans were Anna Louise Strong, Prof. Dana, Albert Rhys Williams, Mary Reed. I said a few words, and Miyakovsky remarked that I was the first American who admitted, after a short stay in Russia, that he did not have definite impressions and conclusions; he said that usually after a few days in Moscow, they write whole books about the country, and seem to have learned everything.

Opposite me sat the President of Gossizdat, Hallaten, an amazing figure: very dark, with large, brilliant, childlike black eyes, a flowing black beard, a little Caucasian cap on his long waving black hair, black leather short coat, dark shirt with rolling collar, full red lips, and an inscrutable expression, half innocent, half cunning, and amused. I could not keep my eyes off him and began asking him questions: finally he consented to sit down by me and speak about himself. He is an Armenian, and only 33 years old, and before the revolution led a very active agitator's life. I could not seem to get at the man; when I asked him a penetrating question he added another responsible post to his innumerable positions—head of production during the war, now member of the Central Soviets, member of the Scientific Commission, each question about his life was the signal for another voluminous title. I gave up and went with him to another room, where a flashlight photo was taken.

It was two o'clock when we road home through driving snow in an izvozchik.

Moscow Nov. 19th, 1927. *Grand Hotel*

At 4 p.m. I went to interview the Commissary of Trade, Mikhayan, whose spacious offices are in the large building of Narkomtorg (People's Commissariat of Commerce) in the Chinese Wall. I sat down in a very large deep leather chair facing the Commissar, who *was* very imposing *and* military in his khaki uniform and black mustaches. On either side of his desk sat a very meek looking little man and a pretty, innocent looking girl, both of whom knew some English and took turns helping out on translation. The *girls voice trembled as she translated.*

First I asked what were the functions of his department.

1. Interior trade
2. Foreign trade

Importation is small because it has to keep pace with the export. He buys for all Russia, first supplying the government and cooperatives, and then, if there is anything left, private business can have it. Private business can buy goods only from the government. Concession*aires* are allowed to import in accordance with their agreement with the Government. Private business is permitted to buy abroad if the materials are for use in plants and not for selling. No privileges are shown in transporting foreign goods after it enters the country. For instance, if the concessionaire has a license to import goods he can transport in Russia freely.

In importing, what class of goods i.e., necessities, luxuries, are given first place? There is a definite plan of importation on a quarterly basis. There is not enough money to buy all they need (in accordance with our export) and so they buy first for productive enterprises, second, the necessities of the people,—and luxuries not at all.

Do you never use the policy of stimulating buying by selling luxuries?

No, we cannot supply the necessities as yet, but the people use luxuries. We produce ourselves many more luxuries than before the war. However, Russia will never be a luxury consuming country.

Do Soviet agents abroad buy with the same shrewdness as private? Yes, more so, because they have the interests of the Russian people as a whole to consider. All foreign agents are under the Commissar of Trade, They buy under specifications from our consumers, the factories, mass demand, etc.

About complaints of consumers? Very few, because buying must be done according to specifications

Interior Trade.

The Government buys grain products from the peasants, food products, industrial materials. There are two or three great organisations which buy special articles, like cotton, or grain. Prices are fixed to a maximum or a minimum. There is a price plan which is strictly adhered to. Such prices as in America are impossible. A certain level must be maintained, not too high, which would be hard on the worker, not too low for it would ruin the peasant. In America, prices fluctuated greatly during the last year; in Russia, they have remained stationary for two years.

Does the Government demand a profit above wages and upkeep?

Yes, the government *takes* a minimum profit.

In the grain trade there was last year an income of 700 millions and only 8 million profit. The Government takes only amortisation from the profits of industry and 40% from the profits of state organisations, which it uses for the national operations of the country.

From here in a droschky—(which same I delight in). I went direct to the Moscow Art Theater to meet Stanislavsky.[49] I found a tall, magnificent looking old man with white hair, brilliant dark eyes, and in general a face striking for its large strong features. His secretary, a small, dark woman, speaks some English. *I am told he is 80. He looks & acts about 65.*

My first question was in regard to the conditions of his work under the new order. He said that of course it had not been easy to adjust themselves, there had been difficult days, but already they

---

49. Konstantin Stanislavsky (1865–1938), famous Russian actor and director, cofounder of the Moscow Art Theatre. Stanislavsky is remembered for his theories on acting, presented in such books as *An Actor Prepares* (1926) and *Building a Character* (1950). His approaches are known as the Stanislavsky system or as "method acting."

Konstantin Stanislavsky around 1931. (From the Russian State Archives of Film and Photo Documents, Moscow)

were entering upon easier times. The line of art is eternal, and passing conditions do not fundamentally change it. There have been deviations, especially to surface forms, but now the role of art is again on the right path. From the revolution, we must take the good and use it.

As a parable, to illustrate this thought: a group of children stray from the main road into the woods to gather mushrooms or flowers and return with their treasures to the road again. And of their findings there is finally left one small crystal for the immortal urn. During the revolution we strayed far off to look for the new, and that of value which we found becomes a part of immortal art.

What of the old have you discarded, and what of the new have you adopted?

The chief role of the Art Theater has been to maintain the tradition of the art of the actor. Decorations and settings are only important as a background for the actor's art. This is the theory of inner as opposed to surface art. The Art Theater *in Russia* is the only theater which has worked in the province of inner creative art; the rest have occupied themselves with decorations, settings and other surface forms. The revolution brought much that is new in these surface forms and also in new contents of plays. The aesthetic character of the old play has given place to political in the new. For old hymns and new, we must have different voices, and all this is now adjusting itself and goes forward at normal tempo. But, said Stanislavsky, I do not understand and cannot feel that the old plays of Shakespeare can be done according to the present manner. True, I do not say that the new youth does not see Shakespeare through other eyes. And they should produce as they feel. But to tamper with Shakespeare, do the plays over—this is complete lack of understanding of creative art. Art consciousness is a living thing. A person cannot cut off his hand and put it in place of his foot. But *still* we profit by all this experimentation. The worst condition for art is when it stands still; it is better for it to move, even *in the* wrong *direction, than to stand still.*

The union of the new with the old stands out in greatest relief in this theater. When we returned from America we found that the young people looked upon us as aged. But last year, and especially this year, they have begun to understand how much they do not know and how much they could learn from the old. They have come to me from all the theaters, asking me to tell them my secrets. For this reason I have decided that it will be most practical for me to give a series of popular lectures on the art of the actor. I notice, said Stanislavsky, a tendency everywhere to revert to the inner forms of art; people seem to be tired of the surface forms. They are not necessarily bad, some of them are very good: cubism, futurism, impressionism, and a lot of nonsense and stupidity. So we must throw away the bad and keep what is good. For instance, decorations and settings have been much enriched since the revolution, but to the inner art of the actor, the revolution has brought nothing. To the surface actor's art has been added,—movement, gymnastics, dancing, singing, all very valuable.

Surface forms arose out of painting and has gone further than the culture of the actor. The actor stands still. He cannot convey more than the painting. Futurism, etc. cannot be expressed. Therefore many surface form theaters *have gone* ahead of the actor's art. When we learn to use paintings in our technique, they will be of great value. But so far in other theaters the decorations are very advanced, premature, and the actor tries *to* act according to the new settings but is not able to and only spoils the effect. Either the actor plays in the oldest style and the decorations are the newest or vise versa, and therefore there is no harmony. Our theater uses only such decorations as support the art of the actor: for the futurist actor we use futurist decorations.

"Has communism produced any really good plays?" *I asked.*

"No, but as chronicles The Days of the Turbines and 'The Armoured Train' are good, and a new play in preparation in our theater by Leonov, *is really of the best.*[50] *How soon I would be able to do it I cannot say.*

And then he added:

"Art itself is organic and therefore slow to change, but the revolution brought many changes in content. Art will play, and is already playing, a big role politically and educationally *in Russia.* In every factory there is a theater, in every workers club a theatrical circle. All Russia now plays.

After the conversation we went to look at the museum of the Art Theater. Here are valuable collections of manuscripts of plays, old portraits and photographs of actors, costumes, miniature stage settings, props, etc., *gathered during the life of Stanislavsky. As far as I could gather Chekhov was one of his intimate and admired friends and worked with him for years, writing plays for him and aiding him in their staging. He also knew Tolstoy.*

---

50. Leonid Maksimovich Leonov (1899–1994), Russian playwright.

Sunday Nov. 20th, 1927. Moscow–to Yasnaya Polyana

At 12:45 we attempted to board the train to Yasnaya Polyana but found that every car was packed. We had tickets in a 'Maxim Gorki' car, with no place cards. My interpreter went to see the G.P.U. man at the station, and by telling him that an American writer was on his way to Tolstoy's home, a delegate, etc., he arranged for us to be given places in the first car, which happened to be for employees of the railroad. But by the time he had made these arrangements, the train began to pull out. We ran and climbed on the second coach, which was full to overflowing with the real Russian masses. There were three tiers of them lying and sitting on the shelves in the dimly lighted, smelly car, and looking up I could see rows of Russian boots hanging from the three shelves; one fellow had taken his boots off and his bare feet were in close proximity to my face. We stood jammed in the aisle for almost an hour, waiting for a stop; when one came, we jumped off and ran to the first coach where the conductor had already prepared places for us. This was a third class coach, a little cleaner and with definite sleeping places. We lay down on the wooden benches and I slept intermittently, lulled by the slow motion of the train and by the chorus of snores in various keys. At seven in the morning we arrived at the little station of Yasnaya Polyana.

Here was a real winter scene: everything covered with snow and all about thick woods of pine and birch trees. We went into a little house near the station for tea. This house had two rooms and a kitchen between. A family lived in each room, and on either side of the walls were large brick stoves on which the two families cooked, and which warmed their respective rooms. Our host was a young fellow who lay sleeping on a bare wooden bed, fully dressed and with his *felt* boots on. The four children were playing about the bed; presently he aroused himself and took the children up on the bed and gazed drowsily but fondly at them. The young wife heated the samovar and cleaned the table on which she had just made a batch of rye bread.

When we had finished our breakfast, we took a sled filled with straw to Tolstoi's home. We bumped over the road through a good sized village and down an avenue of trees to a two story white house. An old watery eyed caretaker opened the door and agreed to show us the museum—certain rooms left as Tolstoy had lived in them— These rooms were unheated and had a very dreary aspect. They had all the plainness and ugliness of an ordinary American farmhouse: a large living room and dining room with long table and a grand piano, family portraits by Rapine on the walls, his stuffy little study and, adjoining, his bedroom with simple narrow bed, an old wash-stand, his shabby old dressing gown *still* hanging *on the wall*.[51] How frugally he must have lived.

It so happened that today was the 17th anniversary of Tolstoy's death. We followed a path with signposts pointing the way to his grave. It was beautifully situated in a grove of birch and pine trees with no tombstone, according to his wish. But the villagers had *already* covered the mound with evergreen branches. We struggled back through the soft snow, now thoroughly chilled, for the temperature was 10 degrees below. In the village was a big white cement building, a 'Sovkhoz' (government farm), and here we inquired about a place to stop. As soon as they found out that an American writer had come, they made a fuss over us. We were conducted back to the Tolstoy home on the order of Tolstoy's youngest daughter, *Olga*, who had come from Moscow to attend the anniversary. The living quarters of the house presented a more cheerful appearance; in the living room were dining tables, shelves of books, plants and in the corner a tiled stove with a low chair against it which made a very cosy seat. A niece of Tolstoys, an elderly woman, received us most kindly and gave us tea and bread and cheese. Then a sled was called to take us back once more to the grave to attend the memorial services. As our sled came down the path, we followed a procession in single file moving through the snow to the grave, perhaps two hundred peasants of the village and children from the school in Tolstoy's name. They gathered about the grave and decorated it with autumn flowers. The children sang beautifully the old Russian dirge: 'Everlasting Remembrance' (Vechnaya pamyat). Milukov, a friend of Tolstoy, spoke; his daughter spoke, and a quaint little peasant with a shaggy beard and kindly smiling face recited thoughts after Tolstoy's death. Again the children sang the same refrain, and the procession filed quietly back again through the woods.

Returning to the house, we were put to bed upstairs, since we had scarcely slept the night before, and after more than two hours I

51. Ilya Repin (1844–1930), considered the leading realist of his generation. A friend of Tolstoy, he painted many portraits of the novelist and his family.

came downstairs to dinner. There were a number of guests, among them Milukov. The niece speaks English, but is out of practice, the daughter speaks quite well. The niece lost all her wealth in the Revolution, was put in prison for two months, came out with only one dress, but seems philosophical about the new order. She is content to be permitted to live in one room in the house for the rest of her days.

I entered into a lively discussion with Milukov, who seemed to know much about the Russian peasants, on the question of the incompetent peasant, but could get no satisfactory answer from him. He wanted me to deliver a letter to Pres. Coolidge from the peasants of the village, asking him to prevent interference with Russia.

In the evening, the villagers all came to a memorial program in the living room where Tolstoy had always dined and received guests. The old niece was very active in the program. Records of Tolstoy's voice in English, German, French, and Russian were played. The niece played Chopin's Funeral March, the school choir sang a song on his death; a woman read extracts from biographies and reminiscences of Tolstoy's life at Yasnaya Polyana, including one from Stanislavsky's Memoirs. His favorite piece, Beethoven's Pathetique, was played by his niece. The gentle Tolstoyan *peasent* who had recited in the woods now came forward and shyly recited his own poem about Tolstoy. He was a janitor in the school, his coat was shabby and dirty, a little knapsack was slung over his back, he had huge felt boots, and on his simple face was a childlike smile. He was practically illiterate, it seems, *only learned to read & write seven years before*. One of Tolstoy's unpublished stories about his little nieces was read, and every body laughed. There was more music and singing, and the guests went downstairs for tea and sandwiches.

I had a wonderful conversation with the daughter, who told me all about her work.

To avoid the 'Maxim Gorki' train, we rode in sleds to Tula, a large city only about 20 versts from Yasnaya Polyana, leaving at ten o'clock in the night. We were given huge sheepskin shubas, which completely enveloped us from head to foot, and thus arrayed we keep warm in spite of a cold wind in our faces. The horses jogged along slowly toward the light of the city, which was reflected on the sky above the snow fields. On the outskirts of Tula, a city of 200,000, we took a brand new street car, which only recently has come, and rode to the station. There we were able to buy tickets in the Inter-

Ruth Kennell's sketch of the Russian janitor. (From the Theodore Dreiser Collection, Special Collections Department, Van Pelt–Dietrich Library Center, University of Pennsylvania, Philadelphia)

national coach and ride in comparative luxury to Moscow, arriving at 6 in the morning.

<u>*Monday. Nov. 21st 1927– Grand Hotel, Moscow*</u>
Because of lateness of arrival RK staid. I did not get up until eleven. At that time I was notified by VOX that Klimokon, Vice President of the All Russian Co-operatives, would recieve me for an interview. These co-operatives do 50% of all the buying and distributing of goods in Russia, and goods means everything from food & shoes & clothing to ornaments et cetera. They buy for as little as possible in enormous quantities and sell to the people as cheaply as possibly. There is no profit for anyone save the State, which takes expenses of course and something more for necessary but non productive departments such as administrative, corrective, judicial, educational, etc. The interview was at two P.M. R. K and Trevis accompanied me as stenographer (RK) and interpreter (Trevis). Trevis in this instance was unnecessary for Klimokon is a young man, of quiet, rather commonplace appearance, *who* speaks excellent English. He answered my questions intelligently and understandingly.

How much private trade is there in R.?

Private trade	22%
State trade	28%
Cooperation	50%

The cooperatives being nothing more than groups of consumers who seek no profit. The state encourages them to take over all collective buying for small stores & the retailing of all purchases. The state does all wholesale buying & selling as well as all manufactures. But it seeks to place distribution in the hands of the people organized into co-operatives. Naturally the trade of the State as a retailer diminishes as the cooperatives increase their power to handle it. The cooperatives consist mostly of small shops. Private shops get their goods from the State, because the government has a monopoly on foreign purchase. The cooperatives also buy through the state, and are a consumers' group.

What is your controlling principle in trying to sell to people? Do you try to stimulate trade? Do you want the cooperatives to be profitable? Answer: *No we only want them to buy their way. We are working* on a small margin, so that we cannot be very prosperous. We do not trade for profit but to supply people with the necessities of life.

Would you prefer to restrain demand for luxuries?

No, if people can afford them, but *at present* imported luxuries are heavily taxed *because the necessaries of life are now so important & so short.*

I have heard the the private shops use more initiative and are more popular with the people.

No, they are decreasing:

	1922–23	1927
State	31	34
Private	40	22

Does the government try as *hard* as private concerns to get cheaper prices and sell cheaper?

Yes, and we are able to do it because big organisations can buy cheaper. For instance, the government, cooperatives and private concerns buy grain from the peasant, but the government, *because it can buy in larger quantities,* can get the best terms.

Does this private buying produce private capitalists?

Yes, but they are on the decrease.
The agricultural cooperatives organise wheat pools. If the private dealer buys, he pays more, but he can sometimes make a profit by selling in local places. However, such speculation is on a small scale because all transport, etc., is in the hands of the government.

You think there is *any real* danger from the private trader? *Answer: not now.* Once, they might have seized trade with one blow; for instance, during the war, when the cooperatives were weak & private traders were *strong.* But *Goverment* financial pressure deprived them of their capital, and foreign private capital *can now* come in with difficulty.

Capital in the cooperative societies was accumulated during the first period after the revolution. The government told the cooperatives they must compete with private trade and beat it with lower prices.

Do the cooperatives satisfy the needs of the people?

You should go to the stores and see for yourself. The prices are standard, and while perhaps high, the private stores ask still more. If you compare with European countries you will find that the standard of living of the Russian worker is higher. But the prices of goods are higher than in other countries. For instance, the price of bread— 8 kopecks a kilo, and white bread 22 k. Rye bread is 4 k. a pound. The cooperative societies baking rye bread lose on it but make up on fancy goods, so that the bakeries are working without a margin of profit, so you see we try not to starve the people. The Moscow cooperatives have sold meat below cost in order to oust private traders.

But must not all government *departments* be operated with a small profit for overhead?

Yes, and for that reason we are now selling meat higher. The best sells for 84 k. per kilo.

Manufactured goods are dearer here, especially in Siberia, because of cost of transportation. However, the Soviet Union is divided into regions, and in each there is a certain fixed basis for wages and prices according to budget.

Are costs of production excessive?

Yes, especially shoes and clothing,

	High boots	$6.00
Women's shoes		8.50
' ' before		5.00
	war	

There is too much handicraft work, and *we* must import much of the raw material.

When Soviet Russia is rich will you people wear cheap clothing, eat cheap food, etc.?

No, only now we are poor: for instance in the cooperative shops there is always a mass of people buying cotton because they know that if they come late, none will be left. We are supplying only 75% or 80% of the people's needs. So of course if a man has money he can go to a private store and pay more and get the material.

But the government hopes to supply this remaining 20% in five years.

As for the present standard of living in Russia, the demand for white bread has increased 250% since the war. Butter also. This figure is of workers—the bourgeoisie doesnt count.

Don't you think that too much red tape is a cause of *high costs and of delay in production?*

Yes, there is still much red tape, much bureaucracy, but far less than before.

What about private initiative?

That is a question of competition. We must compete with 22% of private trade and also with the state.

The government is removing special privileges to cooperatives, i.e., less rent, less taxes,—except for small cooperatives in villages.

Do you feel that in the course of time these cooperative officials will try just as hard to please customers as private traders? Yes.

Will not absence of advertising and other stimulants to buy take away spirit and color of life?

We do not need these commercial stimulants here. But as to the question of how employees are stimulated to sell to customers premiums for sales above average, competition among stores, different methods. The store which gives the best service, has the least complaints gets a reward, and the employees also get rewards. Most of the state industries work on this basis, a system of compensation based on production power of the average worker, plus work over norm.

How fast do your cooperatives meet new demands?

The manager of a store knows *what the local demand is & how* much goods he sells, and every day *he* writes *a* report to the central office of his district, and every day he receives new supplies on the basis of his needs.

Could not stores be used to suggest new ways of living to public? *Yes. Are they? No.*

Does not the Soviet Govt. try to educate the children to be adherents of the Soviet Govt? just as the Catholic Church educates the children to be Catholics? *Yes, but* the Catholic Church educates the children for the sake of the church, whereas communism educates them for the sake of them*selves—their own later prosperity and happiness.*

<u>Tuesday. Nov. 22nd 1927– Moscow– Grand Hotel</u>
The Jack-daws of Moscow interest me.[52] *They are everywhere. I am told that to Russians they have a semi-sacred nature. This morning, lying in bed, I observed them through the window flying in clouds above this central*

---

52. Related to the common crow, which it resembles in everything but color, this gray and black bird still can be seen in great numbers throughout Moscow.

heart of Moscow—above the Kremlin. And all flying in the same direction—away from the city toward the northwest. A lymphatic bird—they seem to fly with an easy, lethargic social motion. They are always playing about with one another as they fly. One single one yesterday came & sat on the ledge of one of my windows, and I took it as a friendly omen. But these birds hanging over this half-asiatic city give it a more friendly look than otherwise it might wear. Circling above the Kremlin in thick, widespread spirals & circles, they give that ancient pile a some what detached, lovely & decidedly medieaval look. They seem somehow an ancient and baronial part of that old & drastic & gloomy world. Seeing them there I see Tzar Theodore, on the steps of his church, asking of his God "Why did you make me Tzar"? And below their darkling wings I can see Ivan killing his son or being slain by his courtiers.[53] It is a sad, drastic, tyrannical world that is below—but above, these wings seem free—and indifferent—; accidental, age old—detached. Below misery, dogma, mysticism—a pathetic slavery to an age old fallacy, and above birds that are pagan, social, genial and gay. How casual and accidental nature can be—freedom, ease, content may be side by side with enslavement & misery—and the one having no meaning for—holding no light toward the other. Under their wings before this scene (the Kremlin) one might well exclaim "Nature! Nature! What can you mean? What is the secret of your will?"

I had breakfast in my room. At 10 Ruth Kennell came and at $10^{\underline{30}}$ Trevis, my new interpreter. These two have been assigned me, as I understand, for the rest of my trip. At 11—as Trevis explained I was at the office of LUBOVITCH, People's Commissariat for Post and Telegraph, for an interview, and at 10^{45} we left & met him.

Lubovitch is a rather stout man with a pleasant, almost jolly countenance, round and smooth shaven. He was as I learned the son of a carpenter, finished elementary schools and became a telegraph operator, after trying many professions including that of teacher. His present career began when, as a Communist officer in 1917, he seized the Petrograd telegraph by force.

What is your plan for Russia for the next 25 years? I asked.

53. Dreiser is referring to Ivan IV ("The Terrible"), who in 1581 reportedly killed his son in a fit of rage. Ivan was not killed by his courtiers, so the reference is probably to a variant of the story that has the son being killed by courtiers, not Ivan. Or Dreiser may be confusing the story with that of Ivan's second son, Theodore. After Ivan's death, Theodore became czar, but the pious and mentally defective boy spent much of his time in prayer while Boris Godunov ruled as regent. Theodore died in 1598 in unexplained circumstances, leading many to suspect Godunov and his court followers were responsible.

We have a five-year plan, but as technique, fortunately, does not stand still, it is difficult to keep to it, and we find it necessary to change the technical details every year.

Plan of Postal Dept. 60% of the regions have been covered by the postal service whereas before the revolution it was only 3%.

Was all this under your direction?

Yes, I was the originator. I studied systems in Europe and installed the best here. First was the method of the *truck* car moving between villages. In 1925 we installed the European plan of postal distribution. At first, the postman made the rounds only 2 or 3 times a week, he traveled about 25 kilo a day on foot. Today, 60% of the postmen travel on horses. There are still few automobiles used in the provinces, with the exception of the Crimea. In certain places where the roads are better, autos are obtained from a society called Auto Industrial Trading Co., beside using their own post autos.

How long before the remaining 40% of the country will be connected with postal service?

Now *those* regions have a 3rd line of communication not belonging directly to the Postal Dept. But in the next five years these will also be connected by radio, telephone, telegraph, & radio *telegraph*.

Is there one telegraph rate?

We have reduced the special rates per kilo to one flat rate. Long distance telephone is by distance, but in the provinces the rates are 2 times cheaper.

Since the revolution the postal service has absolutely changed. The postman is a walking Soviet encyclopaedia, and incorporates every kind of social service in himself. If he cannot answer questions, he goes to the local Soviet and brings the answer next time. He also takes orders for goods, literature, sells books, takes money orders, telegrams, registered letters.

How is he paid?

By kilo and also a percentage on orders for periodical subscriptions and sales. The average earnings are 60 to 75 roubles a month, but he works only 15 days in the month. This is for the postman with his own horse, those on foot earn less.

Is there civil service?

There are special schools and courses, technical and trade schools at which the postman trains.

Telephone service.

In Siberia there is only one line, in upper Siberia none at all, but we want very much to thoroughly connect *up* lower Siberia. Our first problem is to connect *up* a good telephone line in European Russia. Since the revolution, we have finished a main Leningrad-Rostov-Tiflis *line. Also* The wireless telephone is very useful for us and we are now making connections to Tashkent, Turkestan.

Is the wireless as good as the telephone? I don't know, but it has a great future.

How much is the telephone used?

Very much, especially in industrial organisations and 35% private conversations. There are no telephones in peasant homes, but each village, Soviet and cooperative, *has a* telephone. Out of 5,000 villages there are telephones in 3,000. But we are not satisfied, even though before the revolution there was nothing.

Does the peasant want the telephone? They are not only interested in the telephones but in many villages, cooperatives are organised for constructing telephones and supplying materials for construction *to peasents.*

Does the government use these means of communications for education and propaganda?

Of course we serve first the commercial needs. We are stabilising the telephone, which is replacing the telegraph and joining telephone and telegraph to go over the same lines. In the radio telephone we have a great opportunity. In Siberia a big wireless station is being built. There are 50 large wireless stations in Russia. They are supplementing telephone service not only in provinces but also in cities with the wireless. Newspapers use all the telephone-telegraph service at minimum rates.

What per cent of service is private?

60% of the service is to private individual and concerns, 10% newspapers, 30% government. In telegraph, 55% is government and cooperative and 45% private.

Foreign business is less than before the revolution, but inner business is three times greater. Telephone service between cities is 62% state organisations and the rest private.

In the city telephone service, 30% is to state organisations and the rest private telephones.

Big wireless stations are sometimes in the hands of other Soviet organisations like the cooperatives, but the majority are under the Postal Telegraph Dept.

In the sphere of the radio, the majority of the service is international. The technique of the radio is under the control of the Postal Telegraph Dept. but the social use is not.

Does the government use these means of communication for propaganda?

No, we give the techinical apparatus and social organisations use it as they see fit. We have nothing to do with the ideology, only the technique.

Wages of telegraph operators and mechanics?

The average wage of mechanics is 66 R. in Moscow, and technicians 132–150 R.

Telegraph operators, 89–120 R.

Are all expenses covered by this department?

Yes, we have our own budget. Last year we gave nothing to the state and the state gave nothing to us, but for capital construction we receive 4 to 8 millions a year from the government.

Do you expect to give any surplus to the government in the future?

Yes, If it were not for the capital construction.

Perhaps you would like to ask me some questions?

Why didn't the Congress on Telegraph now being held in Washington invite us to participate? We could help them.

Because those in control fear the Soviet influence on the workers.

If the American people wanted culture they have the most complete apparatus in the world for it, but they use it only for luxurious material living.

The average American loves his government and if anyone speaks against it, he yells Bolshevik and wants him arrested. Why? Because he gets good wages, auto, wonderful roads, every farmer has telephone and radio, every farm girl silk stockings.

The Commissar remarked: Democracy exists but under the pressure of the financial rulers.

The Commissar said that he has a brother in America who

worked in Ford's plant. He was ashamed of his brother in Russia and after long controversy they ceased to correspond. Sometime after, another brother in Odessa received a letter from him in which he wrote that he had been out of work for 1 year and that he needed $200 for an operation. His brother in Odessa answered that he also needed an operation which was done free of charge, not as in democratic America. The capital inherited from the old govt. post was *214 million.*

Now the capital is 300 million

After this interview I dismissed Trevis and Ruth Kennell & myself proceeded to a new type of institute for Education called the Institute for Labor Education *which Scott Nearing had recommended to me. Physically it proved* to be a very large brick building, up to date and orderly. The principal of the school, a youngish, sandy complexioned man with a kindly careworn face, took us into his office. In the large corridor a number of boys and girls were taking gymnastic exercises, and the office was full of boys and girls who wanted to consult with the principal. I asked the principal if this was a school for the homeless?

He replied that he did not wish to speak before the pupils. When they had all gone out, he was ready to answer my questions.

This is a special institute for the teaching of wayward children, who have committed actual crimes all the way from petty thievery to murder. One of the 100 boys from 10 to 16 years at present in the school had killed his mother. These criminal children are sent here by a special commission. An interesting feature of the school is the fact that normal children are also sent here by their parents and study along with the criminal element, with remarkably successful results. For instance, the principal's own children attend this school. There are in all 203 students from 7 – 16. There are the usual courses with special emphasis on technology, and science. There is a special department for the psychological study of the child which uses the American tests.

Do you find it necessary to punish the boys?

Yes, but we never use corporal punishment. They are deprived, for instance, of their daily walk, or their holiday excursion outside the grounds, or participation in the children's organisations.

Do you have self-management in the school? Yes we have the

same student committee which functions in every school, wall news-paper, etc.

From where do you get your funds?

From the Moscow Soviet and not from the Educational Dept. We have 450 R. per each boy. This is too little, and so the food is not adequate. We have 12 roubles a month per child, 1 lb. of meat a day, 1 lb. of bread, milk not every day, tea with sugar, mush, potatoes.

What do they do when they finish here? Either they go into higher schools or into industry, no student is permitted to return to the streets.

We then watched the gymnastics in the corridor and the prin-cipal told us that we would find it hard to pick out the boys who live in the institution as against those normal children who attend by the day.

The walls were covered with their drawings, and wall news-papers.

I went away with a fresh impression of the tremendous amount of disinterested labor which is going into the building up of this new society.

In the evening RK & I went to the Stanislavsky Theatre to see The Armored Train—a fair but somewhat melo-dramatic Red-White War drama. Obviously Stanislavsky put it on to curry favor with the Soviet regime. Every element in Russia must now propagandize for the Soviet idea. Afterwards Stanislasky's secretary wanted to know if I would not give them a play. I suggested the American Tragedy (N.Y. Play form) and promised to submit a script.

Wed. Nov. 23rd 1927 – Moscow – Grand Hotel

Another gray day. Certainly bright days are rare here. As usual I have the cold Russian meats & cocoa for breakfast. R.K. comes at 9—Trevis at 10$\frac{30}{}$ There is an interview.

Interview with ⌐   ⌐ Svidersky, Assistant Commissar of Land *at eleven.* He *proved to be* a shrewd looking man of middle age. His father *he said* was a rich land owner. During the revolution he was vice commissar of nutrition and traveled from village to village to commandeer flour. He said that now after six years he could not recognise the villages so greatly had they improved.

What is the *present* peasant population of Russia? 100 millions.

How is the land distributed among them? It depends upon the

district. In a central industrial gubernia each eater has 1.8 dessat. In the Volga district 5 dessatins, in Siberia 15.[54]

Does the government expect from each peasant a certain return in production? No. Only the agricultural products which the government buys, but no fixed amount as he is free.

Why not from peasant if from worker? Because we pay the worker definite wages and can expect a certain amount of labor from him. The peasant does not have the land free of charge. There is an agricultural tax amounting to 400 millions a year.

On what is the principal tax?

There was a proposition to tax only income and not land, but it was rejected. The inspector comes to the peasant and decides what his taxes are to be. The taxes are according to the number in the family, if a large family then a larger tax. It is considered that the larger the family the richer is the peasant. The peasant receives say, 1 1/2 dessatins for each member of his family, 5 people, but *if* only the husband and wife can work, the tax is less. For instance, if he has 8 acres of land and only 2 persons are able to work, he is poor.

Why do you not take the land away if he cannot work it?

Because after the revolution, every member of the family had a right to a piece of land. The government helps the poor peasant with credits, etc. because it cannot take away the land even if he is not able to work it. And if we did take it away, he would get poorer and poorer but if he has it, he can at least rent the land he does not cultivate. But if he rents it more than 3 yrs. the government seizes it.

Would it not be better to use Henry George's theory for the state to own the land and lease as much as the peasant can use for a certain return to *the* state.[55] If he took more than he could give a return on, he would have to give it back and if he worked very badly, he would have to go into some other work.*? Answer* No, such a system could not exist here. The peasant would become a worker and sell his power. *But* For this factories are needed. *And as yet there are*

---

54. A *dessatin* of land is equal to about 2.7 acres.

55. Henry George (1839–97), American economist who argued that land could be leased to the people and that a tax should be imposed on land owned by monopolies and speculators. Industry, in turn, would give back to the community its share of the land value it helped create, thus alleviating the poverty that George felt was caused by the accumulation of great wealth by the few.

no others—not factories to employ such free labor as there is. There is an adage in Russia that the peasant is jealous of the worker. *and it is true*

If we followed Henry George, the peasant would own land according to his ability. George also believes in nationalisation, but according to his system, there would not be equality among the peasants. *Those who could farm such land would get it & those who could not would have little—and we would have what we are trying to avoid here—rich & poor more. In Russia we feel* that the land belongs to all the peasants. There are some families who are very strong and can work well. So we try to help the poorer peasant by giving him the possibility to work with other peasants *and so maintain his stature after a fashion. To this end* the cooperatives give credits to the poor peasants to buy equipment. *But if in the instance we find that* we cannot help the poor peasant, then your theory is right. *But as yet we are* testing the system. That is the difference between a capitalist and socialist system. If we will help the peasant to develop, we can build up our industry, and if not—the bourgeois power will come again.

Before the war the condition of the peasant was worse. His standard *of living* has improved, his *consuming power has increased.* But the peasant is not satisfied with his standard of living, especially his clothing, although it is much better than before the war. But we must improve his condition. It is on this question that there is all the trouble in our Party.

Is his general equipment better?

In some regions worse, in others better. For instance, in Volga region worse, principally because of the famine.

What do you do about the incompetent peasant? For instance, a man not fitted for farming, but born on a farm.

He must take the initative to get out. But in the villages the peasant youth is anxious to leave the farms and go to the factories. The Young Communist organisation is taking care of them.

If a peasant is competent, does the government help to keep him on the land, and on the other hand, if the factory worker would do better on the land, does it try to send him there?

The individual is never guided. In the first days, the policy permitted everyone individually to go to the Land Dept. with his personal problems, but now the Young Communist organisation handles such problems. The Dept. of Education has peasant schools for the young peasants who are trained to be social workers in the villages. There are factory schools to train the industrial worker and he can, if he wishes, be transferred to the agricultural schools.

How does the Russian peasant compare with the peasant of western Europe?

Whom we call a peasant and whom western Europe calls a peasant are two entirely different types. On a trip to Germany, I became acquainted with the peasant school in Konigsberg and saw young men in uniform. I asked who they were and were told that they were peasants. They pay 100 marks a year tuition and live in private homes costing 300 marks. Even in our richest condition, we could not have so much money. Here were altogether different values. Our peasant is small, his enterprise is small. But we are lifting up the poor peasant in great measure. The peasant who comes to me now from my district had in my time no boots, no samovar, no manufactured goods, no schools, no hospital, no cooperative organisation. Now he has all of these things.

Are you reaching all the peasants with the new education and equipment, including all nationalities?

Yes, everyone, even the smallest nationalities whose culture is very low are being reached through the Party, trade union organs, cooperatives, radio. For example, this morning this incident occurred: There is a wild people from the Kazakstan Republic who sent a delegation of 15 to me. These people are like nomads and travel with their herds from place to place. Now they are gradually coming back to the land and they came to me asking for tractors—not horses, but straight away tractors! And not one tractor but many. They had to talk to me through an interpreter because they don't even know Russian.

Does your department actually *sustain itself out of* the revenue from the peasants or does it, like all other departments as far as I have seen, *borrow from the government.*

Answer. We are not self-sustaining and borrow from the government. But the income of the government is used for cultural work, education, health, literature. The state's budget is derived from taxes, forests, mines, etc. and from this income it gives to the different departments like agriculture. Besides *this,* each local department *or state* has its own budget. *It* receives money *from its people or* pays the central government a certain sum *to help in this farm work*. This is called autonomy.

How much *Central Govt.* budget *money* does the Land Department receive?

6% of the national budget *but* this is supplemented by local budgets for local work in the different Republics.

How long do you think it will be before the peasant will have a decent standard of living?

The peasant himself during the war met foreigners and became acquainted with their customs and standards. This tended to increase his own demands. Now he wants the American *tempo*.
We in the Central Soviet Government have a five year plan for his general improvement but it contains too many details to be entered upon here—his education, good roads, good machinery—I cannot tell you what all but is a vast scheme. Personally I think the process of development will take 10 years.

What factors would stimulate development?

Of course, different factors, but first of all industrialisation, especially electric stations, good roads, *automobiles, farming machinery. We have so little money to buy farming machinery with.*

Is it not better to build roads for auto buses and automobiles than railroads.

No, not for us, *as yet. We need long haul transportation so much now—the long haul railroad is cheaper. But* There is a special commission on auto roads and construction will begin in March.

What do you think of autos in place of street cars?

For us it is not practical, because we must buy the autos abroad *and we can & do build the short cars & rails here.*

What about the tempo of the Russian peasant being naturally slow in comparison with *that of the* American?

There is no fundamental difference. It is only an old fable. There are many legends about the Russian peasant, but it is plain that he had enough energy to kick out the czar and put in the Soviet power. He has acquired 30,000 tractors in 3 yr. We were afraid that the peasant could not run the tractor, but our fears had no foundation. *He has brains in plenty to operate machinery.*

Has birth control any place in your program?

No, it is a capitalist problem. For instance, in France, they try to reduce the birth rate so that the inheritances will fall into fewer hands. *Here followed a long argument between R.K. and M. Siverdosky in which I took little part although I believe in Birth Control.*

In the evening I saw my first Russian Ballet at the Bolshoi (Grand Opera). It was beautiful—Pantomimic interpretation of Hugo's Notre Dame, with music by some Russian composer whose name I have forgotten—but the music was not good. But with suitable words & music this pantomime would make a rare Grand Opera. And yet as I saw it I thought how strange. In perhaps only here & in England would this opera be permitted. For in America, France, Italy & perhaps Germany—the Catholic Church would have sufficient influence to prevent a truthful presentation— most of all in America—the Land of the Free. The leading role was played by Geltse—a charming ballerina said to be 58 years old,—but as active & graceful as a girl of 20.[56] *Many of the other dancers were marvellous.*

During the pantomime—Resnich, the representative of the Associated Press here in Moscow, told me how the Associated handled the story of Lenin's death & of the fight between the various correspondents for place at the telegraph desk once the foreign office permitted the news to go. It was held up from midnight when he died until 2 p.m. the following day. He wanted me to see Otto Kahn & get him to take the Russian ballet to America.[57] *After the show we went to the Gypsy Restaurant & I saw the most beautiful flower girl I have seen in years. Incidentally he told me the story of his recent life—a love affair with a Lesbian who almost wrecked him. It was sad and in a way beautiful. From here we went to the writers club restaurant where it was crowded. And here I told him of Leopold & Loeb—the psychology of that case.*[58] *He wished me to make a novel of it. At 2*$\frac{30}{}$ *I hired a droshky & returned to the Grand Hotel.*

Thursday. Nov. 24–1927– Hotel Grand–Moscow

I got very little done today, as no interviews were arranged. I went in the afternoon—to the large sculpture museum on Volhonka.

---

56. Yekaterina Geltser was a prima ballerina for the Bolshoi ballet; she is remembered today for her loyalty to the new Soviet regime and for remaining in Moscow to dance when many of her Russian contemporaries left to dance elsewhere in Europe.

57. Otto Kahn was an American financier and art impresario, much involved with the Metropolitan Opera during this period.

58. Nathan Leopold and Richard Loeb, college students from well-to-do American families, kidnapped and murdered the adolescent Bobby Franks on 21 May 1924. The crime was without apparent motive, undertaken as an intellectual exercise. Leopold and Loeb were defended in a widely reported trial by Clarence Darrow, who argued that they were mentally diseased. Darrow helped them avoid the death penalty; they were imprisoned for life.

This is an enormous, magnificent building. One section is devoted to old foreign paintings, among them many of the Dutch paintings which I consider have never been equalled. The remainder of the great structure is filled with reproductions of classic sculpture, some in heroic size. Here again, I remarked that nothing so perfect as the Greek sculptures has ever been thought of. This is pure beauty unmarred by grossness or material conceptions.

In the evening, Serge Sergeivitch Dinamov came to draw up the agreement with Gossizdat, but as I had meantime learned that the majority of my works are being published by Land and Factory, I considered that a contract with the State Publishing House as my official exclusive publishers would be meaningless. So unless Gossizdat can publish these books, I shall not be interested in making a contract with them.

I got into an argument with Dinamov about individualism, or rather, intellectual aristocracy, as opposed to mass rule. *The little brain & the big brain came in for their customary share in the argument—how to place them—and where. As opposed to Communism and its enforced equality I offered international, benevolent capitalism as very likely to achieve the same results. He did not agree but could not dissolve all of the difficulties of communism as practised here in Russia. In weariness we finally desisted.*

Friday–Nov. 25-1927- Moscow–Grand Hotel

Grey & very dusky. I am irritated by delays in obtaining important interviews here & decide to go to Leningrad—allowing Vox—in the lapse of time, to arrange the interviews I want (Stalin, Buhkarin,[59] [unreadable]. Pending my departure at midnight I visit the Tretyakovsky Gallery, the largest Russian gallery in Moscow and get an idea of Russian art.[60] There were two rooms of Rapine's paintings, including the large picture of Ivan the Terrible after he has killed his son. *This last was really powerful. Most the pictures assembled here are very good & lightly interpretive of Russian life & manners during the past 200 years. A sombre world up to now—forrests, poor roads, meagre equipment, snow—heat.*

59. Nikolai Ivanovich Bukharin (1888–1939), Bolshevik leader and coeditor of *Pravda*. Bukharin headed the Third International (1926–29); later he was expelled from the Communist party but subsequently was reinstated. He was suspected of being a Trotsky supporter during the mid-1930s, was brought to trial during the purges of 1938, and was executed in 1939.

60. The Tretyakov, a famous art gallery in Moscow, was founded by P. U. Tretyakov and donated by him to the city in 1892.

But highly individualistic & colorful. No attempt made to interpret any of
the Russian names into English so that I was at a loss as to who painted
what. But the art itself—Russia as expressed here—remains with me.

Afterwards I walked back to the hotel. Enroute I found a horse-shoe. I
rested until 6—then packed—wrote letters. At 9$\underline{30}$ R.K. came. At 10 Trevis. At 10$\underline{30}$ we took a taxi to the station & at 11 boarded the sleeper. Trevis desire for R.K. caused him to hang around her until 12—but evidently
he lost out for he returned & silently bestowed himself in the upper berth.

Before leaving the hotel I had a talk with Ole Svensen—a rich trader
of Seattle. His business—furs—is centered in Kamchatka.[61] He told of
customs & conditions there—food, clothing, housing. Most houses made of
snow. An inner tent—very small—can be heated with so little as an oil
lamp. Fish, reindeer meat, sugar & blubber principal foods. Fats & sugar
absolutely necessary. Husbands & wives—kill each other on request—
when physical suffering becomes too great. Life easy, food plenty. Men,
especially Americans, become addicted to it. Cannot endure states because
freedom & ease here too great. Natives admire & make life comfortable
for Americans. An American then is a sort of king among them. They
buy all sort of American goods. Best clothing is made of double reindeer
skins—for inside (next skin) & out side. Boots & cap too. Easily cleaned by
freezing & beating when all ice is shaken out and dirt with it. Very warm
country very healthy—People fatalists.

---

61. Kamchatka is a region in Siberia on the Bering Sea, known for its severe climate.

LENINGRAD

Saturday, Nov. 26– 1927– Leningrad– Hotel Europe

On Saturday morning at 10 a.m. we arrived in Leningrad. The head of the Leningrad VOKS and another representative met us at the station. There was an automobile waiting and I was carried off in grand style to the Hotel Europe. Enroute I was struck by the beauty of the city, the broad streets and fine buildings, the air of smartness and alertness which Moscow lacks. The hotel proved to be much more imposing and comfortable than the notorious Bolshaya Moskovskaya in Moscow. Lackeys opened the car doors. We entered the handsome lobby through revolving doors. There was an air of grandeur and obsequiousness and order soothing to a soul harrassed by the shabby lobbies, wretched service and leaky plumbing, despite the ancient magnificence of the rooms, in the 'Grand Hotel'. Each of us (three) was given a spacious room with bath and then we went up to the restaurant on the roof for breakfast. This was a really charming place with potted plants and bright colored walls and shaded lamps. A brisk reporter promptly appeared and interviewed me as I ate my breakfast of cold meats, rolls and cocoa.

After breakfast, I was taken for a ride about the city in an open car. I do not think I have ever seen a more beautiful city. The gray fog which habitually hangs over Leningrad partially enveloped the wonderful old buildings and the domes of magnificent churches. The marble columns of buildings and monuments were coated with frost which gave the stone a wonderfully soft tone. We passed the Winter Palace which has been restored this year to its original colors of white and dark green. We stopped at the great Cathedral of *St. Isaac.*[1] Inside within the lofty dome was a steel scaffolding erected before the revolution for the purpose of constructing a number of pictures in mosaic work. Only eight of the figures were finished when the revolution stopped the work. Now money cannot be spared to complete it so the scaffolding which spoils the interior of the cathedral is *to be* torn down. A priest took us up to the altar where four great mosaic-work pictures were placed on either side of the golden doors leading to the inner shrine *which weighed* 300 poods of gold.[2]

1. One of the largest domed churches in the world, St. Isaac's stands in the central part of St. Petersburg next to the Neva embankment. Built between 1818 and 1858 by the French architect Montferrand, it was constructed in memory of St. Isaac the Dalmatian, a Byzantine monk whose feast day, 30 May, coincided with the birthday of Peter the Great. The Soviets transformed the cathedral into a museum in 1931.

2. A *pood* is a Russian unit of weight equal to about thirty-six pounds.

We stepped into the inner shrine, but my secretary had to stand at the door, because no woman is permitted to enter here. There were slabs of malachite, a green stone, and other valuable stones in the walls. There was an object under a glass case on the altar which made me ask 'Is that a bird's nest?' It proved to be a crown of thorns brought from Jerusalem. While very rich and magnificent, the general interior of the church is not inspiringly beautiful.

Outside as I drive we passed many interesting neighborhoods and finally a rubber factory employing 7,000 workers. *There were* bridges over canals, *churches, broad mains. Finally we* swung into a court and came to the home of VOKS, — rooms in a very beautiful mansion near the *Neva* river. After visiting a while here with the representatives, we crossed the river to the Fortress of Peter and Paul.[3] First we went into the old church *which has a very high slender golden spire* and were shown the tombs of the czars and their wives of the last three centuries. They are of marble with golden crosses. Crossing the courtyard through the snow we entered the ruined fortress which ran along the water's edge. Inside *ranged* cell after cell, in chill monotony, each a large stone room with a high barred window, an iron cot, an iron table and a washbowl in the corner. In each heavy iron door was a narrow slit with glass in it through which the guards could see into the cell, and a small door on hinges through which the food was passed. Here the prisoner was completely isolated, no sound came to him through the thick stone walls, but the prisoners learned to communicate with one another by tapping on the walls. One cell was used for solitary confinement because the adjoining rooms were warehouses and the *prisoner* could not even communicate by tappings. Another cell was used to confine prisoners for punishment. A solid wooden door could be dropped over the window so that the room was in complete darkness. Here was the cell of Vera Figner, of the Decembrists and other famous revolutionists.[4]

3. The fortress built by Peter the Great on Hare Island (Zayachy Ostrov), it is the historic heart of St. Petersburg. For more than two hundred years it was officially called Fort St. Petersburg, but it later acquired the name of the two apostles to whom the fortress's cathedral had been dedicated. Dreiser describes seeing the tombs of the czars, who from Peter the Great to Alexander III were buried in the church. Until 1917, the fortress also contained the prison that Dreiser describes.

4. Vera Nikolaevna Figner (1852–1942). A revolutionary and sister of the famous tenor Nicholas Figner, she became a legendary figure for the Soviet government. She had been exiled in 1904 and had spent her time abroad lecturing about her experiences in the years before the 1917 Revolution.

On the way home we passed what seemed to me the most beautiful church I have yet seen. It was a Tartar Mosque with a large cone shaped dome curiously made of china blue and white material like porcelain and at each corner two miniature cone shaped domes of similar workmanship.

In the evening our assidious hosts bundled us off to the opera 'Evgeni Oneega', which was so boring in spite of good music by Chikovsky, that we left at the end of the first act.[5] The plots of the old Russian operas are very insipid. Cabaret was in full swing in the roof restaurant and here we met our hosts. An imitation jazz band was making a great racket and the guests were bravely trying to dance the fox trot and Charleston. Here was "NEP" and the new bourgeoisie in full bloom.[6] *The NEP men are the private concessionaires—(their wives, sweet hearts and children whom the communists here hate & watch because they feel that they tend to undermine the communist regime. They are spied on and taxed for their gayeties.*

Sunday, Nov. 27-1927- Leningrad - Hote Europe
Gray and damp.

In the morning we drove about 15 versts out of Leningrad to Tsarskoye Selo (Czar's Village) now known as the Children's Village.[7] Here is the summer palace of the Czars and the town itself is made up of handsome homes where officials of the Imperial Government lived, among them 15 Jewish families which were granted the permanent privilege of living here by one of the Czar's because of military services *performed by their ancestors.* There is an extensive park, pavilions, churches, army barracks and finally the palace itself, which is not more imposing than many of the other buildings in the town. *I did not like it at all. The whole thing—village and Palace, had the air of a cheap resort.* The palace is now a museum and is kept as

---

The Decembrists were those who took part in the failed uprising of December 1825; they were subsequently executed or exiled. Among other famous revolutionists jailed at the fortress were Maxim Gorky (1868–1936) and Lenin's brother Aleksandr I. Ulyanov (1866–87), who was imprisoned there before he was hanged for his part in an attempt to kill the czar.

5. *Evgeny Onegin* is Pushkin's famous novel, written in verse. Tchaikovsky wrote an opera based on the novel.

6. The New Economic Policy was the state program in effect during the 1920s; it moved away from a strictly communist economy to a modified socialist-capitalist system.

7. Town in Leningrad (St. Petersburg) oblast. The Pushkin Memorial Museum and the lycée attended by the children of nineteenth-century nobles are both located there.

the last czar left it suddenly on Monday, July 30, 1917. On his desk is a large loose leaf calendar pad whose last leaf is this date.

Our tour of the hundreds of rooms occupied the better part of two hours and my conclusion at the end was that it was the worst palace I have ever seen, a tremendous effort to expend as much wealth as possible in order to create an atmosphere of grandeur, *yet resulting in* bad taste and ugliness depressing to contemplate. I could understand quite clearly why it was necessary to get rid of these people. The rooms of Nicholas were particularly unharmonious, cluttered up with furniture, bric a brac, and rugs, very broad Turkish divans which were out of keeping with the rest of the furniture, walls simply covered with paintings and photographs, as if he had made an effort to display all the presents he had received. His bathroom proved to lack, as all the other bathrooms in the house lacked, a real bathtub. There was a great tiled swimming pool but if the poor man wanted a bath he was compelled to take a sponge with the aid of a porcelain bowl and pitcher on a stand. The only comfortable beds in the palace I found in the sleeping room of Catherine, which was a broad soft looking bed and in the little bedroom of the sailor assigned as playmate to the last young heir to the throne, Nicholas III.

On the second floor were the children's rooms. Besides in one of the grand reception rooms downstairs, one of the Czars (Alexander II a doting father) had ordered to be constructed a grand slide for his children. Here also were large toy automobiles and other playthings *which gave the room a queer look. Yet he was Tzar and could order it. On this same second floor were class rooms for children of different ages. Perhaps those of the relatives of the Czar as well as his own*, one or two of them really artistically decorated and furnished. *Also* the living rooms of the daughters of the last czar, their wardrobes and the extensive rooms of the last heir, who although a lovely child, was a cripple *were interesting.* There were several rooms full of his playthings, toy animals, mechanical toys, automobiles, ships, engines, wardrobe after wardrobe of the poor child's uniforms, his bedroom with a very uncomfortable looking little bed, his bath room, with only a bowl and pitcher in it, and a toilet, and on the tables all his braces and straps which he had to wear.

The boudoir of the last Czarina was a bewildering maze of furniture and objects. *It looked more like the boudoir of an actor or stage manager than that of a Czarina.* The various dressing tables and bureaus were crowded with small ornaments, vases, and photographs and the walls were covered with small photographs and paintings. The guide assured us that the room was as she had lived in it. Her wardrobe occupied a large room and was full of hideous long gowns of satin, velvet and lace and large hats, which would not be likely to excite the envy of a modern shop girl. The czar's wardrobe of uniforms was even more extensive. There must have been hundreds of different uniforms for all his different orders. — *K.P. —Shriners Elks, etc.*[8]

There were also rooms full of royal presents, a wonderful display of large plates presented to Nicholas by the peasants on one of his tours, and presents from foreign governments.

It was a relief when it was over and we went down to the entrance hall again where a bright open fire was burning. A sled drawn by two gray horses and driven by a soldier stood at the entrance and we were given a fast ride about the grounds. The flying hoofs kicked snow into our faces and as we dashed through the grounds, now a public park, the indignant pedestrians, not accustom to being disturbed by vehicles, stepped off the paths into the deep snow and hurled curses at us; one old woman even suggested *that we be hung to a tree—of which gave me a Tzar-like feel. I was stirring the proletariat to ire.*

Then we drove home in the car. On the outskirts of the city are the houses of peasants who work the land, log houses which look fairly good, many of them new and with trimmings on windows and doors of carved wood painted in bright colors. But the country about is flat and desolate looking, vast stretches of snowy plains.

In the evening we went to the State Circus. This is a permanent building, with seats constructed in a circle about the pit and very lofty ceiling *about half the size of the old Madison Square in N.Y.* The program changes weekly, the management making contracts with traveling troupes, the majority of which are foreign. The State Circus comes under the general Department of Education, and under the sub-department of theaters.

The actors, if Russian—are limited to about 10 roubles a day: If foreign they have to be paid foreign rates and are so paid. I was interested by one thought. If a Russian Circus actor had a good idea for an act—and

---

8. K.P. stands for Knights of Pythias, an American fraternal order similar to the Shriners and Elks.

only recieved 10 roubles a day, wherever would he get the money to stage it? The particular act which prompted this thought was called an "American Attraction," although it was really Italian. And the reason for calling it an "American Attraction" was that Americans despite their Russian war record are so popular in Russia whereas the Italians are not. But anyhow the "American Attraction" consisted of an immense cannon—possibly paper maché from which a young man dressed as an aviator was shot high in the air and landed in a net—perhaps 75 feet away. I was fascinated. But, I said, supposing now a Russian circus actor had such an idea. How would he get the money to finance it. Finally I got it cleared up. He would go to the local Soviet of his city or state. If the idea were approved—that is if it were good for the Russian people, the local Soviet would either finance it itself—or get the state to do it. So you see how things are done in Russia today.

But to return: Our seats, were the best, and located in a box near the pit, cost 3.50 (roubles).

The program was excellent, not one poor act. There were about ten numbers and three intermissions during which the spectators went into the buffet and drank tea and beer and ate sandwiches and apples. The crowd was more proletarian and rough than the usual theater crowd in Russia. Nonetheless:

There were marvelous acrobats, jugglers, performing horses and riders, two very funny clowns, one a dwarf, and as the final climax, the so-called 'American attraction'. The great cannon was moved on a large auto truck and it took some time to prepare for the act, placing the cannon at just the right angle, etc. During this time some of the spectators sat holding their ears. But the report was not loud. I think springs did the work.

One thing I noticed—the same silly clownings that tickle an American audience tickled these Russians. The laughter was loud: the applause noisy.

While so different from one's childhood memories of the traveling circus in tents, there was a similar atmosphere, and the odors arising from the dust and smell of horses in the pit were reminiscent of American circus days.

We then returned to the hotel and I slept soundly in the huge queer room which had been assigned me.

Monday, Nov. 28-1927- Leningrad - Hotel Europe
Another gray and slushy day. And the usual Russian breakfast—cold meats & hot chocolate. I am entirely surrounded by VOX-men—the

Leningrad branch of the Soviet Society for Cultural relations. I do not know their names—but they provide cars, arrange interviews & tours. Come & get you at the proper hour, usher you in and out of cars & so on and so forth. It would be easy for a fool to get a false impression of his importance. And so often—nearly all the time—and in the midst of it all, I wish I were out of Russia and at home—in 57ᵗʰ Street—in the little house at Mt. Kisco.

At 10 a.m. interview with Ivan Ivanovich Kandrataev, Vice President of the Leningrad District Soviet. *He* Is a plain looking young man who was a metal worker before the Revolution. *And then questions & answers:*

Are you elected from this district?
I am elected by the local Soviet and by the Congress of the Soviets as Vice President of the region.

What are your activities?
I am, the administrat of the city and of the gubernia, like the governor of a state. I direct the work of the local Soviets, but as Leningrad has no city Soviet, this is the regional Soviet.

Do you have control of factories, stores, etc.?
Yes, there are two classes of industries: those of state importance and those of local importance (here 35% are of general *or* state *importance.* The industries in Leningrad Gubernia are valued at 300 million roubles. There is a separate production and supply department. The general state industries here are ship building (commercial), construction of machines, turbines, textile manufacture, etc. Our local industries are to sustain local needs; shoe factories, paper, building materials, but more and more the government is giving the Leningrad district more heavy industries to operate. The Leningrad Soviet has much initiative in the management of *its* industries. We receive many orders from the government to supply materials, machinery, etc. Unfortunately, we are unable to fill all these orders because of lack of materials and money and machinery. We use the bulk of our capital for extension of industry. Our 15 millions profit last year was all put back into industry, as our demands are growing so fast.

Did *using* this 15 million *in this way cause you to be glad?*
Of course, we neglected many fields, but if we had 150 million profit we would put it all back into industry, because we must satisfy the demands of the country. If we had more money we would invest in new commercial enterprises, i.e. new factory for artificial silk. We have been built a new wood turning factory as *heretofore* we have had to buy these *things* abroad. In the chemical industry, we must

import from Germany, *and if we had the money we would like to build a large chemical plant. But it will come.*

Does this industrial development program take from the building of workers houses, sanitariums, and other social needs?

Yes, it affects our social welfare work, but still we *set aside* a certain percent for this work, too, because the city is growing in industrial population and so the demands of the workers are growing.

You yourself are a worker. What difference do you notice in the energy of the worker today as compared with under the czar?

In the whole mass you feel a great enthusiasm. Worker feels that he is the boss, that his wish is the wish of the government. The whole administration is changed. The worker, even if he is not politically intelligent feels this. Under the czar, the welfare of the worker was not the business of the state; under the czar the worker had no interest in production.

What about women in industry now as compared with former times?

There are many more women workers now.

Does not this cause unemployment?

Yes, of course, but the enlargement of industry is decreasing unemployment. There are 136,000 unemployed in Leningrad. Of these, 96,000 are women of which number 60% are seeking employment for the first time.

How soon do you think you can liquidate unemployment?

It is difficult to answer, on account of the abnormal conditions, because not only national but international conditions affect the question. Also the increasing demand of women to work in industry. But nevertheless we are short of skilled workers and must train workers to fill these needs.

What do you do to train this 136,000 unemployed?

There are special labor collectives (labor schools) in which 11,000 workers are studying various trades in a 7 to 8 months course. These students are then put in factories as apprentices.

Are only young workers? No, both young and old. For the youth are special industrial schools in the factories.

Are the unemployed hungry?

Here are the figures from the report of the Leningrad Soviet. They receive a subsidy from the government (35 roubles for a man with a family) and from the trade unions 28 roubles and all the usual trade union benefits; also only a nominal fee of five kopeks for living quarters. *That* we also organise communal work on streets, and railroads, heavy work for men and lighter for women, for which they receive 1:60 to 2.00 roubles a day–*but many* prefer the subsidy to work! (This is only an example to show they are not starving). About 60% of these unemployed *are* members of families, *some of whom* work. Still there is a significant part really hungry, *and another part deliberately idle* because there are certain people whom you can't make work. And what can you do with them. They have the vote!

Why not take the vote from a man who does not want to work?

Our business is to see that the unemployed are not starving. Many unemployed are wives of workers and they refuse communal work and want to go into industry, or they do not want to accept dirty work.

What is the Soviet Government going to do with the loafer?

If he consistently refuses to work, we can take up the matter of putting him out of the union. But we are more patient with qualified workers who do not want to accept unskilled labor.

What becomes of the loafer eventually—beggar or bandit?

There is very seldom such an occurrence. Among the criminal element we are doing educational work and there are special institutions in which they are taught to work.

What about the housing of labor? In Moscow I saw that the living conditions of the workers are very bad. In new quarters even they are living five and seven in one room without separate bath. Doesn't the government want to raise the standards of the workers? Isn't it better for workers families to have separate quarters?

When the workers made a revolution, they didn't do it for bathtubs but for political power. We are poor, there are many tasks before us. We can satisfy the cultural demands of the workers only through the broad masses themselves. But we feel it is necessary to do all this. The conditions in Leningrad are better than in Moscow. For instance, before the revolution, even the most cultured people not only did not have private baths, but they had only a toilet in the yard. We would gladly build three room apartments with bath, but we must spend 12,000 roubles for such quarters, and with this same money we can supply housing for many more people. Furthermore, the Russian is accustomed to the public bath (banya-steam bath) and prefers it to the private bath.

The demand for education on the part of the worker is tremendous since the revolution. Before the revolution it was only the church for the woman and vodka for the man. If we had to deal with a people already educated the problems would not be so great.

What about roads?

Our program is modest, we use the U.S. as an example, there is a department for the improvement of auto connections, but we need machinery to construct roads *and we havent it yet.*

Will the auto be collectively or privately owned?

Privately owned, just as apartments and houses may be privately owned—for the life of the worker. He can sell—or will his house. On his death such a thing is usually sold & the proceeds divided equally among his wife & children. A car could be sold. But of course people with a home or a car pay higher taxes—much higher than do others.

Kandrataev then called the head of the Commission for Construction of Workers Dwellings of the Presidium of the Leningrad Soviets and asked him to show me what is being done by this department. He was a fair, rosy faced young man who seemed very eager to show the new workers houses. The Soviets furnished a car to take us about.

We went first to a large apartment house constructed by a cooperative building group. On the outside, it *was* a very attractive structure, the plaster tinted in soft colors of gray, lavendar and red. The building had 415 rooms and cost one million roubles. It was finished only a short time ago and the courts *were* not yet in order. The apartments *were* 1, 2 and 3 rooms without private bath. There *was but one* bathroom *to* each section, that is, one bath to 40—persons, and each entitled to only 2 hours per week! It is proposed to keep these bathrooms only for the children and build steam baths (banya) in the courtyards, *because, so they say, Russians prefer them!*

I can never understand that—the herd instinct in these people—but it is true. They appear to have to work and live in groups. Their village, factory and apartment life is communal

One thing that illustrates this was to be seen right here in these new apartments for workers.

Each corridor or section also had a community kitchen. Here the large cook stove was full of pots and pans, soup boiling, meat cooking, and about the stove stood half a dozen women *neighbors* stirring and watching their various kettles. The hours from 5 to 8 in the evening *were* reserved for the working women to do their cooking.

The first apartment we looked into was two rooms, the walls of course *were* fresh and attractively colored, but the furnishings were of the most heterogenous and cheapest. Five people, a man and wife, grandmother and 2 children lived here. In the second two room apartment lived 4 people, husband, wife and 2 children, in the third, 1 room, of a three room apartment, lived 5 people, husband, wife, grandmother and 2 children. The husband and wife both worked and earned between them 115 roubles a month, paid 13.98 per month rent and found it difficult to live. Across the hall 6 people lived in two rooms, the husband and wife earned together 100 roubles, paid 27 roubles a month rent and according to the grandmother who was at home, they were very well satisfied. It was always a mystery in a Russian *home for me* to understand where they all sleep. But in one of the small rooms was a crib, two children's beds and a couch and in the other room, the woman pointed with pride to a good new 'double bed'. 'Of course, we are satisfied,' she said, 'before we slept on the floor in a little damp room. Now we have a nice warm, light clean place, two rooms and look at our beautiful new bed!' How a husband and wife can sleep on these narrow beds is a wonder to me. I should think they would have to strap themselves together.

On each floor *of the building was* a large alcove for social life, a 'Lenin corner'. *If I have not explained before now the nature of the "Lenin Corner" I should. It is the seat or centre in every apartment house, club, factory, shop, school, theatre—anywhere where a group of employés or residents or citizens can be gotten together where the young and the old are instructed not only in the doctrines of Marx and the virtures of the communal life as practised here in Russia, but the dangers of a world war against Russia, the need of the mass sticking together, learning to use rifles, bombs and also to practise first aid & and self help in times of disaster. And everywhere in these places pictures of Lenin and Stalin (no longer any of Trotzky. He is out). And cartoons or lithographs—(most lurid in color of enormous, hog like plutocrats with their fat heels on the necks of the chained workers lying at their feet. And other cartoons of red workers in solid array—their guns leveled, their bayonets sharply pointed, repelling an oncoming horde of plutocratic soldiers. And mottoes—"All for one; One for all" "Down with Plutocracy". "Remember the White Guards; the Red October". And maxims or quotations from Marx and Lenin. And always pictures of Marx and Lenin. And a statue of Lenin. I figure the Lenin Statue Population of Russia to be at least 80,000,000. And often actual revolvers, guns, bombs, bullets and the like, with cards or small strips illustrating the proper use of the same. And gas masks—with details of their proper use. And always some comrade to come nightly and lecture or explain—firing the masses with pictures of the danger in which they stand. Here also educational programs are undertaken—illiteracy liquidated for one thing. There may also be lectures on dietetics, sanitation, the care of children or the house—even lessons in some trade or art. Maybe a radio with lecturer, speeches or patriotic songs coming over that. Never, never, anywhere have I seen the equal of it. There is something strange, almost mystic in the fever of these people to consolidate their gains—make themselves sure that what they have attained shall not be taken away from them. And always in every house, shop, store, school, factory, club, theatre a communist or two—members of the party in good standing whose business it is to see that sentiment in each group is rallied to the Soviet idea. They are what are known as Party workers & in order to get up in politics and so attain power & position (the only avenue to power and position in Russia) one must be a communist in good standing in the Party—ready to do any duty assigned one—with a long record of services rendered in one field or another. It is like party workers in any close organization anywhere. One must work hard, do anything in order to get up. And so, in these "Lenin corners" every where, these party workers shine. I wondered all the time I was in Russia what this propaganda for communism, was, faith in the future of the party & the worker in Russia forbodes for the future of the whole world. I wonder.*

In this building the dormitories of the factory students, those young workers—many of them orphans because of the great war—who are being taught by the Soviet Government to be skilled workers. They have also almost a religious regimen to endure—early or at least regular hours, respectable habits, diligence in the prosecution of their political as well as their practical studies. And all watched by the local Soviet which gives them their chance in order to see that they are going in the proper mental & moral direction. Could the Catholic church do more—I ask you.

We found one of the boys at home in the long, clean room with several comfortable iron cots in a row. He was a sturdy, dark faced boy of 16 with bright brown eyes and a turned up nose. He said he came from White Russia, that his brother works in a factory in Leningrad and *that much his* family was too poor to take care of him, his brother *later* sent for him to come to the factory school. He was studying to be a machinist, 4 hours work and 4 hours study a day, received 22 roubles a month and paid 2 roublés a month for his room.

Every three months his wages were increased and he hoped in a few years to be earning good wages, perhaps 200 roubles a month. He was writing a letter to his family, and after some shyness and hesitation, consented to let us read it. He wrote a beautiful hand, and began his letter 'My Dear Ones'. He wrote how satisfied he was in the school, how nice his living conditions were compared with what he had known at home: 'I live with two other boys in a large, clean room heated with central heating, I have a comfortable bed, and find it very nice after sleeping on the floor at home'. *Can you wonder that the young Russian worker is for Soviet Russia—or that he is likely to do as he is told—if necessary fight & die for his native land.*

We next visited *some* attractive looking new buildings which I had noticed the first day, very large cement houses joined together with arches with large courts inside, and colored in attractive shades. Nearby *were* the old working class houses, *of old Russia,* old frame one-story structures falling to pieces. But inside the new buildings I encountered the familiar Russian smell, a pungent odor combined no doubt of cabbage, sheepskin and tobacco. In a 3 room flat 2 families were living, they had a separate *or rather communal* kitchen in the flat and a toilet, but no bath. A neighbour was visiting and she invited us to come over and see her room. I commented on the hospitality of the people everywhere. We followed her to her room in another adjoining building; it was also part of a three room apartment. She lived in this one room with her husband and daughter who was in high school. *Once there though* She complained bitterly that her daughter did not have a separate room and called attention to the damp wall. (These houses *were* built, as is a large part of Leningrad, on marshy land, and dampness must be a great problem). We tried to escape from her complaining. 'Thank you,' she said 'for coming and examining the conditions, and I hope you will be able to do something about it'. She thought we were an inspection commission.

The head of the department said that the building program for next year would provide housing for 15,000 people.

In the evening I went to the Sovkino and was given a private showing of three pictures.[9] *These related—one to rural or village life in Russia—a really beautiful picture—the best cinema photography I have ever seen. I want to have it shown in America. The other two related to*

---

9. The Soviet film studios in Leningrad were known as the Sovkino.

the Red-White wars between 1918 and 1922—When Denikin, Yudenich and other paid mercenaries of English, Japan, France & the United States invaded war worn Russia. (A fine reward for all their earlier fighting for the Allies).[10] They were interesting pictures—very—one in particular of a red sailer who afterwards became leader of a regiment was now cut off from the Main Army & tried to make his way to the Black Sea in order to aid the Red Army there. It showed how he was made a fool of by an attractive woman bandit & her band—and what he did to her afterwards— killed her.

A second war picture related to the secret service men or spies—of the two opposing armies red & white—and how a red spy finally got the best of a white one, although in the beginning it looked as though he was sure to lose his life.

Tuesday, Nov. 29– 1927– Leningrad – Hotel Europe

In the morning I went to visit the rubber factory, 'The Red Triangle', the largest in Russia. We were shown into the office of the Red Director (one who has risen from the workers and been trained by the new government) Alexander Adamovitch Isnen, a short, heavy set man with curling moustaches, heavy arched brows, keen eyes, his broad face shrewd and good natured. He walked with a limp and was shabbily dressed in a baggy old gray suit and dark shirt. He had worked 21 years in this factory as a worker and only since the revolution rose to be Chief Director.

The factory employs 16,000 workers. Here the whole process of rubber production is carried out—tires, gloves, machine goods,—God knows what, but the largest production is rubber overshoes. Rubber tires are manufactured in small quantities, only enough to supply the needs of the country. From the political point of view the line of work of all factories is the same.

Is this only a branch of the rubber industry of Russia?

Yes, it is one of 4 such plants of the All-Russian Rubber Trust,

---

10. Anton Ivanovich Denikin (1872–1947) was a Russian general during World War I. After the Russian Revolution he was jailed for supporting a revolt against the socialist government, but he escaped and established an army in the south of Russia. Denikin's White Army (as opposed to the Red Army) was a powerful anti-Bolshevik force until 1920. Nikolay Nikolayevich Yudenich (1862–1933) was a Russian general during the Russo-Japanese War and again during World War I. In 1919 he commanded the White Army units based on the Baltic; his attack on Petrograd in that year was beaten off by the Red Army. Both generals were supported by the British and French with troops, supplies, and weapons during 1918 and 1919.

1 in Moscow, another in Odessa. Our system of organisation is different from a United States plant. We do not sell our products, we only produce and have no connection whatever with the sale. *The government arranges the selling.*

Do you employ foreign specialists?

Of our 108 engineers all *are* Russian, but we have had specialists from America and we make regular trips to America for investigation and study.

Would it *not* be better to divide such a big plant *instead* into smaller *ones* on account of transport?

If the raw materials were Russian products, it would be better if the plant were more centrally located, but 90% of the materials are imported, mostly by water.

Would not Odessa be a better place, it is an open port all the year?

But Odessa is also far from the center and our port is open enough during the year. In technique we are up to date in general world methods. Last year we would have liked to buy a half million roubles worth of material in America, *but we had no money to spare.*

Is what Rykov says true about production being two and one half times dearer in Russia *than elsewhere?*

No, not *quite* so much. *It is some dearer here.*

And Why.

Because we have many expenses unknown abroad. For every rouble of production, we spend 32% for the social welfare of our workers, insurance, vacations, pregnancy of women, cultural work.

What is your salary?

225 roubles and a 4-room apartment. There are certain workers who receive more than I do.

How much does the best technician receive?

600 roubles a month and quarters.

And the lowest paid worker?

60 roubles. We have the piece work system here, and there are only about 18 workers getting as low as 2 roubles a day. We have an 8-hour day and if the work is dangerous or injurious 6 hours.

You were a worker under the czar. Is the worker now better qualified and more intelligent than before?

The qualifications of workers in 10 years could not change much, but we have technical schools for the training of a new army of qualified workers who will take the places of the old ranks. Before the revolution, 60% of the workers in this plant were illiterate, now only 1%. 51% of the workers are men and 49% women.

How do women compare in productive power with men?

We have here a kind of production which demands the work of women, which requires not so much physical strength as delicate craftsmanship. *In that respect of course they are better than men—they can do little, delicate things which men cannot do as well.*

Do you consider women as valuable as men?

Certainly. There is no difference in pay as in capitalist countries, where women are used for work because their wages are lower.

What about the social life in America (question of Director).

The basis of the American government is the welfare of the masses and American workers are the best off in the world.

Question by the director:

"When you consider what Russia accomplished in spite of the fact that the capitalist system had never developed *here*, that we had an imperialist war, revolution, civil war and famine, under an administration of simple workers, what do you think she could have accomplished under the Soviet power if she had had the industrial development of America before the revolution? *I answered that I knew that Russia had accomplished wonders & could & would do more. However since he proceeded to attack America* I answered at length about the unselfish work of scientists in America and the achievements of American financiers in building up industry, 50% income tax, gifts of rich men to country, improvement of social conditions to a high point . . . "And perhaps the next step" *I added* "will be the Soviet system, and I believe if this system were put to the masses in America, they would accept it."

Are not *the above* steps being taken *merely* to intrench capitalism and deceive the masses?

No.

The Director then personally conducted us through the factory. In all it is 40 versts in length.[11] I did not of course go through the whole plant, but we walked for almost two hours and saw the process of preparing the raw rubber and all the different products being manufactured: tubing, water bags, tires, combs, parts of telephones,

---

11. A *verst* is a Russian unit of distance that equals approximately 3500 feet.

waterproof cloth, rubber balls and dolls, overshoes enough for all Russia, with the new Ford system of 8 to 36 persons working on the whole process on one overshoe. *At one point* the Director blandly led me into this room where a score of girls were innocently rolling *rubber protectors or "overcoats" for males* on black sticks. This reminded me of the story of the fellow who came into a drug store and bought one, then came back *in 30 minutes* and bought two, then half a dozen, and finally *all in a dingle* came back and bought 6 dozen. He said he had decided to stay all night. We went on down the aisle, the Red Direcor shouting with laughter over this story. Trevas *my red guide* was also very much interested in this branch of the production *as I noticed.*

When we had returned to the Director's office, he ordered tea and platters of bread and bologne and I started off on the subject of his salary again.

Is it true that you receive only 225 roubles?

Well, besides I have the right to use one of the factory automobiles day or night for business or private purposes.

Why does a Soviet director receive 225 and not 1000 roubles?

Marx has said that 'life develops the mind'. If I as a director would get ten times more than the workers, it would withdraw me from their psychology.

Do you want to be near the workers as a Communist or as a person?

Our policy *is to* develop *ourselves* along with the intellectual development of the masses.

If you had the choice would you rather be at the bench or here in the director's chair?

Personally, I think under our conditions it is easier to be a worker than to direct a factory.

That is not answering my question.

I am a member of the Party, by birth a worker, but by present conditions a director. I must decide where I am more useful and work there. I consider that I can be more useful to the government as a director than as a worker.

But as a human being, what is your wish? Put aside all your duty to the Party, etc. etc.

Very well, I put aside all considerations of the Party, etc. etc. Here is Janen, a man. Let Mr. Dreiser answer one question: can you as a writer believe that it is possible to look on a man only from the human point of view *and* independent of his environment?

Yes. I see the man as a unit in a mass. There is the mass & there is the unit. And cannot blend them.

Why are you a writer?

I was born a writer.

Then I was born a director.

I laughed but Aside to Trevas with whom I made a bet that Janen would not answer my question: *I said* Give me five kopecks. *And he paid.*

Since he once more proceeded to attack America as a gross, material, reactive land I launched into a patriotic oration about the debt Russia owes to America for her industrial technique, machinery, etc.

Yanen: There is a proverb: Nothing existed in the beginning. God made the first man and hung him on the wall to dry. From where did America learn the capitalist system? America is an international nation. Her capitalists, her financiers, her scientists, came from every country in the world. Her capitalists, as you say, were nothing at the beginning, so that is why America is a democracy. They were poor immigrants, who risked all in coming to the new world, and there the rich natural resources gave them the opportunity to develop and create industry. *Without them where would your capitalists be?*

But without our capitalists, our money geniuses, our inventions & what not else where would America be. I answered and I traced the rise & services of various financial giants — Col. Cornelius Vanderbilt *& the railroads,* Jay Cooke *& the financing of the Civil War;* John D. Rockefeller *& oil;* Pullman *& the sleeping car;* Carnegie *& the steel industry & his libraries,* Ford *& his car;* Hearst; Crocker, Stanford *& others, the Union Pacific;* Armour *& the meat industry* — *a long list. I showed briefly what they had done for a land that needed to be developed and was developed quickly by genius functioning individually and for gain. I insisted that the big brain had powers & capacities for service which the little one had not & which it must reflect* — *though I hold no brief for exploitation and least of all tyranny. The lion and the lamb should lie down within reasonable distance of each other* — *but he would not agree with me. The capitalist must be hobbled* — *or harnessed like a horse & compelled to draw the heavy earthly burdens for the little man. Here in Russia it was so. If a man wanted position he must serve and for the same wages as the little man. I* *agreed that this might be made true if the proletariat continued to maintain an armed dictatorship and could not be outwitted by the strong man with the big brain. It might even be possible by catching all people young (ala the Catholic Church) to psychologize the strong brains as well as the weak ones into believing that communism was right—the only truth—but I was not sure. Nature was by no means entirely collective or entirely individualistic. Here & there was an individualistic animal; also a collective herd. Both did well, only the individualistic animal preyed & thrived in the herd.*

"And should exterminated" he added.

"All right," I replied, "catch your children early—before the religionist or the individualist get them & train them to 'kill the individualist'."

"We will catch the individualist & train him to believe in communism."

"It is the only way you will down him" I replied. But I wrote in his book. "I have talked with and learned from an able man". He wanted my address so that if ever he was permitted to enter America he could look me up.

In the evening we went to the Sovkino again and saw two excellent pictures: 'Storm' and 'Ryazanskiye Women'.[12]

'Storm' is a story of the civil war in the south. A Russian sailor takes part in the October Revolution in Petrograd and then commands a detachment of red soldiers in the fighting in the south. On the march they capture a small group of bandits who are led by a woman. This woman is young and attractive and daring. She begins to use her charms on the sailor and against the advice of his assistant, the commander permits her to sleep in their room. A relationship thus begins between them, looked upon with distrust by the young assistant. In one of the captured towns, she organises her bandits, all of whom have accompanied the army, to rob the old owner of the house in which they are quartered. The young assistant officer discovers them in the execution of the crime and is killed by the woman. When the commander learns of the murder he is stricken with remorse and gives himself up to his men as a traitor who sold his friend for a woman. The soldiers do not want to punish him; the woman leader and the bandits are led out, and the sailor himself gives the order to shoot them. The plot is interesting and

---

12. *Storm over Asia*, directed by V. I. Pudovkin (1928); *Women of Ryazan*, directed by Olga Preobranzhenskaya (1927).

clearly worked out, the photography is good and the general technique very good.

The second picture is a gem. I have never seen more beautiful photography. The story is compelling, the characters and scenes very realistic. The story takes place in a village in Riazansky Gubernia. The leading figure is a big, stern old peasant with a long beard and keen, cruel dark eyes who rules his household with an iron hand. His eldest son has already been killed in the war which is going on in the year 1916, and he has taken unto himself the widow who lives with him and his wife. The younger son is of marriageable age and the daughter, a willful girl with some of the strength of character of her father, is in love with a blacksmith and goes to live with him without the consent of her father, which of course makes their marriage illegal in old Russia. The father prepares to marry off his son and calls the marriageable women of the countryside to his house to choose a wife. Only by chance a girl who lives with her aunt in an adjoining village and whom the young man had already seen and admired, is brought for inspection. The old man likes her himself and she is chosen. There is the gay wedding, and they are very happy, but shortly after, the young husband is called away to war and the father and the three women are left do do the farm work. After three years, news comes that the boy has been killed; the old man at once begins to pay open court to the young widow, this is noticed by the other two women and brings their hatred down on the head of the unwilling girl. The time comes when the old man attacks and violates the girl and she gives birth to a baby. News comes that the son is alive and is coming home. The girl is in a terrible position, scorned and hated by the two women and taunted and despised by the whole village as an immoral woman, she awaits the arrival of her husband in terror. When he comes, although the women know the truth, they tell the son that his wife has been untrue to him, and has a child by some unknown man. He throws her from him and in desparation she runs to the river bank, near which a spring festival is taking place, and throws herself in the river. When her body is carried into the cottage, the erring sister comes in and takes the child, telling the son that she will take it to the new Soviet children's home and that he should speak to the father of the child, their father, about it. She goes out down the road. The son, realising the truth, goes toward his father with upraised arm. Except for the little incident of the Soviet children's home in the picture, it is artistically perfect. The sweep of the grain fields rippling in the sunlight, the villagers in their picturesque costumes, the village streets, make lovely pictures. And like every serious picture of Sovkino, it has its social purpose.

After the program, the manager of Sovkino theaters, Timofaev, showed us the club of the 400 workers employed by the Leningrad Sovkino which directs 800 movie theaters in the gubernia. It was an extensive club with all the activities and sections to be found in every workers club connected with his place of work: wall newspapers, Lenin corner, radio, meeting hall, library, shooting circle and medical training corps, work with the villages, aid of homeless children, etc. It is to be noted that everything in the life of the worker centers about his place of work: first the job itself, then his insurance department at the place of work, the local of the Communist Party, the medical dispensary, the cultural department, then his trade union club which not only has educational circles but also has entertainments, etc., he also votes from his place of work. Timofaev said that he had just come from a factory meeting of 800 Young Communists who had gathered to discuss the kind of pictures needed. It was a big debate in which the Sovkino representatives took part. The evening before there had been another big meeting of workers in the Red Triangle Rubber Factory at which the workers expressed their demands as to pictures, and criticised the past achievements. For instance, they needed more pictures about young people, or about village life. From all these demands, the manager said that Sovkino sifts out a general public demand and trys to comply with it.

<u>Wed, Nov. 30th 1927 – Leningrad, Hotel Europe.</u>
Leningrad is in some ways more—in other less interesting than Moscow. Its streets are so much wider & more regularly placed—and in consequence and because of its division into islands and the width of some its waterways—the vistas are more striking. Water links always achieve perspectives for a city which a lack of them presents.

As for my entourage—the group which has been assigned me here is vigilant & genial but a little boring. There are so many fixed things the Soviet is determined the foreigner must see—usually (always, I might say) things which relect glory on the Soviet labors. In consequence I am hauled

here & there all to speedily. As for touching or sensing the intimate, com-
monplace life of the city—not a taste. And as for time to idle out about &
dream in out of the way places—not an hour.

And now as to Trevis—my chief guide. What a sly, opourtunistic
Jew. I am sure that at heart he is no more a communist than I am—but he
talks it all the time. Also I think he is making money on the side. He claims
he is only receiving 225 roubles a month but, unless I miss my guess, there
is a rake-off for him in the bills he compiles & keeps so carefully. But if you
talk to him—oh, what service the grafters & private concessionaires—are,
these snakes worming their way into the heart of this great Soviet System.
They ought to be shot. But that he is a grafter in a petty way I not only
guess but have pretty good reason to know.

At about 11 this day we started out on our at times—to me—tire-
some rounds. Museums—God—what a pest they can become. And today
was to be—(principally) Museums. There was—(1)

The Hermitage, a museum of art treasure just adjoining the
Winter Palace. Our guide, Alexander Vasilevitch Suslov, a man of
cultur gave very interesting information about the different works
of art. The first rooms were devoted to old ornaments and jewelry
excavated in the Crimea and dating back to the fifth and sixth centuries B.C. They were made of pure gold in intricate designs, some
so miniature that they could hardly be seen. There was a display of
crown jewels, diamonds, pearls, rubies, emeralds, which might easily
be sold to buy tractors without robbing the world of art treasures.
A large part of the enormous collection of cameos of Katherine the
Great was on exhibition, some of them done by the Empress herself.
Due to her devotion to art, there is a marvelous collec. of foreign
paintings, for instance, 40 Rembrandts, Rubens, Raphael, Leonardo
De Vin, Corot, room after room of rare pictures. Passing the border of the old museum, we entered the palace itself which is now
also a museum. From the windows of the salon of Katherine, I had a
sudden beautiful view of the river and on the other side the church
near the Fortress of Peter and Paul, its slender tall spire shining ra-
diantly in the light of the hitherto unseen sun of Leningrad. On the
other side, the window of the great rooms looked out on the square,
which was the scene of the greatest battles of the revolution in 1917
and where now the official demonstrations are held, as in the Red
Square in Moscow.

When we had finished our tour, I sat down to rest in the entry below.

From the Hermitage we went to the studio factory of Sovkino. This is the largest of the Soviet Moving Picture Studios in Russia just now—although a large one is being built in Moscow. This one covers about seven acres and is a small imitation of the same thing in Hollywood. They are getting ready to do great things so they say—and already you get a sense of how seriously they take themselves. Large salaries are not allowed nor palatial homes for directors or movie queens—(the chief director—Mr. Greenfeld—a Jew—only gets 300 roubles a month.—The highest star 300 roubles a week)—but just the same there are cars, office boys, sub-servient sub-assistants—a great show & clatter of direction— and so as much as anywhere they feel their oats. You cant get in unless you are somebody. They may "Tovarisch": (English—"Comrade") each other all they please—but I notice that a "comrade" in a lower position takes off his hat & bows & scrapes about as much as he does anywhere. Equality— a better day for the poor dub—he is going to run things—we'll wait & see.

The main building is very large and was before the revolution a great amusement palace with skating rink and other amusements. Now the rink is the main studio, and here 40 scenes can be taken at one time. There were sets standing for street scenes and interiors while on the side small scenes were being taken, close-ups etc. for instance, close-up of a Red Army officer with a revolver. The property rooms were like a vast junk shop, all kinds of furniture, pictures, dishes. In a separate building, rooms had just been completed which were especially light for their sculptor to make furnishings, statues, etc. on order for the sets. Using plaster on wood he was able to imitate very well stone structure.

By the time we returned to the comfortable offices, the director, Greenfeld, had arrived—a small, shrewd, middle-aged man, Jewish, speaks English fluently, and was much amused at my request for vodka and my surprise that a kino factory could run without it. He says he works about 16 hours a day, has been in the work only 3 years. Finally, vodka was found and I drank it in my tea, thus discovering a wonderful drink. We then went to the studio and had our pictures taken.

At 6—as usual we had dinner in the hotel dining room. I tried to persude someone to take me to a simple Russian restaurant in Leningrad—but no—foreigners must see only granduer—and what pinchbecks—left over granduers.[13]

At seven P.M. I have an interview:

Interview with Platon the Cardinal of the Russian Reformed Greek Church. *This was at my request and was arranged for me by the Leningrad branch of* VOX *—the Soviet Society for International Cultural relations. The reason I desired to talk with Platon was this. I heard that backed by Soviet influence he was trying to reform the Greek church from within;—to swing it—as near as possible, into some position where its adherents would be at least not inimical to Socialist Soviet intellectual and social programs. Also I had heard that he was in part successful—that so far he had succeeded in capturing 1/3 of the followers of the Orthodox Greek Church and that whether he personally proved successful or not it was likely that the movement headed by him would cause the remainder of the Orthodox Greek leaders—communicants, to adopt or accept a more liberal—or less dogmatic religious viewpoint. Hence the following:*

Platon, when he came, was dressed in simple long black robes. His long brown hair fell to his shoulders and above his long beard was a calm, beautiful face with large, brilliant gray eyes. He had that Christ-like expression so often noticed in priests.

- - - - How many people did the old Russian church represent?

80% of the population.

Was this the national religion?

Yes, it was obligatory on all citizens.

Do you represent the whole Russian church or only one part?

Only one part.

What % of the entire population are now adherents *of your part?*

32% of the religious population are my adherents.

What per cent of the population believes in the old church?

Two thirds in the old church, one third in the reformed church.

What per cent of the present population adheres to the churches?

50% of the former adherents.

You mean in other words, 50% of the former 82%.

Yes.

Why did your part separate from the old?

---

13. A *pinchbeck* is something sham or counterfeit.

After the October Revolution, the situation of the church was not in conformity with the new order. The leaders *of the old church* thought to use the old church to build Christian life in accordance with the old faith. This leadership of the church came in conflict with the new form of government. As a result, there came a full break *with* the old church and *this* aroused a political terror on the part of the government. The general lines of the old church after 1917 were laid out in decisions of a Congress of the old church. Tikhon, the leader, showed that he wanted to save Russia. After this discussion, some of the leaders of the church addressed in 1922 a petition to Tikhon in which they stated that if he continued the old policy it would have a very bad influence on the Russian church. The Patriarch replied that until the calling of the new Congress he would abdicate from his seat. I must say that this petition was inspired by the wish to organise a church which could satisfy more adequately the living needs of the masses.

What were the new principles of this movement?

The so called reformed church is a result of a movement which began in 1905 and these people were its successors. In order to understand the line of the church movement it is necessary to remember that the better representatives of the new church in 1905 wanted to change the superstitious mind of the people and give less emphasis to formalities. The new leadership had a new social outlook as well as new religion view and for this reason a certain number did not join the new reformed church. The religious mass was reactionary and conservative in their political point of view; some of the leaders were an arm of the czarist government and so were opposed to the idea of a political change. The illiterate masses belived that the new church was a political attempt of the Soviet Government to destroy their church. In the present *situation* the government is not interested in *my* church and *my* church has no connection with the government.

Will the state allow *your* church to develop as you wish, or does it interfere?

I shall continue with my explanation. The old church realized that it must repair the old mistakes, and in answer to the anathema of Tikhon made a statement that it legalized the social revolution and supported the Soviet Government, and so the Soviet Government gave full legal rights to this reformed church, and after six years we can say that there is no interference of any kind on the part of the Soviet Government, and on our side also no interference with the government.

What does the new church offer which the old church refused to give?

I must say that the old church did not and does not refuse to give the church reforms, but in the political struggle *which came after the October Revolution of 1917, the Orthodox leaders were so busy with politics & have been since that as yet* they have done nothing *toward real* reforms. The old church was generally led by priests in monasteries and episcopates *who had* lost ideological contact with the masses. They still wanted to hold the direction of the church and make martyrs of themselves if the government persecuted them. One of the ideals of the new church *is* to liberate the believing masses from *this* influence of the monastic group. But that does not mean that the new movement is entirely against monastics, for in general it supports the system. But in regard to marriage among the priesthood, the Congress of the new church made it possible for married priests to become lawfully high dignitaries.

"Is that what you consider one of the important reforms of the new Greek church?"

"I know what you are thinking. And I will answer you presently. Dogmatically this is an important reform. Married priests were not permitted to aspire to the highest places of the church. With this dogma the synod of the new church does not agree."

Two days ago, the Plenum of the Holy Synod, in preparation for the next Congress, was finished. At this, a resolution was passed concerning married priests—that there should be no difference between simple priests and high dignataries in their rights to marry. Of course, this organisational question is not by any means the principal difference between the new and the old. One of the principal aims of the new church is to educate the people, decrease illiteracy and in general bring the masses nearer to culture. As to dogma, we stand on strict eastern forms and close contact with the Eastern Greek church.

Then there has been *no change* in dogma?

None. Mine is a purely orthodox church. The orthodox Eastern churches have their official representative to the new Holy Synod *of my church, and by them he* is considered *the* real representative of the real Russian orthodox church.

------ Do the dogmas of the Greek church coincide with the Roman church of the west generally?

Many are the same, but the Roman church departed somewhat from the old beliefs. The Eastern Greek church represents more closely the fundamental principles of Christ.

"*To you the Pope at Rome is not the divinely authorized Vicar of Christ on earth?*"

"*No*"

"*And never has been*"

"*No.*"

"*Your general sacrements are about the same?*"

"*Yes*"

"*Confession?*"

"*Yes*"

"*Communion*"?

"*Yes*"

"*Baptism?*"

"*Yes*"

"*Marriage*"?

"*Yes*"

"*By the way is your reformed church growing or is it failing?*"

The reformed church, as far as recognised as the real representative of the orthodox church, is getting stronger. The old church is only recognised by the Soviet Government in July 1927 and now will be legalised. But *at present* there is a conflict for power among the leaders. In the reformed church there cannot be this struggle for power because the plan of the new management places it not in one head but in all the high dignitaries, and the body of followers has a voice in electing the high priests.

Then you are sovietizing the church?

No, we are only returning to the old customs of the church when the dignitaries were the elected representatives of the congregation.

------ That was only for 300 years. *after Christ*

But the church itself never destroyed the system, it was the state which put her own high officials into the church in positions of power. Now that the church is again free from the domination of the state it can again put in this system.

------ Does *your* church do any social welfare work?

In every *one of our* church organisations *of my faith* there *is a*

body of followers who do welfare work in their own community. Besides, the followers themselves must take care of the church, do the
cleaning, etc. They must also do intelligent Christian charity, help
their neighbors—

-------- What is intelligent Christian charity?

The old church did not try to give material support to the followers, but we try to organise brotherly material help.

--------- How will you help materially? With hospitals etc. like the
Soviet Government.

The Christian religion demands an attitude of brotherly love
among its followers in an intimate way *but* we consider all the charitable organisations of the old church harmful. Therefore, when the
government wanted to take away from the church the right to organise charitable institutions, we agreed with the state.

------- How then do you help?

We don't consider this a special problem and do not take active
part in the organisation of institutions, but teach brotherly love. For
example, when the earthquake occurred in the Crimea, we did not
give direct aid, but when the government made an appeal to the
people, the church proposed to collect money in the church and
give to the fund. During the famine, the government demanded help
from the churches. The old church said, if we give church treasures
for famine relief we must do it officially through our church and not
give these treasures into strange hands—but the new church said, it
is good that the state has organs to help the famine, and we will help
through them.

"*In other words the church seeks to support the state instead of de-
manding that the state submit to the church?*"

"Yes"

"*But is not this abdicating the supreme rulership and direction of the
God you worship?*"

"*No, The ideologic view of the new church is different. We see the
spirit of God,—his hand—in certain necessary social changes—changes
that oppose evil and aid good. Thus we feel that certain social improvements can spring from the will of the people,—can even be created by
social revolution and that this can bring about a society or social condition
not unlike* the reign of God on earth which will come some day. This
belief in the social revolution is an important fact because this is
why some are leaving the new church, because they say that revolt is

not right, that it is never right for classes to go against one another. But we say that revolt of the oppressed against their oppressors is a natural development, and we are against not the oppressed but the oppressors; in this we follow the old prophets of the Bible.

-------- Is your church content to leave the education of the children to the state or do you want—to influence it?

We think thus: that the intellectual development of the individual must be voluntary and not in any way forced, and therefore as long as the state takes care of education we think it dangerous—*as long as that education is in line with the social welfare of the mass to dictate the religious principles which must govern.*

"Yet the church expects at some time to influence the individual (when he is grown)?

The church does not leave the child without its influence. It gets this through the Christian family. The child is also permitted to participate freely in the mysteries of the church. When the child is grown and has attained cultural development *he* begins to take an interest in all sides of life, and *it is then that* church must on its side make its propaganda.

------- But suppose the child is educated in the modern way, science, Darwin, history, philosophy, how will the church approach *him when we are,* what will it offer?

If a person so educated has not at the same time lost interest in the church, the church has all kinds of materials to present of a scientific nature in which he can find truth. Social academics of religious science which will produce religious scientists exist.

------ But You maintain belief in the direction of a divine Power.

"Yes."

"Yet in my reading of the present Soviet or Communistic faith it does not believe in the direction of a divine power. There is a public sign in Moscow which reads "Religion is the opiate of the people".

"I know of it. None the less we believe that the direction of the divine power is visible in many—most of the idealistic principles of the present regime"

"But the present Soviet regime will not trust the education of the child to any religion—yours included.

"That is true"

Do you agree with that?"

We are a practical church organisation and have not taken up the question. But my personal opinion is that such training in general culture, true cultural development, *as is now given in Russia* does not conflict with religious—education.

"*But if the education of the child were in your hands, how would you proceed to educate it.*"

"*Naturally the principles & dogmas of our faith could not & would not be ignored. But since we are faced by a condition which gives a general and helpful education to the child we content ourselves with work—or perhaps better yet the influence of the church in the home. When the child is old enough We give all material for and against to him and the child decides for himself, for we believe that the individual must develop himself.*

-------- Don't you believe that when a man is educated in the Soviet schools that your dogmas will conflict with his education and contradict them?

I answer so:

If a man finishes a broad cultural and material education and cannot agree with our dogmas, then it means that the church will die. But if we could believe that such a thing could happen, we could not go on with our work, for the need of a faith in something will always remain.

------- Don't think that I am asking silly questions. I have always believed that religious emotions need not conflict with science. In the United States the Catholic Schools confine the education of the child to subjects which will not conflict with religious dogmas, *in short* only practical subjects are taught.

"*So I understand. But as you see for yourself there is no possibility of such a situation here. We are not permitted to educate—merely to influence the child—if we can.*

"*And still you believe religion will not die*"

"*I am sure of it. Indeed as regards* the eternal conflict between the Hegelian theory and the religious theory, between the theory of the divine mind and the materialistic mind, if the thesis of materialism predominates, an antithesis will arise in the matter of the spirit.

----------Will there be *then, do you think,* a new interpretation of life from two points, the spiritual and material?

"I have studied philosophy, but it is difficult in a few words to discuss these questions. I think it is better to finish first our discussion of the church movement . . . Now the minority is with us because we don't want big crowds. What we want is well trained and cultured people who will spiritually understand *and accept* our faith. Our material conditions are bad; the old church organises a material boycott against our church, and even deprives our followers materially when possible, so we are very poor. But our organisation is very strong and has connections with foreign churches and nucleuses in Greek orthodox churches abroad. So with full faith and peace we face the future.

Thursday Dec 1–1927– Leningrad–Hotel Europe

Although the day started badly, (there was not enough on our program to make it worth while spending another day in the city) nevertheless I had a very interesting day. In the morning we went to the Leningrad Public Library, which, with the Library of Congress, is counted the second largest in the world, 4,600,000 books. After the revolution, the acquisition of large private libraries doubled the number of volumes. The building itself is very old, in fact, the entrance to the administrative offices was so dilapadated that I was sure we were making a mistake. However, as we progressed in our journey through the many rooms, the appearance greatly improved and the library began to wear an ancient dignity and grandeur. The endless leather bound volumes were closely placed on shelves reaching to the ceiling, and rare books stood or lay in glass cases, for instance the entire library of Voltaire, purchased by Katherine after his death. There were many original manuscripts of Russian writers like Tolstoy and Dostievsky. I inquired about the philosophy department, but it was so vast that I had to ask *for* some specific branch, so I chose witchcraft. I was led into a room and the director of that department, and his assistants began to bring me aged volumes of magic, sorcery, etc. in French, Latin, Greek, and I had some difficulty in escaping from the eager helpfulness of the librarian, for I had no time to pore over these fascinating old books. There was a special exhibit in one room of material from the October Revolution, placards, manifestoes, newspapers, etc. which would have been interesting to examine. Through a window above we looked down on the long reading room full of people sitting at the tables or waiting in line at the desk. However, it is quite evident that the reading room is not large enough for the patrons. A new building which will be finished in the course of a few years is now in process of construction to house this great library. As we went out, I met the chief librarian who is the father of the head of VOKS—*a little plump man with eye-glasses who comically resembles his son.*

One of things about this library that impressed me was the Sovietization of the same. In the office of the librarian—a large portrait of Lenin. Also one of Marx. In the reading room—(main), portraits of Stalin, Bukharin, etc. In one of the great chambers an exhibition of posters, pictures, pamphlets, books etc relating to the "Red October" and its triumph. In the library at large a special department filled with books relating to socialism, communism and the new Soviet ideology. In short the kow-towing of the intelligentsia to the workingman & peasent with the gun. And all the employes—from director down, extremely civil to everybody—especially the proletariat—everybody a Tovarisch—or Comrade, to everybody else; Marks, Engel, George etcetera, great & finest thinkers on this business of living & thinking—in short the intelligentsia kowtowing at present to brother farmer & worker, since they happen to be armed and directed by idealists who tell them that they are all there is to this business of living— that bread, potatoes and art come first for the worker—artisan really— and last for everybody else.

Oh, Aristotle—where art thou?

Our guide was a very solicitious and energetic young man; he insisted on my seeing the Academy of Sciences, and I didn't feel the slightest interest in it. But he had already telephoned the director that we were coming so I reluctantly submitted on the condition that we would escape as soon as possible. Fortunately no more important personage than the assistant director wasted his time on me. I asked him a few polite questions and he (a very energetic looking man with fiercely curling fair moustaches) disposed of me quite efficiently by packing us off to Pushkin's House. The main reason for my impatience with libraries, academies and museums was the fact that it was the first sunny day in Leningrad and the city looked so radiant with the bright sunlight shining on the snow and on the golden domes and spires that it seemed a crime to go inside. The chauffeur had put down the top of the car, and we went off to Pushkin's House again on condition that we would not stay long. The museum had been moved only recently to a very attractive gray stone building with large windows. The director himself very graciously conducted us about; I was glad to learn that the museum was devoted not only to Pushkin but also to all the Russian writers of his period. There were portraits and original manuscripts of all my favorite Russian authors, but the main exhibit was about Pushkin, which showed the different periods of his life from childhood to death. It seems that his grandfather was a negro, a page in the czar's court, and in his portrait one sees a resemblance to Pushkin. There were also pictures and articles concerning the duel in which he was killed by the husband of his wife's sister.

When we came out again the winter sun, which had circled low along the eastern sky, was almost setting. We crossed the bridge and drove for some distance to another part of the city to the Buddhist Temple. It is surrounded by a high wall, an exact reproduction of the temples in India, Siam and Mongolia. A friendly little Mongolian who came out at that moment agreed to show us the interior. Strange and impressive as was the outside of the fine structure, the inside made a tremendous impression on me as I entered and saw facing me a great idol of brass. The walls of the temple were hung with long strips of oriental silk and wierd paintings of Chinese looking figures were on either side the door. Here in Leningrad, old St. Petersburg, I had hardly expected suddenly to be transported to a mystic Indian temple.

As we drove back across the city in the early twilight, we passed a red wagon with a coffin standing on it and behind a few mourners walking. The coffin was wrapped in red cloth,—the funeral of a Communist. *Not far beyond this in the snow loomed up the blue & grey dome of the Mohamedan Mosque with its twin minarets standing before the church on a broad platform—quite the lovliest single building I have seen in Russia thus far. The early evening sky was so sleepy—with a faint pink glow on some clouds just above the horizon. Something at once gay & sad in the air. I fell to thinking of America—New York & singing Victor Herberts "Kiss me—Kiss me." R. K. who was along said—"Ah, that brings back California. I felt a touch of homesickness—ached if you will believe it to be out of Russia."*

At 7 P.M. we went to the theatre for Young Spectators. This is one of those propagandist ideologic theatres fostered by the Soviet Regime and intended to effect a change of social psychology in the mind of the young. All of these things—as I was beginning to feel, were redolent (odoriferous if you will) of the Catholic church & it's policy toward the young—its desire to color permanently the psychology of the same. I have said—and repeat—that the Soviet Central Committee got rid of one iron dogmatic faith only to erect a second & to me more dangerous one in its place.

However that may be I was enthusiastically greeted by the Director, Alexander Briantsev, a little man with a round fair face, mild blue eyes and a scant little beard which looked absurd on his childlike face; the stage director, Eugene Hackel, a thin young fellow; and a more sophisticated looking man, with a Shavian face, Waldemar Beyer, the decorator. The entry was buzzing with boys and girls ranging in age from eight to fourteen. The play of the evening was Schiller's 'The Bandits', and the stage director was eager to give me the outline of the plot before the play began. He had revised it somewhat for the children, had written a prologue to each act which connected the play with the life of Schiller, and was very proud of the results. The theater was exceedingly well built for the young audience, the broad seats in a semi-circle like an amphitheater, so that no spectator was far from the stage. I liked the stage sets very much, the scene was very quickly changed by shifting long silver pillars, swung on ropes into different positions, and some slight change of properties. But my first impression of the play itself was very bad. It seemed *to be* old fashioned declamation, but after the first act, I began to get accustomed to the shouting and came to the conclusion that the style of acting suited the play. Judging from the deafening applause, the laughter, sighs and tears, the young audience liked it. At the end of the first act, the stage director took us back to the director's tiny office. He introduced me to the pedagogical head of the theater, who studies the needs of the children and their reactions to the plays. There are forms which the children fill out giving their opinions and these, as well as observation of the spectators during performances, are the basis for their conclusions.

After the play, we returned to the director's office. On the way, we went behind the scenes and met the actors still in their grease paint and costumes. They gathered about and greeted me. One girl stepped up and said, 'We want to go to America'. I told them we would be very glad to see them all in America as they were good actors. In the little office of the director we were served tea and perozhniye (french pastries) and I asked a few questions.

------ What morals do you teach the children?

Not only communism but general principles of personal conduct, not to strive for personal good fortune but for the benefit of the community. But our chief aim is not to teach morals but to give pure art. Every community is made up of human beings and we must teach them to live together. Our theater is 'for young spectators' and we try to get our inspiration from our audience. We were the first, but now we have many followers.

------- Does the Soviet Government wish to make this kind of theater a part of the educational plan?

This is a provincial theater and so does not get direct support from the center, but our local Soviet supports us. (The theater costs the government 250,000 roubles a year). We try to educate the spectator so that when he grows up he will be trained to go to the new theater. The local Soviets try to organise more of such theaters and apply to us for advice so that the general idea will spread.

--------From where do the actors come?

First the founders were a small group, including the actors, who had been dreaming of this idea a long time. We at first got money from the Central Department of Education in Moscow, and then after two years from Leningrad. During the famine, we got only bread and herring. For two years the actors gave 30% of their salaries to the theater fund. The director had been a teacher in a children's school and had been a well known stage manager. Besides this first group there is a whole line of actors who come to the director and apply for places, but we cannot take casually, we take only specially qualified graduates of Actors' Universities and those who have the ideal of the children's theater. We have no school, but all actors receive special training here. In the craft of the actor it is necessary to follow one school. We follow the system of Stanislavsky as do most of the Russian theaters, including Meierhold.[14] We do not imitate him, but accept his discovery of the fundamental principles of the theater. The art of the actor has different expressions, he must convey emotions to the audience, his speech must be perfect. The rythm of the actors should be the same, and so vocal training is very important, especially choir training. The third requirement is motion—the actor must be nimble, graceful, and for this we have

14. Vsevolod Meyerhold was an actor and director who founded the Society of New Drama in Russia in 1902. In 1920 he became head of theater in the people's commissariat for education. He began his own theater in Moscow and had a working studio with student directors, one of whom was Sergei Eisenstein.

rythmic gymnastics, physical culture, dancing, fencing, acrobatics. Every day before rehearsals they have two lessons. According to the trade union law, the actor's working day is 6 hours, but our actors work 8 hours and even more. There are special meetings every week to discuss all aspects of the work.

In the matter of stage setting, We do not create special settings for each play but have a certain stage setting which we adapt. It is an original idea for a stage and was worked out by myself (director). We chose this particular building because of the possibilities of the stage. I decided upon the amphitheater and arena because I had always the idea that for the youth the stage must have a dynamic character and demand the freedom of the actor. So it was necessary to find a form of stage that would not restrict the actor's expression or dynamics. To give an uninterrupted view to every spectator, the circle is necessary. Of course, such a stage is poor for a play which demands many changes of scenery, so we added some principles of the medieval stage.

We then fell to discussing the present craze in Russia for Sovietizing all plays—twisting the psychology so as to inculcate communistic ideals. Seeing a stage setting for Uncle Toms Cabin *& inquiring when & how that was done, I finally asked—"How does your production of it differ from the American standard. Have you preserved it intact?"*

"No" was the reply—and I immediately sensed international complications.

Here We must adapt plays to audiences. In Uncle Tom's Cabin the attention *should* not center on Tom who is a passive character but on the active hero, George. But of course certain traditions of the book must be kept, only the direction is changed. *"You dont say", I thought and added aloud*
-------- I'm afraid that when my government hears of this there will be trouble. I shall do my best to prevent war.

Sinclair does not exist in the play. The sentimental part is thrown out. Eva doesn't exist—
--------- I'm afraid that I can't prevent war! Shelby is a good man to his negroes until he sells Eliza and her daughter (not son). There are their adventures during the flight and Tom, Eliza and her daughter are sold at auction. George, Eliza and her husband run away, and the engineer of a factory (invented) helps them. He appreciates George who is a clever worker, and Mr. Legree buys the daughter

and Tom. Tom and George help Eliza and her daughter to escape.
(There is no ice)—

--------- (I'm not even sure—that I want to prevent war!)
But there are three real wolf hounds, and at this point all the audience cries bitterly (we had to drop the music to decrease the weeping). LeGree flogs Tom. The daughter of Shelby gives Tom a revolver. LeGree sells the dying Tom, and the little negro boy (Ben)
takes the revolver and kills LeGree.

Leningrad, Friday, Dec. 2–1927 Hotel Europe

*In the morning I visited the Red Putiloff—the Great Engine Works of
Leningrad. This was built, so I understood, in 1835. Before the war—
under the Czar it employed 35,000 men. Today, under Communism it
employs 11,000. Two years ago it employed only 9,000. They make engines, tractors—an exact copy of Fords—also some special machinery—
on order. They make very large & I am told powerful engines yet with
this plant here capable of housing 35,000 men orders for engines are given
to the Baldwin Co. in the U.S.A. (Phila Pa) and some big company in
Switzerland. I looked over the Plant which is more or less meaningless to
one not of a mechanical turn. I did not like the idea of deliberately steal-
ing the Ford Tractor & copying it. Afterwards I talked with the Red
Director—the man who looks after the interests of labor & tried to get a
general idea of the state of the work here. As usual he painted a fair picture of progress—but knowing about the foreign orders for engines I could
not believe it. Also he stated that the technical directors were German &
Finnish—a fact which is not promising.*

*There are too many foreign directors in Russia—and too many local
labor authorities over them—for that is what it comes to. The emphasis
is always on the rights and the proper care of labor—never as it seemed
to me, at least not sufficiently, on the labor or productive power of the
workers—the technical skill & speed. The tempo of the place was slow.
Too many men fooling their time away over one small job—six men for instance pushing a small hand-car accross the yard—a hand car with 3 small
logs on it. One man could have done it. And when I inquired as to the
whyness of it—all I could gather was that there were certain union rules
which made groups in certain cases obligatory—and that these rules would
first have to be modified by the union leaders at Moscow before anything
could be done here.*

But the director (for the general state of affairs) had the usual excuses.

Insufficient machinery; no money to buy more—or not enough—or not fast enough. Not sufficient technical men in Russia. "Well, then", I asked, "what about,—temporarily—reducing the building program for laborers— all the millions paid on the new apartments and cottages with all improvements and putting that money into machinery". "All well enough to suggest but the state of the worker was so bad that his housing improvement could no longer be delayed. Besides he would not work as well as he did if his physical state were not improved. Besides the revolution had been based on a program of improvement for him & so it was only right & just that the first expenditures should be in his behalf. "But supposing all this expenditure on everything but this very necessary machinery results in the inability of Russia to meet all the needs of all the people—is not that likely to bring on unrest & counter revolution?" "No—because the general state of men in Russia was not so bad but that—knowing that the Central Government was doing all it possibly could for him with what it had, but that he would be content to wait until it could catch up."

"And so no real danger to the Communist goverment lurks in this slow or delayed service". "I think not".   I left him after another explanation as to why America would not loan Russia money—our American Banker goverment. Also why Sacco and Vanzetti were hanged in Massachusetts—the very peculiar Elements which might explain why the American people—in the main—was indifferent to their fate.[15] He shook his head. I am sure he was convinced that I was a materialistically infected bourgeois—or blood-sucker, not fitted to either grasp or sympathize with the ills of the underdog.

P.S. This interview lasted from $11^{\underline{30}}$ to 5 P.M. After dinning at the Hotel Yevro Parsky—with my five guides & mentors I left at 11—accompanied by Trevas and Ruth Kennell for Leningrad. There was, I learned afterwards, a sharp quarrel between Trevas and Ruth because she would not sleep with him. Her statement to me was that she was sure—unless she chose to yeild to him—which she did not, that he would force her out of her position as travelling secretary to me—he having more pull with the Cultural Relations Society than she did.

15. Nicola Sacco and Bartolomeo Vanzetti were Italian immigrants and political radicals convicted of murder and robbery, despite conflicting evidence and testimony. Their case became a cause célèbre in the United States during the 1920s and sparked demonstrations and riots; the two men were electrocuted on 23 August 1927.

RETURN TO MOSCOW

Moscow, Saturday, Dec 3rd 1927 – The steady unchanging cold & snow of Russia is always fascinating to me. It is so much the one thing—in regions outside the cities vast level spaces covered with snow—and occasional patches of woods—and occasional snow banked villages with their one church & their flock of jackdaws—the cities with their creamy white houses and bright church towers. . . . . Once you know Russia as it is today, at least and if you are of a sanitary turn of mind, you will always resent the dirt—the underlying, nagging thought that never leaves you (once you are in the country) that there may be bed-bugs or a cockroach in the soup— or something unclean about the bedding or the water—or what you will. And it is always amazing to me that a nation— 150,000,000 strong, could have come along with modern Europe next door & not have developed a disgust for uncleanness. Yet here—on this best line—between Leningrad & Moscow, I am troubled by this thought. Also by the thought that in Moscow—or any where in Russia, I will be unable to obtain really pleasing & palatable food. It all has—alas—a heavy gluey sameness—an almost unendurable thought for me. Already—& after so short a stay, I find myself turning to Vodka—vodka plain, vodka in tea, vodka over a desert in order that I make a go of things. And worse—& so far from home—the only two people I take any comfort in are Ruth Kennell and Scott Nearing— Ruth because of her fine understanding & broad philosophic acceptance of life—Nearing for his undiluted if mistaken devotion to salvation of the underdog. Whenever I think of him here—and more especially because I know I shall see much of him, I have a feeling of companionship in so great & and for me alien a world. He is supposed to come round today with some news. And Ruth is supposed to hear finally whether she, along with Trevas, is to be permitted to accompany me on my tour through Russia. I distinctly hope so—for by now her intellectual as well as diplomatic competence have been clearly proved to me.

At the station we all go into the restaurant for tea. Trevas, representing the foreign office as well as Voks & probably, (I hear) the G.P.U. retains the gay spirits which should characterize a diplomat who is also a spy or watch dog of sorts. His humor & attentiveness is never failing. On the other hand Mrs. Kennell is somewhat more temperamental but in the main optomistic & cheerful. We order vodka, tea & for myself—an omelette confiture—the only type of omelet I can endure here. While we are breakfasting as many as five different and most amazing beggars arrive— creatures so diverse or compound & still fluttery in their rags that they hold me as a picture—and as something new & strange. I get a kick from just *looking at them. In one case I give twenty kopecks (about 20 cents of our money). In another I offer the beggar his choice of fifteen kopecks—all the change I have, or a glass of vodka—out of the bottle on the table. He takes the vodka—as I felt he would. . . .*

After breakfast Trevas left us to go to VOKS, promising to try to arrange for my departure for the south, if possible the same day. *Instead of* the pretentious suite I had before at 20 roubles a day I took a modest room without bath, which was more comfortable. I heard nothing more of him until late in the day when we were asked to go to VOKS to make final arrangements. *As Ruth had predicted—and solely because she would not accept him as her lover during the trip, a fight on her had developed. Previously in America and here in Russia—and by Trevas himself—I had been assured that the question of a private secretary for myself as well as one for the goverment would be—and already had been, arranged for by the foreign office. Now however—and because of his anger at Mrs. Kennell, the question of expenses came up. And now Korenetz, the Secretary of Voks, that the Society for Cultural Relations had not sufficient to pay for two secretaries and that one would have to represent the government. And since Mrs. Kennell was not a* Russian *Communist it could not be she.* Whereupon I told them that unless they could make satisfactory arrangements I would leave the country at once. They promised to take the matter up and give me an answer on Monday.

That night Mrs. Kennell & I took a walk & dined at the Bolshoi Moskofsky, after which we went to a Russian movie. Later I posted these notes and about 1 am turned in.

Moscow, Sunday, Dec. 4- 1927 – Russia

Another Sunday. And as my time is short & to me valuable I had hoped to arrange for several interviews with principal officials for today. But, as usual here, there is no getting anything done. "Oh, yes, yes. Immediately. You will most certainly see two & maybe three officials on Sunday." Yet here it is Sunday & no officials. I some times think that Russians like the negroes are in that less developed state called by the psychiatrists L   ⌋, *since instead of having to accumulate & organize and execute in a constructive way they prefer to dream & play & talk like children. It is very likely so—and explains their present social backwardness. At any rate—here I am—marooned in a strange capital & no important work in hand. At Ruths suggestion therefore and at about noon I agree to*

take a sleigh ride with Ruth & her friend O'Callaghan.[1] *This is her odd
& highly intellectualized Irish friend who can do nothing but inform you of
what other people have done—and make bright & usually caustic remarks
in regard to the same. If she had real personal charm this might prove un-
irritating. As it is her constant biting at everything gets on my nerves.*

We rode out Tverskaya to the race tracks near Petrovka Park. It
was very cold, but I enjoyed the air. Crowds of people were on their
way to the races which began at 2 O'clock, but as I did not care to
see the races, we walked back for some distance along the avenue
where children were skating and skeeing, and took the auto bus at
Triumphalnaya Square for home.

In the evening, I went to the Mierhold Theater with Serge
Dinamov and saw 'Revizor'. Meierhold has produced Gogol's old
play in a radically different way from the classic presentation of the
Art Theater and caused a great controversy in theatrical circles last
season. He has much extended and altered the play, putting in whole
new scenes, enlarging the text and adding a mysticism and symbol-
ism, all of which he claims are according to the original manuscript
and spirit of Gogol. The sets are miniature and are rolled onto the
great bare stage on wheels, all ready for the action. Although the
acting is very good, I was not impressed by the staging. At eleven
o'clock, there were still two more acts ahead, and so we left without
seeing the end.

Moscow, Monday, Dec 5- 1927 - Russia

I was told in the morning that Bucharin might give me an interview after the session of the Party Conference at 5 o'clock, so I
waited in the hotel for a telephone call. At 5 p.m. Trevas came to
take me to Bucharin. At last, I entered the Kremlin, but was given
no opportunity to see anything. As we went through the inevitable
disrobing process in the corridor—overcoat, overshoes, etc.—my
secretary discovered that I had again forgotten my tie. I was quite
upset about it but Trevas assured me that probably Bucharin would
be in the same condition. We were ushered into a large comfortable
room and soon a quiet, little man entered. He had fair hair getting
thin on top and brushed back from a very high forehead. His face

1. May O'Callaghan was a technical worker who lived at the Lux.

was boyish, his blue eyes large and childlike and he had a charming, affectionate manner. I began my attack without delay.

-------Does the Soviet Government follow Marx closely *or* how have you diverged?

We have not diverged at all. But I think we have modified Marx according to our problems

-------If you have not diverged, why then does the individual own land, horses, houses, automobiles?

The doctrine of Marx is not a set doctrine which lays out a plan for the future *of* society. *I have written a book which covers that.* Marx never denied *a* transition period. In the works of Marx and Engels, 'The Peasant War with Germany', the Communist Manifesto, can be found straight declarations in accordance with our problems and programs.

"*You then insist that you are following Marx completely—that his transition period accounts for all lacks or unsocial phases of your present communistic state here.*

Marx's plan is by no means a definite, detailed plan, *Rather,* he recognised the transition period. In the Communist Manifesto are 11 or 12 points which deal with the question of the transitory period, during which the socialisation of industry would take place.

------- We are moving toward that in America.

Yes, but under the dictatorship of the capitalists.

-------Here you have also a dictatorship.

Yes, but of another class.

------- Is there any difference?

Yes, but we must consider it from the standpoint of the development of all society. Capitalism also had its various forms: primitive, industrial, etc.

-------- Religious?

Yes, but I speak of the economic structure.

-------- Well, isn't religion economic?

Yes, from the standpoint of the church. *But* socialism is not a fixed order, and as capitalism had in its history various forms, so will socialism develop.

-------- Like a tree?

Yes, and the present form is the dictatorship of the proletariat. I read various *forms of* economic literature *much of it confusing &*

Nikolai Bukharin. (Courtesy of Stephen F. Cohen)

wrong. For instance, Thomas Nixon Carver.[2] Carver, *An American,* *says* that the economic revolution is taking place in America, not in Russia; that this economic revolution takes the form of labor banks, employee stock ownership, etc. which are transforming capitalism entirely.

-------- *Well I think* This is true.

No it is an illusion. You have several layers of society in America —you have skilled workers, you have unskilled workers, you have poor farmers, rich farmers, negroes, and the standard of living of some of these classes is very low. You have in America only 3 million organised workers, *out of* 25 million workers. And these labor banks are only for the labor aristocracy, these privileges only for a few. Such an exception situation is due to world economic conditions, such as affected England earlier. Now England no longer has such exceptional conditions for the workers, which was the economic basis for the evolutionizing process of the English laborer. The exceptional situation in the United States now is the basis for the machine process the benefits of which chiefly accrue to the capitalists and the labor aristocracy. But the present situation in America is only a moment in the constellation.

------- Do you maintain that the situation here is final?

No such thing. It can change.

------- But in what direction? You don't think it could change into an intellectual despotism?

No.

------- But are there not millions who don't agree *with this government as it is now?*

No, not so many.

------- *Let me ask you a question.* If 51% of the population *here &* *now* were Communist and 49% not, what would the government do? The Government has an intellectual theory of life. What would it do with the 49% who do not agree?

Yours is an absolutely abstract point. We must look at problems concretely and not abstractly, because we have no abstract situation. It is not a situation which can be stated as for and against commu-

2. Thomas Nixon Carver (b. 1865), American economist, whose books include *The Distribution of Wealth* (1904) and *The Present Economic Revolution in the United States* (1926), the book to which Bukharin refers here.

nism, because the leading force is communist. The great number are with us, the rich peasant is against us, a third section is neutral.

----- *You are sticking to the mechanics of the present situation. But please answer my theoretical question. 49 against 51?*

But *that* is not possible in such a simplified form. *In the present instance* 51 have all the great industries, 49 are only unskilled labor.

-------*I ask you to answer the question theoretically.*

But it is not a right point of view *as you put it* because you cannot argue on mental grounds *alone* but *only* on actual social conditions.

"*I do not agree that my question does not represent a possible social condition—not even here in Russia*"

--- "*But our relationship to the peasents is not to be stated in your way.*

"*Then you do not admit to an intellectual tyranny?*"

"*Decidedly not. Our peasents are led by us—not driven*".

------ But your peasants do not always agree, and if they don't you lead them anyhow?

Your mistake is that you think only in a static and not in a dynamic way. In great questions the peasants are with us, and from this important basis of agreement we lead the peasantry to other questions. For example, I received today a photograph of myself when I was in prison twenty years ago. I can recall that at that time if you spoke against the czar, a peasant would knock you down, because all the traditions were for the czar. But we made such propaganda that we were able to show the peasant that only fools would support the czar. We came to the peasants and said: 'What do you suffer for?' 'We need more land'. Then we showed the peasants that the czar had most of the land, and so little by little from this we led the peasants nearer and nearer to us.

"*Very good. That was work or instruction in line with the peasents interests. But let me state the problem in another way. Communism was not heard of let alone understood by most of the peasents—say 90 per cent, up to fifteen or twenty years ago—and certainly it was not accepted. There was unrest among the skilled workers—say 10 or 15 percent of all the citizens of the country. And it is possible—I do not know—that because of radical propaganda in Russia all of these had heard of and even accepted the main tenets of Marx. But today Communism, as preached by Lenin & especially Trotsky & yourself, calls for a complete re-education & if possible alteration of the human mind so that in the future self interest shall disappear & state—or communistic interest take its place. You want that.*

You want only communistically minded people. But do all Russians want that? Do they even understand,—even a fraction of them—that there is such a dream as that extant."

"I think most of them understand it."

"I do not agree with you. It is not possible that they should have. Too many are still too ignorant—illiterate. More—you yourself say that many are against you & your theories"

"By no means a majority—only those capitalistically minded."

"Well let me state my proposition anyway. Isnt it true that you will do this with the child—take him & teach him—perforce—certainly principles about which he knows nothing—concerning which he cannot even reason, & so dogmatically & tyrannically even force a certain viewpoint or mental condition on him whether he wills it or not."

"But I insist that the majority are not against us but sympathize with our ideals & our program because these are for their betterment".

"If the majority were really with you I could not object—but I doubt it. Besides—your program—unless all desire it, is exactly that of the Catholic church or the Greek Church—or the old Czaristic Goverment or any form of tyranny or propaganda of which you can think. You take the ignorant and make them believe your way because you are sure your way is best. But is it? Do you know yet"

"Yes—as to that—we know it is the best—fairest form of human goverment yet devised. It is for all against the few. Our dream is to help all— not just a few—make all happy—as against a few who are happy while millions suffer.

"I am for the millions as much as you are if they can be made happy & life still go on. Or if these cannot be made happy—I am willing that all life should end. But intellectually I think your proposition needs a clear & clean defense & must have one. Personally I think good often needs as much tyranny to establish & maintain it as evil—a benevolent tyranny— at least until all men have brains sufficient to appreciate good. Why not adopt that as a defense."

"Because I do not believe it. Left alone humanity moves in the general direction of its best interests."

"Well—maybe. Still as yet the Russians—& particularly the Russian children, know nothing of your theories & still you are driving them by a military dictatorship into an acceptance of your theories."

"We are warding off enemies to our theories or truths—the while we explain them to the masses.

"The child is not forcibly educated in one way?"

"On the radio you can receive on one line or another, and the apperceptions of one class are one thing and *of* another class another. And when we transform the child we have to break through the force of resistance and we have the problem of various tendencies *in* the child

------Isn't it true that if you take the child and say this is true, it is, and doesn't the success of communism depend on changing the psychology of the child? Didn't the Catholic Church do this?

The most important question is the *mental* position *of the teacher. Ours is for the welfare of the many.*"

"The welfare as you see welfare"

"Well, put it that way. But history & science I think will show that we are correct. Yes, we inherited that.

------ Aristotle is as great today as he was then.

No, not as great. Do you know that in the Chinese we can find almost all the processes of Greek civilization? In fact, it is a big question whether the writings of Plato were before Christ or in the Renaissance.

------ Now that is a theoretical question.

Modern capitalism puts this problem before us. If we have two or three more world wars, we will disappear, but there is only one force which will save — the dictatorship of the proletariat.

------I must explain that I am not against the Soviet system, but I came to see if it can work. Question: Should the big mind rule the little one?

Ah, this is the question of intellectual aristocracy. In answer, I will explain the real communist society of the future and then return to your question.

----- But what about the big mind and the little mind right now.

If we need the advice of a statistician, we go to a good statistician. If you go to a doctor you go to a good doctor and follow his advice. It is not possible that all people have the same nose, eyes, or the same quantity of brains.

------Yes, you are right, there are a few gigantic minds and many little ones.

But if we take the present capitalist society, there is a standard of intellect, a monopoly of education, and it is necessary to finish higher schools, university—

------ No, that's not true.

But it is a fact that in capitalist society, the proletariat is oppressed culturally, and if you will compare the quantity of brains of the oppressed class with those of the capitalist you will find that there is no difference.

------ From where do you get these statistics?

From scientific sources.

------Can you mention a great mind from the proletariat?

Statistical law is of big figures, not the exceptions but the average. Part of our great minds are from the intelligentsia and part from the proletariat to whom the dictatorship of the proletariat gives more opportunities.

------Do you think that the intellectual class in capitalist society is a separate class?

No, but all great forces in bourgeois society are against the proletariat. They do not have advantages of education. The dictatorship of the proletariat makes for the first time in history the field of selection larger than before. This is the principle of selection. In capitalist society the intellectual forces are separated from the laborers. As class they are against the proletariat. But with us it is the opposite, we give more advantages to the working class and we have here an intellectual laboratory. We are always getting new forces from the woking classes, and that is not possible in capitalist society. In the latter if you have strong people (in Germany Steinetz, Hindenburg, etc.) they are against the working class.[3] Here we have big minds which do not work against the working class. Take me for instance, I am the expression of the dictatorship of the proletariat against the bourgeoisie.

-------- Is Marx ruling your mind?

Yes but this relationship is not analogous. If your question is that the more clever should rule the less clever, it is no question, but a more important question is class relationships, it is not the same thing that the proletariat has more intelligent people or the bourgeoisie more intelligent.

3. Paul von Hindenburg (1847–1934), German field marshall during World War I and second president of the Weimar Republic from 1925 until his death. He used brutal tactics to suppress leftist uprisings in Germany after the war. Carl Friedrich von Steinmetz (1796–1877), Prussian general who led German troops at Gravelotte in 1870; he authorized such a murderous assault on the French there that he was dismissed from command.

------- Yes, but if in Soviet Russia the clever mind rules the less clever, you have an intellectual aristocracy.

But the idea is entirely different. There was an intellectual aristocracy of Judea based on privileged classes. In Egypt the rich were the intellectuals.

------ But in Soviet Russia there are two classes the intelligent and the less intelligent. But they are not classes.

------Yes they are. Now in the street there is a street cleaner of very low intelligence. Do you mean to say that his position in society is the same as yours. (I'LL die but I'll get this out of him).

Yes, in our social system he has the same opportunities as I have and the same rights.

-----Then what are you doing here? You agree that you would rather be here?

Yes, but we can class all men like brunettes and blondes, rich or poor, fools or intelligent, etc. I am not the same as the man in the street, we agree, but in politics we make it a policy that all manual workers must be educated from the same standpoint as the intelligentsia. We must look into the future. For instance, ten years ago we had in the Central Committee of the Party 5 or 6 intellectuals to 2 or 3 workers, and the intellectual differences were very great. Now we have 60 members of the Central Committee, all are workers and there is no intellectual difference between them and us.

-------These came up through a special path.

Yes, but there are masses of them.

-------You can't tell me that these 60 men are a general example.

No, but I'll give you another example of great masses of our workers. I worked among them a great deal and our masses of workers are very intelligent.

------- I think big minds will always sit in high places and have comfortable rooms and lead the little minds in the street.

If you talk of material compensation, then it is an economic question.

------- If we get rich and everybody has money, who will sit here and who will work in the mines?

There is a general line of development. We will die, and the new generation will be a generation of workers.

------- Yes, but who will do the dirty work? All can't sit here.

Read p. 309 of my book 'Historical Materialism'.[4] (Bucharin brought his book—I read the pages indicated).

- - - - - -Incompetence always will be.

Oh, my God, I can't stand this. Well, in that case no one forces me to trust my doctor. I think Anatole France was a great writer, but between me and France there is no common economic basis.

There is a more important question, of the dictatorship of the proletariat and the liquidation of the dictatorship of the proletariat.

We always will have differences in intellectual qualifications, but when there is such a situation that a big scientist says to me, you must produce more in your branch, there is no oppression in this.

We think that through big development of economic forces we will succeed in machine production without capitalist competition. There will be the same competition between two workers as between two writers.

- - - - - - You think there will be no unhappiness, no disappointment, no tragedies?

There will always be unhappy love, individual tragedies, idiots and defectives for whom we will build hospitals. But individual ambitions will disappear because they will have no basis. There will be another type of personal ambition; to best serve society, and not for material means, only spiritual.

We Communists today are a product of the old society. We must often fight against old traditions in ourselves. When a child learns to read he must make an effort, but later he reads unconsciously without any effort. And this relationship between man and man will finally be as easy as reading.

- - - - - -You're going to have a perfect world, against human nature, and you think God will accept it?

(Here Adam Smith was brought up by Bucharin as an example. Notes not complete).

6/XII Tuesday.

In the afternoon, Serge went to VOKS to straighten out my affairs. He telephoned that everything was being arranged for my

4. Nikolai Bukharin, *Historical Materialism: A System of Sociology* (New York: International Publishers, 1925).

departure and that we should come at once for an interview with
Kameneva. We took an izvozchik over, and although only three
o'clock it was already twilight when we reached the fantastic stone
house which is the headquarters of VOKS. As we went in the door,
we met Kameneva just leaving. She seemed confused at seeing us,
said she had not expected me but of course was glad to have me
come. She returned to her office and sat down at her desk. She then,
after a few polite questions about my visit in Leningrad, asked what
I wanted of her. I said she had sent for me and that she knew better
what we wanted to discuss. She then explained that she was help-
less to do any more in the matter of paying expenses as she had only
2000 roubles left out of the fund entrusted to her. I said that I would
like to take that money and return to New York. She replied that
as there had been nothing said about VOKS paying my fare to New
York, she would have to ask the committee about it. I said that the
secretary Korenetz had promised me in the presence of Biedenkapp
that the return fare would be paid, and I asked if Korenetz was not
empowered to make such promises. She said he could not be held responsible. We parted coldly with the understanding that she would
find out from the committee about the financial arrangements.

This, it seems, was to be my day of defeats. We walked along
the boulevard toward Strasnaya Ploschad. The moon was shining
and the air was crisp and very cold. We looked in at the monastery
on the Square, whose beautiful church has five star-studded domes.
From there we continued down the boulevard to Tsvetnoy Square.
The children were out on their sleds and skates. Taking an A car
back, we were almost crushed in the tremendous mob and barely escaped from the car with our lives. We went to the little dining room
in the Dom Gertzena (House of Herzen) where all the writers' organisations are located.[5] The dining room was deserted and we had a
quiet and, because of very slow service, prolonged dinner.

I had an appointment with Stanislavsky at 6 p.m. Seated in
his comfortable office, his secretary called Stanislavsky who came in
looking very serious and dignified. He said that my manuscript of
the play 'American Tragedy' had been carefully read by the commit-

5. So named for Alexander Ivanovich Herzen (see p. 109n), the journalist and political
thinker who helped to lay the foundations of agrarian socialism.

tee, and he had been given a synopsis in Russian. He said that he liked it very much and personally would be very happy to produce it, but that his censorship specialists had decided that it could not pass the censor, first because of the religious sections, and second because of the relationship between employer and worker in the play. He said it was exceedingly painful to him to have to reject it, as he would have liked very much to produce it.

So that was that. The secretary in parting assured me that all who had read the play thought it wonderful and added that perhaps in five years they might be permitted to produce it!

As the new Soviet ballet was on at the Bolshoi, we tried to get tickets, but all seats were sold. Again defeated, I had the brilliant idea of leaving for Nizhniy Novgorod that night, in order not to waste any more time. We sent a man to the station, but he telephoned that there were only 'hard' cars available, without place cards (Maxim Gorki), so that scheme had to be abandoned.

7/XII Wednesday.

I had an appointment with Meierhold at 10:30 in the morning. His living quarters are in a court; on the outside door there is a sign 'Living Quarters of the Meierhold Theater'. Like all other organisations, the workers of this theater not only work but live together. Up a flight of dirty stairs, a narrow corridor, and in a large room with many iron cots (Is this where the actors sleep?) we met a red-haired young man who profusely apologised for Mr. Meierhold, who had been unexpectedly called to the Party Conference early in the morning to give a report on some scandal in the theater and so could not keep his appointment with me. He would of course be very glad to have the meeting some other time, etc. We walked out and down a very handsome street, Vorovskogo, 'Ambassadors' Row', where the foreign embassies are located. As the Headquarters of the Quakers are nearby, we dropped in there. A young woman by the name of Miss Davis received us and talked about the work of the Society in the villages, about sanitation, cockroaches, bedbugs and other important Russian subjects. We walked down to the Arbat Square and at last found the French Gallery which I have been wanting to see all along. Here is a small but very valuable collection of French and a few English pictures: Henri Matisse, Van Gogh, Gaugin.

Later in the day, I was summoned to VOKS where the final battle took place. Korenetz was on his dignity, he assured me that he was a responsible man and wanted to keep his word, that he had telegraphed to Biedenkapp about the fare to New York and had received the following reply: 'Dreiser paid Five Hundred Fifty Dollars for fare to and from Russia. All other expenses in connection with his visit in Russia VOKS must pay.' I said all right, I'd go back and get it out of Biedenkapp. Korenetz said then we could not talk about the trip within Russia. I said I didn't want to talk with them any more. That VOKS could go to hell, he could go to hell, and when he begged me to see Kameneva, who was waiting for me, I said she could could to hell also. Korenetz said they would all go to hell in good time, but first we would talk about the trip. I rose to go. Then another man, Yaroshevski, head of the Foreign Affairs Dept. of VOKS, gently persuaded me to come and talk with Kameneva. I went in and we had a stormy scene. They insisted that I must not leave Russia, but must have my tour, and promised to telephone me the decision at 8 o'clock. To cool down, we walked home through the clear, frosty air by way of the Boulevard and Petrovka. Of course, we could do nothing in the evening but wait for the telephone call from VOKS. Serge came over and was there when Yaroshevsky telephoned. They had a long conversation in which it was agreed that I would pay the expenses of my secretary and VOKS would pay for me and one other person. It was decided that we would leave next evening for Nijni.

Thurs. Dec 8 – Waiting about for Vox. A great strain. Rainbows on mall in open. At 3 PM. I am invited to go to Vox. My temper gets the best of me. A great row. I tell all severally & collectively to go to hell. Great effort to calm me. All is to be straightened out. Do I not want a lovely trip to Nizjni Novgorod. Beautiful scenery. I say I want nothing save permission to pay my own way & leave the country. But they insist they must carry out the original understanding as near as possible. I give them until 8 PM. to prepare their plan & submit it. It is 11 before they call. Meantime R.K. & I walk. The beauty of Moscow on a starry night. We stop at a telegraph office. I cable Bye to cable $1000. Then dinner in hotel. Dynamov comes. Gossizdat has accepted my terms for my books—$1000 down, 10%.

8/XII Thursday

We made all arrangements for departure this evening. VOKS has finally found someone to accompany us—a woman doctor, nurse in the Hotel Lux, Devedovsky,—eminently suited for the job, having seldom traveled in her life before, and of a disposition and intellect admirably adapted to my needs. Thus competently chaperoned by the nurse and librarian of the Comintern, I set out for Niji at 8 p.M.

THROUGH RUSSIA

9/XII Friday

We arrived in Nijni Novgorod at 9:30 in the morning. The station looked clean and lively. We sat down in the restaurant and I watched the people passing through the station while we ate sausage and bread and butter and tea with vodka. A tiny girl of four in a huge shuba touching the floor, her head enveloped in a shawl, went toddling about smiling genially at everyone. Outside, we took the street car which carried us a long distance to the House of the Unions. It was a bright, cold day. We stood on the platform of the street car and looked at the passing city. Nijni seemed to be a very attractive, up-to-date place, with broad clean streets, we passed the fair grounds, now deserted, very extensive wooden buildings, then crossed the River Oka which flows into the Volga. The other side of the river with its old buildings and beautiful churches and hills, with the wall of the Kremlin and the old towers, made a wonderful view from afar. Near a fine square called 'Sovetskaya Ploschad', with the wall and towers of the Kremlin on one side and a lovely white church with silver domes in the center, we found the hotel 'New Russia' and were given two musty, shabby rooms, mine especially imposing with its black upholstered chairs and couch, which gave it the look of a gambling hall. Devedovsky had gone to the local Soviet, where they were much excited at the news of our arrival and soon a representative came over to show us about the city. First we took a ride about the city in a little automobile, one of three which I saw during my stay in Nijni. We drove along the bank of the Volga, which looked a mighty river, the middle current still flowing although boats can no longer navigate. The more I saw of the city the better I liked it. There was a snappy, bright atmosphere about it along with the charm of old churches and other buildings. We stopped at a very handsome new building of flats for workers and went in. What a man's work is persists in being the most important fact about him. On door leading into one flat was a sign which said that here were living railroad workers, including the master mechanic Vorosov and assistant mechanic Kraskov. The corridors and rooms were attractively finished, the floors highly polished and everything as yet spotless after one month's habitation. The first was a family of 4 living in 2 rooms, and a family of three in 1 room with a common bath and kitchen for both families. The first family paid 15 roubles a month rent, out of a salary of 75 roubles. One four room apartment was almost up to

American standards. It was occupied by a scientist and his wife and child; the rooms were large and attractive and there was a bath. They paid 40 roubles a month. We passed a large section of new workers houses built of logs and quite good looking, built in the factory district. We went into one and found it quite comfortable: a family of four living in two of the rooms and a soldier and his wife, who also worked in the factory, in the other room, with a common kitchen and no bath. They all claimed to be highly pleased with their new quarters and that living conditions have greatly improved.

We visited the textile factory, 'Krasni October' employing 3,700 workers. This is a very old factory with on the whole old equipment and machinery, which takes the raw flax and makes it into cloth of a coarse grade. As we entered, a shift which finished work at 2 p.m. was just filing out. There were many women, some with little tubs on their heads, as they go to the banya (steam bath) from work, and all looked very gray and tired. For of course this labor in the dust from the raw material is very unhealthful. The workers get a month's vacation and a special ration of butter and milk, but tuberculosis is very prevalent. Inside, almost the first thing which was called to my attention was the new ventilating system, just installed this year at a cost of 400,000 roubles, and at the demand of the workers themselves through their union. As the ventilators are not all working yet, it cannot be said how much they will help the air, which seemed pretty thick with dust. But it seemed to me that the 400,000 might just as beneficially have been put into new machinery.

On the way back we visited the gubernia hospital, which seemed to be a very large institution, well managed, clean and orderly.

We had dinner in the hotel dining room, deserted but for us, a balcony overlooking the large billiard room. After dinner, we went to an evening school for workers. Here was a lively little world, boys and girls hurrying through corridors to classes, gymnastics, wall newspapers, boys anxious to show me the art room and to present me with any drawing I happened to like, physics room with instruments which the students made themselves. Here are trained factory school leaders; everybody tremendously in earnest and very enthusiastic.

It was a glorious night, the moon cast a radiance on the snow, on the white church in the square and on the Kremlin wall. It was so cold that the snow crunched underfoot.

We stopped at the great central workers club, formerly a club for the aristocracy, and while this also was a buzzing little world of working men and women, with tea room, lecture room, library, and all the other auxiliaries of workers' clubs, we had to go on to the movies. I had tracked the picture 'The Poet and the Czar' from Moscow to Leningrad, Leningrad to Moscow, and now I found it in Nijni. It was an interesting picture, giving much historical data about Pushkin and his time, but there was nothing new in the production itself and no doubt some tampering with historical facts.

10/XII Saturday

We ate breakfast in the little buffet near our rooms; we ordered fried eggs and they brought us at least 13. I argued with my secretary and she talked back to me. I said to her, 'If I ever get out of this country alive, I'll run as fast as I can across the border, and looking back as I run, I'll yell: 'You're nothing but a damned Bolshevik'.

Our faithful guide from the local Soviet came to go with us to a village, and also a lively young newspaper reporter who asked me for an interview. I dictated a statement about Nijni for him, then as we put on our things to go, I said to him (apropos of my earlier questions about pigs and other animals living with the Russians in their houses): 'And now for the pigs!' Pavel Pavlovich Schtatnov, the newspaperman, was so delighted at my remark that he wanted it written in English in Russian letters for his article which he said would bear this title. We started off in the auto in high spirits. It was intensely cold when we got out into the open spaces; my secretary suffered from the cold wind and got down under the blanket. But whenever I made a remark about the passing scenery, the vast stretches of snow, or a village in the distance, she wanted to put her head out and see too, because she was afraid she wasn't earning her salary. A few miles outside the city stood a fine looking big red brick factory, which manufactures telephones. We stopped to look at it, and were taken around by one of the managers. The factory employs 830 workers and is one of four plants of the Soviet Telephone Trust. It was built so far out because it was started to fill war orders and had to be in a safe place. The factory produces telephones only on order for the whole of USSR, the output being 30,000 telephones, the same number of radio, and 5,000 loud speakers a year. The working conditions seemed to be very good. There were many women workers at machines, for instance, making bolts, or polishing mouthpieces, and they as well as men doing the same work received 50 to 54 roubles a month on piece work. A skilled worker, for instance, a filer, received 150 roubles a month.

The village of Blizhne Borovskaya looked very attractive nestling down in the snow plains as we came in sight of it. Although only about 20 versts from Nijni Novgorod, it seemed quite isolated. We went into the office of the village Soviet located in a small log house. Here we talked with the head of the district Soviet (Selsoviet, or Agricultural Soviet) which includes 9 villages, and with the secretary of the local Soviet, both quite young fellows. A crowd of children, some old men and a few women had already heard of our arrival and crowded into the small room and stood watching us eagerly as we talked.

I asked the district representative what was the reconstruction program of the Selsoviet. He said that the aim is to unite small farms, or if necessary to subdivide into smaller, in the interests of the community. The tendency is to keep farms intact. In case three sons inherit a farm, the Soviet tries to see that the most capable has the management of the farm, or if one is entirely incompetent to deprive him of any control, although the land cannot be taken away from him. As to schools and clubs, the direction is in the hands of the higher (volost) Soviet which appoints teachers, etc.[1] The chief work of the Selsoviet is to help the population in their problems and in the protection of their interests. They bring all their troubles to the Soviet: if a cow dies, they get insurance, the Soviet is the carrier of culture and enlightenment to the peasants, it fixes taxes, collects taxes, this money goes to the district soviet which finances the schools, etc. Two of the members of the Soviet are paid and three are volunteers.

------ If the peasants want tractors what do they do?

Artels are organised among the peasants for getting machinery on installment payments.[2]

------What is this particular village now trying to do?

Two problems now, 1, to supply fuel as the woods here are not

---

1. A *volost* is a rural district.
2. An *artel* was a union of workers who shared the income of their collective labor.

sufficient, and 2, to gave a rotation of crops every three years, 3. to organise peasants for communal work in production and distribution. We have already organised one artel for buying implements.

The fire apparatus you see here was bought by the Soviet. The water supply is not good here. This Soviet also gets good seed, good feed for stock, implements, organisation for buying and selling milk, but grain is handled by the cooperative. However, here we have only enough for local needs, and no white flour.

------- Can the Selsoviet decide question of opening a factory?

This is already based on economic conditions, but this Soviet has power to decide whether they want a factory, but it must go to the higher organs for support. If an individual wants to start an industry, if it is a small business the local Soviet can give permission. We have telephones put in by the Soviet. (District). We can speak to Moscow, Leningrad. We have a radio here, the population is very much interested, the cooperatives have radio study circles. The trade unions got the radio for our village, but of course the local soviet manages all the affairs of the village.

------- Have you electricity?

No, but there is a great desire for it.

We then went out for a tour of the village, and an ever growing crowd trailed along behind us down the village street. The first log cottage we stopped at had one large room and a tiny kitchen, there was an entry and then a very low door leading into the living room. The floor was scrubbed clean, there was the big whitewashed brick stove, and in a corner the altar. 6 people lived here, I couldn't make out where they slept. This family had 4.8 dessatin of land, made an income of 264 roubles a year and paid 7.60 in taxes. Besides they owned a horse with which he worked for others, they had no rent to pay, wood not enough, no home industry now and no cow. Their only complaint was that there was no cow, but they have a radio. This was the home of a poor peasant. A neighbour, a little man with a shaggy red beard and matted hair, which was damp because he just came from the banya (today is Saturday), stood against the stove and smiled at me as if he thought the whole thing was a joke. He invited us to his house. This was the home of a poor peasant also, 2 rooms, quite comfortable looking, 8 people. I looked in vain for pigs in the parlour and cockroaches. I began to feel that my trip to Russia had been for nothing.

Next we went to the home of a middle peasant, a very good looking log house with fancy wood carving on the window frames and a little verandah. Adjoining the house was a covered shed for the cow and horse and chickens. Inside were three very nice rooms, a large kitchen, a comfortable living room with upholstered furniture and a bedroom. Five people lived here, The peasant owned 4.72 dessatins and made 403 roubles income a year.

We looked in at the post office and telephone station which connects with 11 centrals, it costs 18 kopeks to telephone to Nijni, 3 min.

We trailed off to the house of the village pope. I was afraid that the whole procession would follow me into the house but the Soviet representative told them to stay out. Nevertheless there were three of us, the head of the district soviet, the secretary of the local soviet and the reporter, making 6 people. The cottage had 3 rooms, a large and cosy living room with some signs of culture about it and a bedroom or study. The priest, a slender man with a thin scholarly face and short beard, greeted us nervously. The interview began with difficulty. I asked him how many followers he had before the revolution and after. Devodovesky translated my question. The priest hesitated.

What nationality are you personally? he asked her. She said she was a Polish Jewess. He said that the translators usually were not Russians. Then he proceeded to answer slowly.

It is a difficult question. The church can exist only with not less than 50 members. I suppose we have about 300 now. How many more unbelievers there are now is difficult to say. The tendency to get away from religion is especially strong among the youth.
- - - - - Do you think the condition of the village is better or worse social and economically since the revolution.

I cannot give my opinion. You must ask the local representatives of the government. But personally my condition is worse than before.
- - - - - - - How does the church exist materially?

We live on the income from funerals, weddings etc. I have no income, house is the property of the church.
- - - - - - - Is there danger that religion will die?

I refer you to Trotsky's interview with the American labor delegation in Pravda for my answer.

We decided to discontinue the interview as gracefully as possible as it was evident that we were torturing the 'Batushka', who could not talk freely before so many people.[3] As we went out, my secretary returned because she had forgotten her gloves. The priest said to her: Please explain to the gentleman that I would gladly have answered his questions, if we had been alone, but before a Jewess, and the government representatives and a newspaper correspondent! If I had given my opinions ——' He drew his finger across his throat.

We then returned to the Soviet House and in the little room of the caretaker we were served tea from a samovar, bologne, black bread, boiled eggs, pickles, candy and wine. The guests sat down at the table, while the hosts and villagers stood behind us and watched us eat. I felt like a new Revizor.[4] When we had finished eating, I asked them to sing. The young secretary of the local Soviet led the chorus. First they sang the Volga Song, and then many others, beautiful songs, all of them. And like all Russians they sang very well. It was delightful to listen to them.

It was already getting dark when we came out into the air again. We trailed across a ravine to the school house and entered the warm, clean school room. It was quite dark, but the teacher came out of her living quarters at the back carrying a lamp and showed us the pupils' work on the walls, the wall newspaper, and drawings. As we got into the automobile to leave, quite a crowd saw us off. The children cheered: 'Hurrah for the American delegate!' The automobile set off across the pathless snow until we struck the main road to town.

We all had dinner in my room with beer. The newspaperman was very gay. He interviewed me again (Note of Sec.: I slept through this, so can't report), danced with my secretary a Russian dance, then recited some of his own poems, and made himself generally entertaining.

They saw us off on the train which left at 9:30 in the evening.

11/XII Sunday.

We arrived in Moscow in the morning. I had dinner with Wood. There was a New York theatrical manager by the name of Beeber-

3. *Batushka* in Russian means "little father"; it is a term of respect and endearment.
4. The reference here is to Nikolai Gogol's 1836 comedy *Revizor* (*The Inspector-General*), in which a corrupt government bureaucrat holds court in a provincial Russian village and accepts "loans" and other gifts from the townspeople in return for favors. See p. 183, where Dreiser sees a production of this play.

man there. I went with him to the Jewish Theater and saw '200,000'.
He is planning to take this company to America.

12/XII Monday.

We went to the bank in the morning and I received the $1000
from Bye. When we returned to the hotel, Serge came and was with
me the rest of the day. While my secretary was at VOKS making the
final arrangements for our departure, I went with Serge to buy some
things—
We hurried through our dinner because it was understood that the
train left at eight o'clock. We stopped at the Lux and got our traveling companion, Devodovsky, and hurried in the taxi to the station.
We were afraid we would be late, but D. said that the train would
leave about 8:25. We said we thought eight, she said she wasn't sure.
The porter carried our baggage to the platform. We found the number of our car, but it was third class. Some inquiries disclosed the
fact that this was not our train, that ours would leave at 11:25. We
returned to the station restaurant, and decided to wait there. My
Sec. was very, very angry (at herself) but Serge and I kept up our
spirits. I suggested to Serge that he might make a lecture tour of the
United States, which I could arrange for him. He was much pleased
with the idea. I asked him to write out his numerous titles and positions. He set to work earnestly, while I remarked that he had better
send the list by express, that I was afraid there wasn't enough time
before the train left for him to finish the list, etc. all of which sent
me and my sec, into paroxysms of mirth, while Serge, pleased to see
us so gay but not seeing the joke at all, continued to write with the
greatest seriousness.

The time thus passed very quickly and at 11 p.m. we boarded
the train, took leave of Serge and at last I had left Moscow for the
last time.
My traveling companion in my coupe was a young Turk, who was
very friendly with us.

13/XII

There was no diner on the train and we had not equipped ourselves as all good Russians do, with food, tea kettle, glasses, etc. The

Turk insisted on feeding us. He had a can of peppers which he would open in spite of everything. He broke his knife on it, almost broke ours but finally his perseverance was rewarded. When I tasted the peppers stuffed with carrots, I understood why he had been so persistent. They were delicious, and we had a good meal of bread and cheese, vodka, wine and peppers.

I then proceeded (having got all his food out of him) to get all the information I could from the obliging Turk.

On the road from Moscow to Kharkov. Interview with my traveling companion, a Turk, on his way to Constantinople. Khalil Kasimovich (Memi Ogli).

Kamil Pasha is now in power.[5] About the changes which have taken place since the revolution: the church is separated from the state. Education was put on a different basis. Before they had only church schools but now they have a good general school and compulsory education The percentage of illiteracy before the revolution was 10% less than in Russia. In regard to economic conditions. What Kamil Pasha has done for the country. Before the revolution, in the course of 300 years, there were only 2 sugar refineries built, but during the last four years of Kamil Pasha's regime, Turkey has added 2 more. They have opened technical schools, formerly if a machine was broken only a foreigner could fix it.

------- How many large cities are there in Turkey?

Constantinople, Angora, Adrianople, Izmeer, Svas, and Mussel. In Mussel is an English concession which has a 25 year contract through the League of Nations.

------- Does religion hinder the development of the country?

Yes.

------- Is Turkey striving for industrialisation as in Russia?

No they are not yet up to that point.

------- About education?

5. Kennell has confused the names of two Turkish leaders. Mehmed Kamil Pasha was a Turkish army officer who served four times as Ottoman grand vizier but who died in 1913. The political leader of whom their traveling companion speaks was Mustafa Kemal, who organized a revolution to establish the modern state of Turkey and became its first president in October 1923. Kemal, also known as "Ataturk," was an autocratic ruler whose policies emphasized republicanism, nationalism, populism, and secularism. He should not be confused with Mustafa Kamil (1874–1908), the Cairo lawyer and journalist who helped found the National Party in Egypt.

The schools are better than in Russia because Turkey has compulsory education.

------ What was done for the peasantry?

The position of the peasant has improved now because of the fact that the big landowners were deprived of their political power which they used so strongly against the peasantry formerly.

-------In your opinion, which government has done more for its peasantry, the dictatorship of the proletariat in Russia or the bourgeois republic in Turkey?

The dictatorship of the proletariat has done more because in the first place Russia is richer, because Russia did not pay its prerevolutionary debts, and Turkey as a member of the League of Nations is paying its war debts. But Russia refused to accept payment for Turkey's debt to her of 17,000,000 roubles.(?) or lire ?

------ Condition of women in Turkey?

Polygamy is abolished and the women have taken off their veils. Formerly the husband had the right to divorce a wife without her consent, but she did not have the same right. Formerly, a man could have as many as seven wives and none of them had any right to the property. If the husband died, all the wives were turned out and the property given to his parents. But now they have equal right to the property. Women have equal rights everywhere, there is co-education and higher education and they are employed in business and everywhere on an equal basis. There is one woman in the representatives to the League of Nations.

------- Is the Mohammedan religion stronger or weaker than before?

I think weaker, the only people who follow the Mohamedan religion now are the peasants and officials, and the peasants are in the minority, 40%.

------- Did Turkey have literature, novelists, poets, sculptors, painters, newspapers, magazines etc. Before?

Before they had only newspapers, but nothing in art.

------Do you know any groups of writers and artists now in Turkey?

Yes, there are such groups in Constantinople.

----- Are there any young poets?

Yes, there are. But I don't know their names.

------ Are there any new publishing houses?

Yes, in the hands of the government.

------Is the country developing now?

Yes.

------ What sources of income has Turkey, what has she for export?

Tobacco, fruit such as oranges, lemons, figs, dates, nuts, silk, cotton, rice, wool.

------ With whom do they deal?

We send wool, tobacco, etc to England: Russia takes tobacco and rice and in return receives sugar and kerosene. We also deal with North America. In former years we used to produce raw material, so our returns were so much less. Now, we are preparing to use the raw material in manufacture.

------ What has the Republic done for the peasant?

The peasantry is very poor, there is no industry, they have only their small plots of land, which is of worse quality than the Russian. There is an abundance of fruit but as there are no means of transporting it, it actually rots in many places. The first thing the government does is to build railroads, and this work is going on at full speed.

Angora is being built now by an America engineer on the plan of New York. It will be called 'Second New York'. They are also building a new opera house. The population is 84,000.

------ Would Turkey be better off if she had a proletarian revolution than as a bourgeois republic?

Of course, the dictatorship of the proletariat is the thing we are aiming for, but at that time we could not have had a proletarian revolution because there was no proletariat, and religion had too much of a hold, and if religion had been taken away along with the sultan, so the bourgeois revolution was a necessary step to the proletarian revolution, and we could not have had it without the influence of the Russian Rev. Turkey will follow in the footsteps of Russia and in my opinion much more easily because our government apparatus works better than the Russian.

------ How old is Kemal Pasha?

48 years.

------ How did he come to power?

He was elected for four years.

Recently he made his report and was reelected.

------ What will happen after he dies?

Just as after Lenin died, his followers took his place, so it will be with him. He was a former general but he is a scientific man.

------ System of voting?

We have equal suffrage.

------ Are there any rich people as before?

Yes, there are, but they have no special political rights as they had before.

------ With what countries have they connection?

Mostly with North America. They get from there machines, textile fabrics, and metal products.

We arrived in Kharkov at 8:20 at last to get a good dinner, but we found that the train for Kiev left at 8:40. So in another quarter of an hour we found ourselves sitting in a coupe on the way to Kiev, hungry and with no prospect of food until morning. However, my two ladies in waiting did get off at an 8 minute stop and buy some Narzan, bread and cheese.[6] There were very few passengers and we rode in comparative comfort to Kiev, arriving at about noon. We had dinner in the unimposing station, the usual borsch, meat and some vodka, while we kept close watch on our baggage. We found a wreck of an automobile outside which took us to the Continental Hotel'. It was a foggy, drizzly day, but from the first sight there was a charm about the city of Kiev, broad streets, fine old buildings, beautiful churches. The Continental Hotel was a handsome old building, the interior quite magnificent, reminding one of the East, broad stairway with soft red carpets and stained glass windows at the head of the stairs, the reception room decorated with elaborate wood carving which made it look like a cathedral. We were first given two rooms, 1 quite tastily furnished which D. pronounced a 'ladies room', and the other a huge thing furnished with fat upholstery of red leather which she thought just suitable for a gentleman. I found it not only ugly but terribly damp and cold. There was the usual wash stand of marble with a bowl and pitcher. The maid with reluctance answered the bell and I managed to get a towel and a glass of hot water for shaving. The room was unbearably cold; I sat in my fur coat. So we found two other rooms on the third floor, mine very warm with a bathroom.

While our D. went to look up the local Soviet, RK and I took a

---

6. Narzan is bottled mineral water; Dreiser and his companions visit the springs from which it comes later in the journey.

walk. The heavy fog still persisted, the sidewalks were frozen, it was bitterly cold, but there was a liveliness and an air of culture about the crowds on the streets which warmed the heart. The more I got to know of the city, the more it reminded me of Paris. The shop windows were attractive, the women well dressed and good looking. We turned up the main thoroughfare and came to a square "La International" and beyond that a steep slope leading up to a kind of park, all deep in snow, where the children were playing with their sleds. In the evening, a reporter came to interview me and during the interview D. ordered dinner, but the waiter brought only one schnitzel. Our guide from the Educational Dept. was a business like looking young fellow in a short black leather coat. In the evening he took us to the opera while RK stayed at home to write her notes. The opera was 'Faust' very badly done. We escaped as soon as possible. When we arrived home, the samovar was waiting for us and we enjoyed a supper of bread and cheese.

14/XII

As usual we were late getting started in the morning. Our guides always so blithely agree to come at nine o'clock and then show up about ten thirty. At ten we set out alone for the old monastery 'Kievo-Pecherskaya Lavra', 600 years old, which stands up on the hills overlooking the Dnieper River. We took a car which ran along by the park we had before noticed, past many fine buildings and churches with various colored domes. As we got off the car, we could see the walls and golden domes of the monastery ahead up the hill. As we climbed up the road in the cold bright sunshine we passed many people walking on crutches, without legs or arms. In the monastery is a home for war invalids and also a factory for the manufacture of artificial limbs. As we entered the archway of the golden-domed tower which led into the monastery grounds, we saw before us one of the most magnificent cathedrals I have seen anywhere. It had the usual five golden domes, four points forming a square with a large dome in the center. The outside walls were painted with pictures. Inside the church an old priest in long black robes and a black hat and a gray-bearded face anything but saintly in expression sold us tapers at ten kopeks each and proceeded to conduct us through a very limited section of the church. Here was a rich altar, many golden ikons inlaid with jewels and the caskets of priests and princes who had been connected with the monastery. He led us through a trap door in the floor down into a dark, dank room, and by the light of our tapers we could see a tomb and the outlines of a figure under the gold embroidered cover. The old priest mumbled a prayer and kissed the cover, then he lifted several layers of velvet and gold cloth and disclosed what was supposed to be a withered hand. This was the most important thing he had to show us, the mummified figure of Metropolitan. We went outside and climbing up the highest part of the wall, got a wonderful view of the Dnieper and the city across the river. Around this monastery the city has been built. The priests of that time had the modest ambition to build the grandest mortal edifice to God. 'Lavra is the highest institution of the Greek church on earth.'

As one of the crippled young men remarked as we leaned against the wall: 'From here you get a direct train to heaven'. The monastery is extensive and contains within its walls several other churches and structures, the latter being now occupied by museums, etc. The Pechersky monastery was founded in the middle ages and is closely bound up with the history of Kiev, which is one of the oldest cities in Europe. During the Revolution there was much fighting around this fortress and much damage was done. On the outside walls of the cathedral are patches of new plaster where damage has been repaired, and they are outlined with red paint, to the superstitious suggesting blood of the martyrs. (See English Guide Book, p. 321).

Our guide now found us and took us to an anti-religious museum containing relics, emblems, symbols and treasures of the great religions of the world, the purpose no doubt being to show the similarities and weaknesses and superstitions of all religions. Among the exhibits are some very fine pieces.

In another building were a collection of church treasures, many rich clerical robes, crowns, marvelous Ukrainian embroidery. One began to get an idea of the culture and talents of the Ukrainian people. Outside we met many priests, all evidently having been to market, for they carried baskets of products; one thin old fellow with a wisp of hair falling below his black hat crossed the path on his way to one of the smaller buildings. He carried a tea kettle of hot water. We spoke to him and asked him about the bullet holes we noticed in the walls; yes, these were from the revolutionary fighting, but God had spared the ikons, not a one was touched.

We next went to the museum of Pototsky. Pototsky was an old Russian General who had collected many art treasures before the revolution. In order to keep them intact, he offered to preserve the collection as a public museum, himself in charge. He was a heavy set, not very interesting looking man with a gray clipped beard. He himself opened the door and he and his wife conducted us through the museum. The rooms were very cold, the collection not especially remarkable. There was a whole corridor of pictures of the various Russian wars, there were several very fine pieces of furniture, carved sideboards, chairs, a lovely fire screen embroidered with beads. There were some rare books, among them a history of Kiev in English written by an Englishman in 1850.

From the monastery we went in an automobile for a drive about the city. We followed a very bumpy road along the river's edge past many wagons carrying lumber for construction, then around through the trading section of the city. We stopped at a manufacturing plant for planting machines made only for sugar plantations, which are numerous in this region. It was a small but up to date and efficient factory, the manager mentioned with pride the fact that of 200 workers, only 19 were employees. They turn out more than 2000 machines a year.

We visited a machine factory called the Bolshevik, an old factory with little new machinery, employing 1,400 workers.

(Note of Sec. As I almost froze to death on this trip, the memory is very painful to me. Hence, incomplete notes).

Toward evening, our guide still insisted on our seeing more— a tobacco factory, but it was already closed, well then, a bread factory—at least it would be warm there. It was comfortingly warm (Notes quite complete on this plant) and the technical director was very proud and enthusiastic about his work. Only two kinds of bread are baked, both a graham. The ovens are German and it was a pretty sight to see the golden brown loaves rolling out of the ovens. 3,500 tons of bread are baked a day, one and one half hours to bake, 7 hours to produce, making in all 20,000 loaves a day. There are 114 workers. Although the latest American methods are still unknown here, it is a very clean, modern plant.

We came home late, had dinner in the beautifully decorated

restaurant of the hotel with our guide and chauffeur, had a samovar after and also another ride to the hill to look at the view, a visit to workers quarters (RK stayed home) and at 10 p.m. we left for Karkov.

J.H. Pierce in Pottsville Journal, Nov. 12, '27.
                    'Gives History of Czar's Regime.
    'Fortunately I know much of the history of Russia under the Czar's regime. Following the Napoleonic war in 1812 and continuously for over 100 years, plots were fomenting against the Imperial family, and frequently these flamed forth into fierce conflagrations and in 1905 swept to the very gates of the winter palace at Petrograd. Always these revolutions had been suppressed but in 1917 the ruling class of Russia had been gravely weakened by an unsuccessful war, and this time the opposition, although no better organized, was successful and the monarchy ceased to exist on Nov. 7, 1917.
    'Russia, half medieval and half Asiatic when the veneer of foreign culture was removed, always lived behind a veil of mystery, terrorism and romance. Its population consisting of 140 million people lived in a condition of ignorance and squalor with barely sufficient to keep them alive, while the ruling class lived in luxury and magnificence from the exploitation of these unfortunate people. Education and self determination were practically denied the laboring classes, and this was the fertile field in which the seeds of restlessness, envy, hatred and revolt were sown.
    'Russia, with the territory and natural resources of the United States and Canada combined, was practically undeveloped; its people through hundreds of years of repression had acquired an inferiority complex. The foreign capital of other nations was welcomed in to exploit the hidden wealth in Russia; her mines and factories were largely managed by foreign engineers and executives. Thus was the initiative spirit destroyed, and when it came time to reconstruct her factories, mines and railroads, the lack of long years of specialized training was not available to properly execute a problem so gigantic. Minds which had yearned for self expression for hundreds of years became over zealous to learn and grasped new thoughts with remarkable rapidity when the fetters were released.
    'We may pass over rapidly the sad story of revolution and counter revolution, of invasion by foreign armies, of famine and

pestilence, but we should keep clearly in mind that prior to the revolution nearly 2,million men had been killed and 5,million injured in the world war, that railroads and factories had been destroyed, that mines were flooded, that morale was at its lowest ebb, and that 140 million people, mostly illiterate, had no credit or any medium of exchange and were suddenly thrust back hundreds of years to the days of barter and exchange. The peasants' potatoes were traded for the merchant's shoes, and crusts of bread were traded for a hard day's labor . . . . . .

Currency on Gold Basis.

'During this time she has rebuilt her railroads and factories, many new indusries have been started tremendous power plants have been built, mines de-watered and put in operating conditions and thousands of splendid homes for workers have been erected. Her currency has been established on a gold basis, her school system has been tremendously enlarged and education encouraged. They have less crime of all kinds than we have in New York or Chicago. They are spending 90 millions per year for social welfare.

How rapid the process of reconstruction has been may be judged by the fact that in 1924-25 the output of manufacture and mining showed a gain over the preceding year of 60%. In 1925-26 an increase over the previous year of 40%, and over the fiscal year just completed a gain over the prior year of 20%. The declining rate of production growth is naturally due to the gradual completion of the reconstruction program. . . At the end of 1926, there were 144 concessions operating, including over 40 industries, 25 mining and 36 commercial. The number of concessions is gradually growing, the largest of them are the Harriman manganese concessions, the Japanese coal and oil concessions, the Lena Gold Fields, an English syndicate, and the Krupp Agricultural concession. The total capital invested in concessions in Oct, 1, 1926 was 41,million dollars, of which foreign concerns supplied 51% and the Soviet organisations supplied the balance.

'The figures I have given are sufficient to convince an impartial mind that there is economic progress. Here also are vast economic resources awaiting capital to exploit them. Where the capital is to come from is the important question. It is a well known fact that the large banks, trust companies and insurance companies of America are accumulating funds at an alarming rate. The bond issues of the United States cannot begin to absorb this money and the various financial institutions have agents throughout Europe striving to loan money, but the supply still exceeds the demand. This money must find an outlet or cease to be useful.

'In the United States we have overproduction in nearly every line of business, and unless some additional markets are created we cannot hope to continue our present pace. Our money should be put to work to create these markets, and our bankers should insist that American credit should be used for purchases in America, if this is not done America will supply the world with the sinews of war to challenge her industrial supremacy.

'In the face of the attitude of the American government it takes a good deal of courage on the part of the American business man to decide to loan money in Russia. Is this foreign policy sound? Is it helpful and sympathetic? Will it redound to our credit when the mists have cleared away and we look back in retrospect? Are we so close to the forest that we cannot see the trees? Is it good policy for us to help rehabilitate Belgium, France, Italy, Poland and Germany as we are doing and turn deaf ears to Russia? We have liquidated greater debts to our allies than the total of Russian indebtedness and we are pouring millions of dollars into Germany, which history records was the instigator, was the cause of the toll of human life and created these gigantic debts for future generations to pay.

'Are we to be super-critical and assume that only we have a perfect government, or are we to be considerate and tolerant? Are we to forget that when this country was ten years old, we also had strange views which we now hold impossible? Do you recall that history records people being burned at the stake for expressing certain religious beliefs in our country's early life, and when you feel especially superior, please recall that only 66 years ago this great nation, which was founded on the doctrine that all men are created equal, was torn asunder by our civil War, because a great part of our country believed in slavery for their fellowmen?

16/XII Friday

It was gray and cold when we arrived in Kharkov again at about noon. I had conceived a prejudice against Kharkov from rumours I had heard, and it seemed confirmed as we rode through the unattractive streets in a dilapidated automobile. At the Hotel Krasnaya (Red) we were given only one room temporarily, a long narrow room which looked like it was meant for a corridor. Evidently prices and service here were on a par with the Bolshaya Moskovskaya, for the room was 8 roubles and there seemed to be no conveniences. While Devedovsky went to look up the local Soviet, we took a walk down to the telegraph office. The streets were very lively and in the open square in front of the hotel stood a long row of izvozchiks, their sleds gay with bright colored carpets and red and green upholstering and little tinkling bells on the horses. Next door we found a branch of Donugol, the travelers' bureau, and went in and got detailed information about the rest of the trip. The man there sent us to Donoogel (the Coal Trust of the Donetz Basin) to see about the journey into the Don Bas. We wandered about in this enormous, imposing looking gray stone building for some time looking for the right department, until we dropped in on the rooms of the American Commission. I knew at once that there were some Americans in the room, for their appearance was unmistakable—five American engineers who had been only a few months in Russia. They had many friendly suggestions to make about the trip to Don Bas, and one of them offered to use his influence in the hotel to get us a better room. We had cocoa and rolls in a bakery lunch room which was crowded with what were certainly business men, officials of industrial trusts, private traders, etc., a large proportion of whom were Jews.

We had dinner in the hotel dining room, with music, during which we tried to raise our spirits by talking about the beauties of Florida and the Black Sea. In Kharkov we seemed no nearer our dream of a warmer clime than in Moscow. After dinner, we were given a large room upstairs for 10 R., which we decided to share together. D. had stirred up the local officials by presenting her letter from VOKS and the article of Serge about me in the Evening Moscow. A very cultured young man came from the Educational Dept. and offered a practical program for seeing the city.

In the evening he took us to the leading Dramatic Theater which was giving in the Ukrainian language a dramatization of Rigoletto. It was a large theater built on the plan of the Bolshoi, with the three tiers of circular boxes above, but almost empty because of a sudden change of program. Later on, several hundred soldiers from the local base crowded in and filled up the seats. I was surprised at the excellence of the production and the playing. The Ukrainian people seem to have a wonderful amount of artistic talent, which, suppressed under the tsars, since the official language was Russian and the masses knew only Ukrainian, now under the new movement of authorizing local languages, seems to be blossoming forth. After two acts, I left with reluctance to go to the opera house. Here, strange to say, another foreign classic was holding forth, 'Carmen', also in the Ukrainian language. Here again, I liked the production very much, the voices were beautiful and Carmen was as good as any I have seen in the role. I was so tired that I wanted to go after the third act, but the director begged me to stay, assuring me that the last act was the best. However, the intermission was so long, more than half an hour, that I was quite out of patience when the curtain finally rose. We rode home in an izvozchik and my opinion of Kharkov was steadily rising.

17/XII Saturday.

In the morning our guide came and we set out in a very good car for the Electro-mechanical Plant on the edge of the city. There had been a change in the temperature and it was thawing and foggy. On the way, I got some idea of the city. There were several broad streets with fine houses and new structures going up. We passed a district of new workers' houses made of red brick, one and two stories, which were very attractive looking. Kharkov like every other center has a housing problem, the city having grown in population from 200,000 to 450,000 in the last ten years. The plant which we visited is the biggest I have yet seen; it was before the revolution a German plant in Riga and was transferred here afterward and newly constructed. It has 4,000 workers and 1,000 employees and engineers, and 400 of the workers are women. Due to the fact that orders have come in faster than expected and they ran out of materials, at present only one shift is working, but none of the staff has been laid off. In state industries it is possible when it is slack in one concern to move workers to another, temporarily. The plant is now working at only one fourth of its capacity. It has a production of 15 million roubles a year with a plan for the future of 40 millions. The technical director, a Lithuanian engineer, took us about; he answered some of my questions, for instance, about the high cost of production in Russia.

He said it was not more than 100% higher, and was due not only to the high compensation and social benefits given the workers but also to a lower tempo of work which conserves rather than wears out prematurely the workers. He counts that production when considered per person, costs 30% less than in America.

As we went along through the great building, noting the crane above, the new German instrument making machines, insulation materials, etc. a crowd of workers gathered about us and wanted to know about America. When they heard that wages and living conditions are so good there, they loyally explained that here the worker is better protected, gets free medical care, the children of women workers are kept in factory nurseries, etc. One worker stepped up and said to my secretary, we should not believe that the conditions of the workers are good, that they live very poorly, that they have not freedom at all, they can't open their mouths to criticise and so on. The other workers were much annoyed, but the sec. answered that it looked as though he wasn't afraid to open his mouth to criticise. As we passed on, two workers ran after us and explained that this worker was a little bit cracked, 'You see,' they said, 'every family has its defective'.

There are 27 such plants in Russia, all a part of the Russian Government Electro Trust, 'GET'. The wages of workers range from 100 to 150 for skilled workers, women at machines on piece work get about 55 roubles and the more highly skilled women get 70 to 80 roubles. Many of the workers, for instance, those in the foundry, get a month's vacation, and the factory is closed 2 weeks of the year for the general vacation period.

I asked the Esthonian his personal opinion about the Soviet system, would it have to be modified in the course of time? He answered that he was sure it would not, it was a going concern, the workers supported it and he saw no reason why it would need to be changed. He said he was not a party member and stayed on simply because he was satisfied with his material conditions and working conditions. He said that he pays 40 roubles for his two room apartment, but a worker would pay perhaps 5 roubles for the same thing because his wages were that much lower.

From the plant itself we went to the day nursery for the children of the women workers, just adjoining. Here conditions for the infants and older children seemed quite as ideal as in the model nursery in Moscow. Nursing mothers come over during working hours to nurse their babies, working 6 instead of 8 hours. The idea is wonderful but I don't want to look at any more nurseries.

Back in the hotel we found the samovar still standing as we had left it, and my sec. and I sat down to lukewarm tea and engaged in our endless argument on the subject of the intelligent fellow ruling the dub.

Our guide came and took us to an exhibit of Ukrainian art which was shown in the new building of the Trusts, where the offices of the big government industrial trusts will be located. We sped through the streets in sleighs, then along a wide boulevard and at the end in an almost open space we came upon a great new gray stone building of eight or ten stories, which looked as though it had been taken out of New York and set down here in the snow plains. It made a most tremendous psychological impression: it seemed to symbolise the industrialisation of Russia. Inside there was no heating as yet, and the white plaster walls glistened with frost. The stone steps were very slippery and my Sec. remarked that if she should fall and be hurt I would have to pay her employee's compensation, in fact, she was reminded that I should be paying insurance dues into the government insurance department for her all along.

The exhibit itself was also unexpectedly thrilling. Here were some really fine paintings and sculpture, an art alive and young and strong. I liked very much a small painting of a woodland scene, done in rich bold colors of greens with a splash of red, the painter A. Simonov, the title 'Reading the letter', as the small red figure is sitting in an open place in the woods reading. I was given the price of 350 roubles for it and will receive definite information about it and about some bowls and vases which I wanted to buy by mail.

There were several rooms devoted to architectural plans and drawings of buildings now under construction in Kharkov and also projects for the future. Here is a city dreaming wonderful dreams; this new building is only the first of a number to be built about a court, one of which will be the headquarters of the government departments. The drawing of the whole project is certainly a beautiful picture. In ten years, it is easy to believe that there will be a Ukrainian Chicago here in Kharkov.

While we were eating dinner in the hotel, our guide, Boris Wolsky, who is himself an artist, came and brought me photographs of the pictures in the exhibit. I then gave him an interview which almost made us miss our train. We walked what seemed miles along the station platform on the slippery ice to our car, and got in just in time. The car was hot and full of people. I was feeling very tired and sick, there was no bedding and we spent a rather uncomfortable night, somewhat relieved by two bottles of Narzan which the conductor bought at a stop. In the four-berth coupe with us was an elderly man, an invalid, who at once entered into conversation with me in German and had a long tale of woe about his sufferings through the revolution. He was a merchant and lost everything and now he claims he and his family are watched by the secret police.

18/XII Sunday

At ten in the morning we arrived in Stalino, in the center of the Donet Basin, a mining city of 110,000. The city itself is 12 versts from the station, so we got into an old carriage, drawn by a big black and a little white horse, and on wheels, for there is a thaw going on and the roads are running rivulets of melting snow. As we rode along over the muddy roads in the chill, foggy air, my low spirits began to rise: this looked as though it would be interesting after all. On all sides rose steep hills of slag like pyramids, where the shafts were, and down the steep incline of one a coal car was moving. The houses about the station were hovels, but as we neared the city, they became better looking. What a desolate waste, and yet how alive. Soon we were on the streets of the town splashing through the mud; crowds were walking, the usual Sunday bazaar was in progress. The hotel proved to be perfectly new and as the porter at the door assured us: 'charmingly clean'. The small rooms were light and comfortable. Here we paid 4 roubles a room, but as we insisted on an upper sheet for the beds, each cost an additional 50 k.

We ate breakfast in the cooperative restaurant next door, where an interesting lot of people were dining, women with gray woolen shawls over their heads, rough looking men, and now and then a well dressed man, and one 'with a cane yet'. We had hot dogs and mashed potatoes with gravy, the first reminder of American cooking, while Devedovsky had her beloved 'gefilte fish'.

While D. was telephoning to the town officials and getting them all stirred up over the arrival of a distinguished visitor, my Sec. and

I took a walk through the muddy streets. It was raw and damp, and the town looked about as dreary and ugly as it was possible. Only the people seemed lively and well dressed. Spread out in the water and mud of a street were the wares of various peddlers, drygoods and notions, books, rusty articles of hardware, picks, bedding, beds, chinz covered couches, chairs, cradles—a wretched assortment. We came to what seemed to be a central pumping station (water is a problem here, and they are only just getting it piped to this section) and women came one after another to the little window, handed in a talon, a yellow slip of paper, put their two buckets under the pipe and the station master turned on the water. Then they hung their two buckets on a pole, balanced it on their shoulders and walked along the slippery streets toward home. One young woman had a great misfortune. She slipped on an icy incline and fell, all the water in her two buckets spilling on her. She rose with a stoical face, picked up the empty buckets and returned to the water station. On the hills in the distance, we could see some attractive white stone houses which we learned are workers quarters housing 12,000 workers and their families.

In the evening, our Stalin guide, a young man from the Education Dept., came and took us in an automobile to one of the workers' clubs. Here was a fine exhibit prepared for the Tenth Anniversary; first the history of the Revolution, photos, placards, documents, the growth of the trade unions in ten years, charts without end—one showing the number of citizens not voting before the Russian Revolution as 95% and the number voting now 94%. A room of agriculture, with chart showing the growth of collectives of peasants in this district as 6 in 1921 and 113 in 1927. Ten thousand peasants are organised in these collectives and they use 3% of the land.

In 1916 there were 120,000 horses in this district, the war and revolution left only 22,000 and now the original number has almost been restored. This is true in like manner of the cows.

A large room was devoted to the mining industry. Here were models of new machinery, smelting ovens on the American plan, graphic charts of development and miniature coal cars of various sizes showing production from 1917 to 1927. In 1917 before the coal industry was destroyed the production was 1511 million poods a year, now it is 1400 million. There were several models of inventions of mine workers, a coal carrier, a coal car on a cable. The various special clothing furnished each worker, strong, high rubber boots, overalls, gloves, etc. In the protection of labor dept. were shown the various safety devices in mines, the electric mining lamp, oxygen pump, posters warning workmen of dangers.

In the Cultural Dept. exhibit were charts showing the liquidation of illiteracy from 1923 to date. Out of 41,727 who attended these evening schools in this district in 1923, 28,983 are now literate, that is, have finished the elementary courses. The school attendance of children up to 9 years is 100%, and from 9 years 82% in this district.

In the same building is the central library; a lively little fellow with an attractive dark skinned face and bright black eyes, who looked not over 20, seemed to be the librarian. The delivery room was crowded with patrons. My Sec. asked him if they had any of my books; he answered at once, no, but we have ordered all that are being published in Russian. She started to explain about Land and Factory and he interrupted quickly: 'Oh yes, I know that Land and Factory was to have published his collected works, but now Gossizdat will publish them. I read about it in the bibliographical journal.' The library has 20,000 books, 250 readers a day in the reading room and 47% of the borrowers are workers.

From the library we went to a club of the Soviet Commercial Employees trade union, which has 1,600 members. The building is old, there is a large auditorium, tea room, gymnasium, library of several thousand books (all libraries here have the American Dewey Decimal system of classification). Here as in the other building was a radio set up in a rest room where the members listen every evening to local stations, Moscow, Berlin, London.

I came home early as I was very tired from the night before on the train. My impression of Stalino was changing considerably for here, in this what seemed on the surface a desolate hole, I was finding lively cultural centers for the mass of the population.

19/XII Monday.

In the morning, our young man came to take us on the usual inspection tour. A nice car was waiting for us; it was suddenly very cold again and the melting snow had frozen, making a slippery surface everywhere. We drove to the Government Farm 'in the name of Trotzky' (Sovhoz), a distance of 12 versts from the city, past mine shafts standing on the flat treeless steppes, each with its little group of dwellings clustered about it. The chauffeur drove at reckless speed across the icy plains, while a bitter, damp wind blew in our faces. The car veered and skidded, bumping over the rough roads and sending us into the air now and then. We passed a carriage in which the manager of the Sovhoz was riding to town. The chief agronome of the district, a Latvian by name of l'Etienne, who was accompanying us, stopped the carriage and asked the manager to turn back. The Sovhoz stood on a slight hillock, a cluster of whitewashed brick buildings. Before the revolution, this farm was owned by an American, Hughes. The farm as it is now operated consists of 3,000 dessatins, 2,000 of which are under cultivation. In winter, there was little to see except the stables, live stock and dairy. We first went to the stables which house 200 working and 150 young horses including a few race horses and besides this number 60 draft horses. There was a special barn for brood mares. We asked if they also get the 2 months before and 2 months after birth given to all working women as leave of absence, and received the quite serious answer that this was true. They breed only in winter, have an extra warm place and special feed. Of course, adjoining, as in all industries, was the 'Yasli', nursery, for the colts, the males and females being kept separate. The agronom pointed out that there was a barrier between them and they could only look at one another at this age. I remarked that this was strict Red morality. We then went to see the cows who were very comfortably housed. When I remarked on their thinness, the agronom explained that these were a German breed who do not give so much milk if they are fat. They feed the cows chopped beets, 10 funts of beets producing 3 funts of milk.[7] This dairy furnishes the neighboring industries with milk to feed their workers employed in injurious work.

I asked why this region is so treeless, and the agronom explained that few trees grow naturally here, not so much because of the soil as the atmosphere. However they are planting some forests. In every district (okrug) there are 10 sub-districts with 4 agronoms to each, and 6 at the center, our guide being one of the 6.

7. A *funt* is a measure of weight equal to just under a pound.

'And now for the pigs!' has become an historic expression which we introduced at this point, also. We slipped and crawled over the icy ground to the hog houses, where we found some fine hogs very comfortably housed and clean. Adjoining was a large space with a high wall about it where the young male pigs were running; the agronom remarked that this was a 'pig monastery'. In the courtyard he showed us the pigs' bath and said that the pigs walked in the big courtyard in summer.

Next we skated arm in arm with the big fat Scandanavian manager to the machine sheds where I was surprised to find so much machinery, plows, barrows, cultivators, mowers, mostly Deering manufacture. There is also a machine shop at the farm.

Although there were still the sheep to see, we were all so cold and miserable that we decided to return to the farmhouse. Inside the large, cosy living room I found a wood grate burning and in front of it a rocking chair which I gratefully sat down in. On the long table were large bunches of white chrysanthemums growing, which I mistook for the paper flowers so prevalent in Russia. I said I supposed the rocking chair must be a legacy from the American, Hughes, but they denied it. We had cereal, coffee, home-made white bread, head cheese, swiss cheese, pickles, wine and vodka. It was all very pleasant and soothing after the long trip out in the cold wind. When we had become melting and talkative from the food and drink, we got into a discussion about relations between U.S. and Soviet Russia and other kindred subjects. In the midst of the discussion, my Sec. burst forth into what seemed to be a tirade against me. When I reproached her with going against me in a foreign tongue, she was very indignant and said: 'On the contrary, I was stirring them up by telling them how wonderful you are, what an important person you are in America and what a powerful influence you can exert for Russia. In other words, instead of deceiving you I was deceiving them.'

Before I left there was the usual book to write my impressions in, but my impression was not very good, because they had said that their profit last year above all expenses was only 3,000 roubles. There are about 200 permanent workers. They explained that they had to put most of the surplus back into the enterprise.

Our open car was full of snow when we came out. We took a broom and brushed it out of the seats. The agronom was wrapped

Dreiser and his traveling party at Stalino, Donetz Basin, 19 December 1927. *Left to right*: l'Etienne, a Latvian, chief district agronomist; Dr. Sophia Davidovskaya; Dreiser; Ruth Kennell; a local guide. (From Ruth Epperson Kennell, *Theodore Dreiser and the Soviet Union* [New York: International Publishers, 1969], p. 18)

in an enormous sheepskin shuba of curly black sheep's wool.[8] Besides, he had brought 'just in case they might be needed' a pair of felt boots. Our young guide who wore only a light overcoat now got into another similar black shuba and thus arrayed and looking like great shaggy bison, they sat in the seats in front of us and protected us somewhat from the bitter wind and sleet. Away we flew over the dreary steppes. On the way, we passed a 'hooter' (an isolated farm or farm building, so rare in Russia) and I noticed a herd of cattle standing out in a wooden fence enclosure in the bitter weather. It was explained that they were waiting to be taken to the slaughter house (so their welfare was no longer of any consequence). All covered with snow, we stopped at a photographers, and thus attired in our

8. A *shuba* is a bulky fur or woolen coat.

fur coats and hats, had our picture taken by an energetic little fellow who almost burst a blood vessel in an endeavour to show 'American speed'. I also had a separate picture taken without my over coat. I autographed two mounting cards and at last, due to the insistence of my Sec. that I must at least see a mine in Don Bas, we were off to a shaft. The chauffeur had let down the top of the car, but our guide was very solicitous about my seeing the sights. He therefore opened one window to the right of me and himself sat down in the seat beside it. Arrayed in the great shuba whose voluminous black wool collar spread out a mile, he completely hid the whole side of the car from my view, so that I could see only one tiny corner of the window. But he seemed so happy at his little scheme for letting me look at the scenery, that I didn't have the heart to disillusion him.

We tore through the town up to the hills I had noticed from the mudhole below on my first day. Here were some fine new stone houses for workers and we stopped at a handsome stone building which had only recently been finished as the club house of the mine workers union. This fine structure contains 67 rooms, is modern throughout and well furnished, with a beautiful auditorium-theater with several thousand seating capacity. Besides there is a nice lecture hall with specially equipped desk-seats, large gymnasium with up to date equipment. The building cost 600,000 roubles; there is still another large metal workers club in the district being erected at a cost of two million.

Now we were off to the shaft. On the way we picked up a special guide who had brought our special clothing along. Now although only about four o'clock it was quite dark: the wind blew the sleet against the windows of the car; electric lights gleamed through the fog and now and then a plant whistle boomed forth. At the shaft, we went into a miners' little banya to dress. It was deliciously warm inside. One of the mine superintendents came, a handsome young fellow with a straight nose which gave an arrogant look to his face. We got into the heavy oiled pants and coat and wide brimmed hats, were given carbon lamps, and thus looking quite like any of the miners we passed, we went out into the wild weather and across the slippery ground to the stairway leading up the shaft. Above in the coal car station were several women working on the tracks. The cage came up dripping the water, we got in and were dropped 140 meters through the earth. When the cage stopped we came out into a cavern electric lighted with tracks. But only this central place was lighted and when we got into the corridor it was lit only by our lanterns. Every few minutes a warning whistle would sound, our guide would call 'to the right', or if the car was coming in the opposite direction, 'to the *left*' and we would throw ourselves against the rocky wall in which the props were imbedded, and a horse would come running down the track drawing two or more mine cars loaded with coal, the driver sitting on top with his head lowered to avoid the ceiling. I noticed that the air seemed quite fresh, in fact now and then as we proceeded down the rocky corridor, I felt a breeze in my face. We passed through a door and at once the air seemed much warmer and the pungent smell of horses came to us. Here were the stables of the unfortunate horses who work in the depths of the earth. They stood in their narrow stalls in the darkness—after several years of this life they go blind. Three times more air must be pumped down for them than for men. I kept thinking of their wretched existence as the odor of them followed us down the corridor. We came out at last to where the coal was being mined. This shaft is thoroughly mechanised and no pick mining is done at all. I saw in action the invention for transporting the coal through the narrow workings to the cars, the model for which I had seen in the exhibit, invented by a miner. A few young miners gathered about and wanted to know about mining conditions in America. They said they were well satisfied with conditions—the actual diggers work six hours but the drivers of the cars work eight; however, they are looking forward to the seven hours promised all workers by the Government. On the way back a breeze was in our faces all the way, we passed scolding drivers and now and then a worker sitting by the wayside resting. Then into the bright electric lighted room, into the cage down which the water was pouring, and were taken above all safe and sound. Again out into the cold, again into the warm banya where we washed the coal dirt from our hands and faces.

On the way back we stopped at a group of new miners houses and knocked at the door of one little stone house with lighted windows. A shrill woman's voice answered—she was afraid to open the door because her husband was not at home. We went on to the next house; here the dogs began barking and a man opened the door. He was quite civil, invited us inside, his wife was a young girl in bare feet. There was a little kitchen with large brick cook stove, a large living room and a bedroom, all fresh and attractive. He said he got the place free of rent, electricity and water because the plant for which he works had built the house. He earns 150 roubles a month as he is a skilled mechanic. There is no water in the house, it must be carried from the water station nearby.

When we reached the hotel, we went down to dinner in the cooperative restaurant next door. We had beet and schnitzel and enjoyed the playing of a Viennese violinist, his wife the pianist and a cellist. He first played, at the request of a young fellow, a lovely Jewish thing and seeing that we appreciated it, he played especially for us some American songs, including Yankee Doodle. While he is not prospering in this desolate place, I think he must be very much needed. Near the piano sat two prostitutes, heavily painted, and they precipitated an argument on the subject with Devodovsky.

The beer made us all sleepy, we were very tired, but nevertheless I got into another argument with my secretary. I had another fit of doubts about this Soviet thing, and she got very indignant at me. I said when I saw that most of these industries were not new but had been running years before under the czar, that some were not even up to pre-war production, that the Sovhoz had only 3000 roubles profit, that those tractors they were turning out in such great numbers in Leningrad were admitted by this agronom to be far inferior to the American and to cost more—then that merchant on the train and his complaints. I said this thing couldn't work at that rate, the industries must show more profits. She answered that she was ashamed to have to repeat again the old story about the war and revolution destroying all the industries, so that they had to be rebuilt, and the explanation of Rykov's statement about production being so high, that is, that so much went to the workers and the tempo of work was lower. How could I think, after all I had seen of the improved conditions of the masses and of the country, that the system wasn't working? Why did I think they must show a cash profit? I thought she wasn't much of an economist, but she didn't think I was. Is the fundamental purpose of production to provide profits or to supply the people with the necessities and comforts of life? Wasn't that what industry was accomplishing very rapidly in Soviet Russia? I was always saying that I knew the terrible conditions of life in Russia under the czar, but she didn't think I knew after all, or I would realise where all the profits in industry were going, when

I saw the great improvement in the standard of living of the masses throughout Russia. Look at the new houses for the workers, the beautiful clubs, the cultural works going on, even in this hole. Look at the new hospitals, the nurseries for the children in the factories (or perhaps I didn't see enough of them)—and surely one couldn't doubt that industry is running at a profit.

(Note of Sec. I didn't say all this but I thought about it after-ward).

Monday Dec 19 – 1927 – Stalin Russia

A blowy, sleety day. I am up at 8:30. Rereading the new Machiavelli.[9] *(English Socialism of the 1900 Period.) We are to do a Sovhoz (Agricultural Farm)—a mine, a miners club & some workers' houses. The local Soviet is to provide an automobile. About 10:30 we start. The driver a chauffuer formerly connected with the Kreml in Moscow. A reckless driver. The Steppes. 15 Versts in a driving snow—over an icy plain. The French-German director Mr. Hughes farm. Blooded stallions, mares. Bulls & cows. Sows & boars. Ewes and* ⌞　　　⌟. *The main office. Mr. Hughes introduces comfort into Russia. Real flowers. The central house toilet. It makes me suggest a national toilet day for Russia. Another long argument although we are supposed to have no time. Cattle out in the snow. Why are they left so. Oh, they are going to be killed. A mine workers club. I remark about the local office workers club. Oh—they don't need anything better. A mine. Horses that go blind after five years. 6 hours working for the actual miners (the diggers). 8 for others. We do it. A miners banya.*

Russia

They seem to believe at times that <u>classes</u> are real and independent of their individuals. Statistics march by you with error and injustice and greed and foolish misapprehension reduced to quite manageable percentages.

+

They want things more organized, completely correlated with government and a collective purpose and with endless government functionaries—but no other

+

9. H. G. Wells' *The New Machiavelli* (1911), a novel concerned with British political life before World War I.

And they seem to understand—at last—as no other modern government does—that they must avail themselves more & more of the services of expert officials. They are not like us who still mix the starkly efficient—on the one hand—with ill instructed and rudderless heirs of the same. They tolerate no inefficient & wasteful heirs of Efficiency, insight and courage.

+

We have not as yet suffused public education with public intention and they have. And they are developing—or trying to—a new or better living generation with a collectivist habit of thought. They desire to & do link hitherto chaotic activities in every human affair. Nothing escapes them for goverment is all.

In America our task is to catch and harness for the good of all that escaped, world-making world-ruining thing industrial & financial enterprise & bring it back to the service of the general good.

+

Our multitude of functionless property owners.

One sees really a country with no abandoned—if as yet wretched poor. No foolish & meaningless rich thank God—flaunting their non sense before the eyes of want; a nation armed & determined, ordered, in part trained—in part in training and officially at least (and with an immense party behind that—purposeful. It's emotions are in the main collective emotions; it's purposes collective—not individual now what our [unreadable word] had.

They are communists because for them individualism means muddle. Their purpose appears to be to subdue the undisciplined worker, just as they have subdued & abolished undisciplined wealth. Order & devotion as in the early church are of the very essence of their meaning. In short, as Bukharin himself said to me, they project a splendid collective vigor & happiness. In short if I may [unreadable word] him he said

Tuesday, Dec. 20th - 1927 - Stalin, Russia

Gray & cold. Sleet & snow. We breakfast in the restaurant of this hotel— The Metalurgical. One impression I get from Russian life & hotels is that they mean well from a sanitary point of view but they do not quite grasp the processes. They put in toilets—but misuse them—neglecting for instance so simple a thing as to pull the chain. The realize that wash basins are nec-

*essary but provide one with so little water that a mere dabbing of the face
& hands is possible. They will have a room with a bath—but hot water
only on Saturday or Sunday—according to their pre-bath tub customs.*

*With us, this morning there is a strained feeling. I called Danedosta
down the day before for trying to make me travel Maxim Gorky (offered
to pay her way back to Moscow) & her feelings are hurt. All of the special
things near Stalin having been seen the day before there is seemingly nothing to do. I start re-read the New Machiavelli. A pig is killed just below
my window by two men—presumably meat for the hotel Restaurant. I
have my hair cut & a shave by the hotel barber. He proves to be a Jew
who worked 11 years in Constantinople. Apparently no subscriber to communist principles he complains of life in Russia—but diplomatically. He
first asks how Russia compares in comfort with America. When I say not
very well he says things here are dreadful. One can make a hundred or two
roubles but his rent costs so much—25 roubles. A razor which in former
days cost 1 rouble now costs 13—Scissors, ditto. Soap & perfumes are very
high. His shirt which quality for quality I could buy in N.Y. for 1^{\underline{50}}$ cost
him 8 roubles 4^{\underline{00}}$. His suit—worth 35^{\underline{00}}$ in America—not more—cost
170 roubles or about $85^{00}. Food & other things were high. In Constanti-
nople where he worked he made 100 francs a month—but could afford 12
suits. Here he has just 1. He would like to get out of Russia but the goverment will not issue a passport. If it does it costs 200 roubles & he has not so
much. Worse, other countries will not recieve immigrants from Russia because they believe them to be communists. "I wish I could get out" he said.*

*Afterwards RK & I walk to the telegraph office. As usual there
is a serious discussion of Russia & her reasons for being here. She is a
little depressed—Russia does not look so good & yet she defends Communism—the new day based on the welfare of the lowest workers. We rag &
wrangle. In the afternoon the representative of the local paper calls & gets
an interview on Russia & America! These people are cracked on the subject of America. Afterwards the representative of the local Soviet calls. I
am to see a steel plant at ⌐   ⌐? R.K. refuses to go. Davidosta &
I go but I dread the drive behind the most reckless chauffeur I have met in
years. We are thrown about, the car skids & spins & I complain but to no
effect. The steel plant, once we are there, proves to be one built in the Czar
time by French concessionaires. It is large but not immense—some twelve
furnaces & smelters. However I learn that a concession for doubling the
plant has just been granted to an American by the name of Farquhar. He
advances $25,000,000 & builds the additions but all is to be recaptured*

by Russia in 20 years. A young Russian engineer who speaks English takes
us around: he is very intelligent, definite and a little condescending but
courteous. At 4³⁰ we start back for Stalin. Another wild ride. Afterwards
(immediately) we pack & leave for Rastov.

20/XII – 21/XII Wednesday morning.

At five o'clock in the evening we left in the automobile for the
station. Our reckless chauffeur was driving and he tore over the ice
and bumped over the ruts until we landed quite breathless. In the
station we found the buffet packed with people, the waiting room as
well, a rare collection in sheepskins and a variety of old fur hats and
caps. We took our tea standing, bread and bologne and nice French
pastry. When the train rolled in there was a grand rush for the platform, and we waited a little. Outside a cold wind was blowing against
us as we struggled along the icy platform beside the endless train of
cars. At the steps of the Maxim Gorki cars a long line of people were
standing waiting to get in; it didn't seem possible that they could all
get into the coaches, and I felt very sorry for them, standing as they
must on the slippery platform with their assorted baggage and bedding in the bitter wind. But we had no sooner got settled in 'soft'
(myaki) when the train started to move, and our conductor said that
all the crowd had got on. We dozed during the three-hour ride to
Konstantinov and arrived at about ten o'clock. What was our horror
to learn that the train for Rostov was due at three in the morning.
The station buffet was crowded and it seemed impossible to contemplate waiting there all those hours, when we had thought it would be
only 20 minutes. I was filled with rage at everything Russian, such a
lack of system, such inexcusable negligence on the part of the official
in Stalin who didn't know when the train left. But all misery passes,
and we adapt ourselves to any hardships. First I drank Narzan and
that cooled me off a little, then later I had tea, rolls and cheese, a
little vodka of course in the tea to lift my spirits. Glory be, the time
was passing. It was now 12:30—only three hours to wait yet. Then
my women folk came back from the station master's with the news
that the train would be late—how late no one knew yet—because
of the snowstorms. This required some more adjustments. One well
dressed young woman with very much rouged lips almost cried; she
had received a telegram that her husband was ill in Rostov and she

must get to him quickly. There was an impromptu conference of passengers about our table: suggestions were shouted in order to drown
out other suggestions. There was a plan to wait in the station until
five o'clock when we could get a workers train to a workers settle-
ment and take the train from there when it came. There were rooms
and hotels there, whereas here near the station was nothing. The
young woman wanted to ride to another station early in the morning
and get a train from there. At this point the chief of the station arrived and stunned us with the news that the train was ten hours late.
We decided that there was nothing to do but sit in the station until it
was light. People were already nodding and sleeping with their heads
on the tables. In a corner, half a dozen or more homeless children lay
on the floor. Now and then the guard came in and made the rounds,
routing out the orphans and prodding the sleepers, telling them they
couldn't sleep here, they must go to third class to sleep. The G.P.U.
man on duty at the station kindly offered me a nice hard bench in
his little room to sleep on which I gratefully accepted. I made a pillow of my fur coat and slept there until morning. The air was thick
with Russian odors; shortly after I lay down, the G.P.U. official put
his head on the table and slept soundly; however, the guard looked
in occasionally and evidently paraded up and down outside in the
third class waiting room where a motley throng of bears and bandits were gathered. By the way, I have decided that the Russians
are more like bears than anything else—they just about hibernate in
the winter, and they look so big and shaggy in their sheepskins and
padded clothes, or like walking mattresses, I think sometimes.

Thus the darkness passed and at seven in the morning R.K.
came in and roused me from my luxurious couch and I went with
her back to the buffet, where I found Devedovsky looking quite
worn and gray. R.K. had adopted the native custom of sleeping on
the table, but D. sat bolt upright all night.

Now that the izvozchiki were on the job outside, we decided to
take a ride to clear our heads. A shrewd old fellow, whom the guard
had tried to protect me from by telling him I was an American and
didn't know anything about the customs (whereupon he answered
vehemently 'What do you mean, doesn't know?') came into the buffet
to ask us again. He had a gray beard, a rakish old fur hat and sheepskin coat. He agreed to take us to the town and back for two roubles,
It proved to be a very interesting ride. In this town are no less than 12
big plants, coke, benzol, glass, steel, mirrors, ceramics, and the foggy

air was heavy with the smoke from their chimneys. The whole town seemed to be newly built; we rode down a long street of new brick and white plaster cottages all built in very good taste, with attractive wooden fences about them, painted green and the wooden shutters of the houses were likewise green. About the steel plant were large, fine new stone houses for the workers. Our voluble driver took us to the bazaar: this is an ancient but dying institution in Russia (— open stalls on the streets or goods laid out on the ground and sold by petty merchants and peasants) for the cooperatives come along and build their big modern stores right along side and drive the private traders out of business. We looked into the new cooperative, a fine big store containing many departments. Surely enough, when we found another new bazaar, there along side was being built a new cooperative store. The people looked well dressed and satisfied.

When we returned to the station, we found D. sitting as we had left her. It was getting on toward nine o'clock. The women were busy cleaning up the buffet, scrubbing the tables, wiping the furniture, cleaning the plants and watering them and scrubbing the tiled floor. The women don't get on their knees but stand up and bend over, pushing the twisted cloth vigorously back and forth. The floor looked very clean—in fact, it was difficult to realise that it had been the scene of such misery and dirt of massed humanity the night before.

Our old izvozchik wanted more than the two roubles, he said five was little enough for such conscientious work, so I gave him 25 kopeks more for his 'conscientiousness'. But I was not through with him so easily. He followed me into the buffet and asked me to 'warm him' with a drink. Finally I agreed, he was given a glass of vodka which he drank at one quaff and I paid 60 kopeks more for his services.

We were the only passengers waiting now, we went into the ladies' room and washed some of the dirt off and wiped off the rest on a towel; breakfast was ordered, and I began to feel at home: I puttered about arranging the chairs at the table. Davedovsky said: 'He's beginning already to take an interest in the place'.

And really the breakfast seemed quite homelike. We had fried eggs, hot milk, rolls, bologne, and quince jam, and afterward we told stories and I got off on my experiences when I was a collector in Chicago. The time passed, twelve o'clock, still no train . . . .

Left Constantinovka at 12:30 noon. We at last found ourselves once again seated in the comfortable two place coupe of an International car. Just to sit in quiet and retirement and look out the broad window was restful enough after the long, weary way we had traveled from Moscow. The snow-covered steppes stretched as far as the eye could reach, broken now and then by villages and new industrial towns. As I have passed through these endless Russian steppes and thought about how they are to be developed, an idea has been forming: it seems to me that the government should undertake to cultivate the land just as it is running the industries, organise big farming units and hire the peasants at wages just as it hires the workers in the factories. This would eliminate many of the unsolvable problems which not only Russia but every country has had to face in regard to the farming class.

The darkness came all too soon and quickly blotted out the plains. There was nothing to do but lower the shades and rest until 7 p.m. when we arrived in Rostov. The Hotel San Remo. The first room we looked at was an enormous thing with a grand piano and a wierd collection of antique furniture including a great black settee. We chose another large room for the three of us, which had several windows looking out on the street and an elaborate marble fireplace—figures of cherubs holding garlands over the unused gate. We wanted to go to the public banya and have a bath but it was too late. We stopped at a 'Bar' in a basement and had dinner. There was a hard looking bunch of customers in the place, an orchestra was playing. We ordered the Caucasian dish shaschlik, which was appetizingly served with green onions and french fried potatoes.[10] We went home and went to bed at 10 O'clock.

22/XII

A sunny morning. We slept until 8 a.m, in spite of going to bed so early. We went down to the post office and I got the answer to my telegram, also changed $100. at a cooperative bank, receiving 194 roubles. Rostov is a nice looking city of 220,000 population, well laid out in squares with wide streets, but it is not very lively, and has no distinctive atmosphere, such as Kiev and Kharkov. It is the chief city of the Northern Caucasus, a rich farming region. There seemed

---

10. *Shaschlik* is a popular lamb dish in the Caucasus.

to be a lot of building going on. We had breakfast in one of a chain of restaurants, cooperative, 'EPO', which faintly reminded one of an American lunch room.

We walked to a tobacco factory, the largest in Russia, 'The Don State Tobacco Factory in the name of Rosa Luxemburg'. It consisted of a number of red brick buildings, most of which were built 78 years ago when the factory was first started. Before the war, the factory worked only 3 or 4 days a week and produced 15 million cigarettes a day. There were 3,800 workers at that time. There are now 4,500 workers including employees, 3,400 of which are employed on cigarettes, the rest on the auxiliary factories, paper, boxes, etc. The output is now 35 million a day, the chief reason for the increase being the introduction of new machinery. One of their professors spent two years in America getting new methods.

All this information I got from the director, Michael Ivan Petrov, a fine looking young man of 29, by profession an electro-mechanic, elected to his post by the workers. He receives the Party maximum for this district of 210 roubles, pays 35 R. a month rent for a furnished apartment.

He claimed that as far as intensity of work is concerned, the factory could compare with America, but the equipment and buildings were old. Yes, he was acquainted with the new methods in New Salem of turning out in one process the boxed cigarettes, but they knew them through France. It would be difficult to introduce them here because it would necessitate the laying off of a great many workers, and in Soviet Russia this must be done carefully and gradually, also the buildings are not suitable. The tobacco is grown in this district, in Georgia and in the Crimea, the last best. The 7-hour day has been in operation in this factory a long time (1922) and we find that the industry works better under it.

-------- Would you gain even more with the six hour day?

We are already considering this.

-------- And five hours?

We don't consider fantastic dreams.

-------- I am not speaking fantastically. Bucharin included such a thing in his program for the future.

Yes, but we do not plan so far ahead.

-------- Do you export?

Yes, to all countries, but very little, 15 million a year. When we export, it is necessary to remove all Soviet labels and emblems from the boxes. The 'Orient' is our best brand for export.

Our workers receive one month's vacation, special living quarters, a club, a nursery, a night sanatarium where those who have weak lungs stay for a period. 71% of the workers are women, and they receive 3 days a month vacation during their menstrual period, because the industry is especially injurious to the mucuous membrane. The babies of nursing mothers are brought to them in a special room at stated intervals from the day nursery adjoining.

-------- How much money do you spend for the welfare of the workers?

Since 1921 we have spent five million roubles on ventilation, sanitation, nursery, club. For the workers quarters we gave a certain sum to the city construction department, 300,000 roubles. 3,300,000 R. were spent by the city on on remodelling military barracks for workers quarters, and 9 million in building living quarters. 10% of the income of every institution and industry goes for building.

Before the revolution, the conditions in this tobacco factory were terrible, no ventilating system, the workers worked 12 and 14 hours.

------- Are your technical specialists foreign?

No, all are Russian and young men who graduated since the revolution. Foreign specialists are not needed as the industry is not complicated.

Rostov is a new city, whose development was stopped by the war. The czar always hampered its growth because Rostov on Don was always a city of revolutionary workers. So there have been great hardships in building it up.

------- What are the wages?

73.20 is the average, the lowest is 45 R and the highest 250. The worker on the lowest wage has about 19 roubles left after all expenses have been paid because not many are without families to support, but their benefits, free trips, medical care, schools, help. But of course at 45 roubles life is not easy, then they can get credit from the factory, but there is poverty here. Then there are the building cooperatives in which 450 of our workers participated this year, 150 individuals are building for themselves.

We then went through the plant. In the first room were the leaves which were being sorted. The ventilation system is new and the air is changed completely every hour. Among the women picking over the leaves of tobacco were several veterans, 1 who had worked in the factory for 54 years, another 37, and they looked quite hardy. They said that conditions were much better now. These workers received 72 roubles.

In the main department there was one shift, 6:30 to 2, in other departments 2 and 3 shifts. New machines for pressing and cutting do more than twice as much. A mechanic invented the appliance on old feeding machines which increased their output 50%.

In one of the rooms which had formerly been the club several mottoes were painted on the walls: 'The Smoke of the Chimneys is the Breath of Soviet Russia'. 'Intensity of Labor, faithfulness of every worker at his post will bring communism—the happiness of the workers'.

Here a pretty young girl of 20, with a fresh complexion, came up and addressed us in broken English. She said she was from Edinburgh Scotland and had been in Russia six years. Her father worked at Odessa, and she spoke English so seldom that she was forgetting it. She was an ardent Young Communist (Komsomolka) and asked me what I thought of the Opposition. When I said that I knew very little about it, she said: It is a shame for you'.

When we returned to the director's office I asked a few more questions.

- - - - - - How much higher is the cost of production here than abroad?

In our factory it is one fourth cheaper. We sell this cigarette for 45 k. a box, 25 in a box, and if we take away all the government taxes, a box costs us 18 k. On 45k. brand we pay 27 k. taxes, on the 14 k., 8 k. taxes. Of course, the statement of Rykov is true of machine industry.

The director then wanted to ask me some questions. The first and last was about the Sacco-Vanzetti case. I tried to explain the attitude of the American public to foreigners who had not been naturalized, and asked him what would be the attitude of the Russians toward a foreigner suspected of crime here. He replied that in the case of foreigners they are always deported. I said that Sacco and Vanzetti did not want to be deported to Italy. He said that they could have been deported to Russia.

We had tea for the second time, I was presented with a wooden cigarette case and several packages of cigarettes. Our guide then took us to the night sanitarium adjoining where workers with weak lungs stay for two months at a time, continuing their work but under special care and observation. It was very attractive place, with nice sleeping rooms, dining room and tempting kitchen. I said I would like to stay here myself. From there we went into another brick building. As we went up the stairs I remarked that I wouldn't be surprised if they weren't trying to slip another nursery over on me, and sure enough it was. R.K. said that if I would come peacefully and look at the day nursery, she would find me a toilet afterwards. So I went through the same thing again, only I must say this nursery was especially fine—I think nicer than the model one in Moscow.

When we got outside again, it was foggy and snow was falling. We found an izvozchik who drove us to the Armenian section of the city, 'Nahichivan'. It did not seem in the gathering twilight to have any very distinctive racial features, the streets were broad and attractive. We stopped at a large church and went in as I was under the impression that the Armenian church is Roman, but as far as I could see from the interior, it was the same as the other Greek. The picturesqueness of these churches is wearing off for me, and now I only feel a depression when I go into their cold, cheerless vaulted interiors, dimly lighted by candles, see the few worshippers crossing themselves and hear the priests chanting their nonsense.

We were quite chilled by our ride and decided to stop at the central banya. There was the problem of my money which I carried with me in two rolls. It was decided that since I had to go my way alone, it was best to give the money to R.K. who at least could speak the language. In the spacious entrance there was a crowd of beggars and hangers-on sitting and standing about the fountain, so we went to the doorway and there I handed over the money. After some fuss, I was permitted to go alone into the men's first class. (Note of Sec.— Unfortunately I was not present so cannot report on this adventure).

We all finally met outside all scrubbed and shining, R.K.'s bosom bulging with my rolls of American bills. We had dinner at the main EPO restaurant, shaschlik again with green onions and french fried potatoes and beer. We went home and packed. The hotel porter was positive there would be International on the train, but when we got to the train we found that not only was there only second class, but also no bedding. I wanted to go back to the hotel, but as there wasn't a fast train until Saturday, and it seems that only the fast trains have the special service, I got on board. At least, the conductor did not put a fourth person into our coupe, and gave me a little pillow. We went to bed in anything but a happy frame of mind.

Friday, Dec 23ʳᵈ 1927–
En Route between Rostov and Kislovodsk
Snow. Cold. The same type of trains. Oil trains. A wrecked one. Canals. 130 Caucasians in their uniforms & foot [unreadable word].

The Jackdaw. An American looking soo big or Caucasian. Peasents on our car. Tea at 10 A.M. At Armavir.
Big battle with Denikeri here
A new town being laid out
Pigs chickens dogs all gathered round the door. A woman with bare legs & arms walking through the snow to a shed
Summer dresses & winter boots
Women & men going with buckets to a hole out in the ice of a stream for water. We buy a duck for 40 kopecks
The crow in this region replaces the Jackdaw
New Towns.
Caucausians driving home their cows in company
Fields of Jackdaws
Mts in the distance
The sun comes out

23/XII

Next morning, more steppes greeted my eyes. If Mineralni Vodi was to be warmer, there was as yet no sign of a change. Snowy steppes and still more snow without end. I felt that I was now leaving Russia proper, the great waste stretches which make up the greater part of it. Now we were drawing near the Caucasus. It was already dark at 3:30 p.m. when we arrived at Mineralniye, which is a terminal station for trains into the Caucasus. Although there was plenty of snow here, the air was decidedly milder. The train for Kislovodsk was to leave in an hour. We had tea in the buffet. Nearby sat a poor woman with two children, who directed her complaints to us when she saw that we were interested in her conversation with another poor woman who sat next. She was on her way to Grosni, toward Baku, and had waited three days in the station for her train, because they were so crowded she could not get place cards in third class. She had now spent all her money. We turned over our considerable accumulation of food to her—bread, butter, apples, cheese, bologne, granulted sugar that had been leaking out all along the way, and the children began eating everything in succession ravenously, while the old woman next sat stoically munching white bread.

The ride to Kislovodsk was more than two hours. We could see absolutely nothing in the darkness, but now and then it was plain that there was still snow along the tracks. Near us sat a man and wife, apparently well to do people with two young children. The older girl cried fretfully all the way, the father tried petting, threatening and pleading but all to no avail. As they got off at Pyatigorsk and he carried the kicking and screaming child in his arms, his patience gave out. 'Svoloch!' he shouted, 'You're nothing but a svoloch.[11] Without conscience!' They disappeared in the darkness of the station. Two young boys very badly dressed like *bootblacks* in the U.S. got on with heavy sacks on their backs and sat down in front of us. They were talking in a strange tongue. We asked them about themselves. They were Armenian students, attending higher school in Pyatigorsk and going home for the Christmas holidays which included Saturday, Sunday (25) and Monday. The sacks, if you please, were their baggage. They were black eyed, swarthy skinned, sturdy fellows, and they planned to go to Rostov and continue in technical school when they finished here. They got out an enormous loaf of white bread and as they talked they broke off huge hunks and stuffing them in their mouths, gulped them down without chewing. Then they wanted to know about us. They were much excited to find that we were from America. They at once wanted to know the condition of the working man in America! One thought Chamberlain was president but the other said no, he's in England, but he couldn't remember the name of our president, although he knew that the capital was Washington.

At 7 p.m. when we got off the train, it seemed that we were in a new world. Although there was snow on the ground, the air had a soft, fresh feel to it, and as we followed the porter, who ex-

---

11. *Svoloch* is an obscenity meaning scum, swine, bastard.

plained that our hotel was so near he could carry our baggage there, we saw before us a winding street, at one side a high stone wall and above a magnificent building, evidently a sanitarium or pleasure palace connected with the railroad. At once, one sensed the soothing atmosphere of a rest resort, the tang of mountain air, a little cultivated beauty and comfort after the coldness and harshness of the working world we had left behind. The hotel was a government pension. We chose a nice large room on the second floor with many windows and a balcony over the street. The price was 6 roubles, in summer months, 12 roubles, but now it was the winter season and few visitors. We were so tired that it would have been comforting to have unpacked our bags for a prolonged stay. We went down to the dining room to supper. The cooking was the best I have encountered in Russia: we divided our portions and had a great variety— there were beets with smyetana, cabbage cutlets, veal with baked spaghetti, and wine and the total cost was 3 roubles. While we were eating, I noticed a distinguished looking man in a simple Russian costume come in and sit down—there was something familiar about that fair, bearded face with the fine, mild blue eyes. 'It looks like that archbishop at Leningrad', I said. R.K. turned and looked at him— 'Of course, it is Platon', she said, 'there is no mistaking those eyes'. At this point, he met our eyes, we smiled and he bowed in recognition. As we went out we stopped and spoke to him. He said he was on vacation, taking the Narzan baths for his heart.

We decided to go to bed at once so that we could get up early and see the town in the daylight.

24/XII

We actually did get up at 7 o'clock. It was not hard, for the sun was already shining into our room. We soon got outside and were charmed by the cold, fresh air and the beauty of the town. On all sides streets ran up to the hills and above were beautiful sanitariums and cottages and rest houses, and a big white building with columns which was a Narzan bath. I was already reconciled to the continuation of winter, for the place looked so beautiful in the snow and the air was so invigorating. We wandered down the winding streets until we came to a busy market, where peasants as primitive as any you would find in a village were selling their wares. There were also permanent stalls selling materials and supplies. We bought some hot milk of a peasant woman. We passed the rest home of the Art Workers Union. Many stone steps led to the houses above, all of which were closed for the winter. We crossed a bridge and entered a charming park. We came to a clear stream ending in a little artificial waterfall. A slight steam rose from the surface and I thought it might be Narzan. R.K. knelt and took some up in the palm of her hand. 'Tastes like perfume', she said. She smelled it. 'Smells like perfume!' She held some in her hand for me to smell. Yes, it did smell like perfume. Great excitement. I also bent down to try it. A shout of laughter from R.K. She remembered she had put scented cold cream on her hands.

At the end of the park was the handsome Narzan Gallery, enclosed in glass with a flower conservatory, fountain of Narzan at which we drank freely the water we pay 40 k. a bottle for in Moscow. Then Davidovsky stopped at the tourist bureau to get information and we went on up to the Kurzal, the big amusement pavilion run by the railroad which we had noticed as we came in. Here was the great building containing theater, concert hall, billiard room, etc. beautiful gardens with concert pavilion and summer theater and along the edge of the hill a fine view of the city. Further, two very nice Russian bears in a cage, of a lovely honey color, and then some eagles, owls, foxes and peacocks. In the shelter of the large building one could sit on the benches in the warm sunshine and believe it was spring.

When we returned to the hotel we met our Davi- very indignant, for she had been looking for us. An izvozchik was waiting to take us to the sanitariums and she was armed with a type-written introduction. It was a beautiful droshky drawn by two horses—in fact, I was to see the last of the little Russian one-horse drosky or sled from now on.

The first sanitarium was for peasants from all over the Soviet Union. There were 65 patients at a time for a period of five weeks. It was all very clean and attractive, nice dining room and social hall, four beds to a room, the peasants dressed in white linen costumes. Their local health department sends them free of charge. There were eight women, one an old Communist, aged 60, Ivdanova Michaelova Borisova, who was at her studies when we looked in. She is a member of her local Soviet, is very active in speech making and is only now learning to read and write.

The second sanitarium we visited was formerly in the name of Trotzky, now is 'October', and is for responsible Party workers. It was a beautiful place, with single and double rooms attractively furnished, bright red blankets on the beds. I was told that Wells stayed here for six weeks when he was in Russia. In summer there are 70 patients, in winter 45. In a separate building were the Narzan baths, well equipped, also electric baths and various other treatments. In the corridor of the baths we met Kreps, head of the Press Bureau of the Comintern, here on vacation.

The third sanitarium we visited is in the name of Lenin, and is the largest institution in Kislovodsk. It is not only a sanatarium but also a scientific institute for the study of diseases of the heart. It is located on the hills and commands a wonderful view of the city and the surrounding hills. It accomodates 120 patients in summer and 110 in winter and takes not only members of trade unions sent by their local clinics but also individuals who pay 158 to 300 roubles a month. As this was the 'dead hour' (myertvi chas) when all patients must lie down, we saw only the rooms of the fat people who walk during this time. In the office of the manager we were told about the town before the revolution. Practically all the buildings were privately owned hotels and cottages before for instance, the present building was a hotel which rented rooms to patients who took private treatments. During the civil war, these buildings were used as quarters for white guards, and their horses were stabled in the bathroom. In the course of the discussion, it was mentioned that children's sanitariums are gradually being eliminated, as it has been found that the children are apt to become confirmed invalids. Instead they are put in forest schools which give the children special treatment and at the same time permit them to follow their education. This is the principle on which the 'night sanitariums' in connection with industries are operated.

When we came out, our izvozchik was trotting his fine horses and equipage up and down the road to warm them. We stopped at the telegraph office where I wanted to send a Christmas telegram, but the usual argument about the 32 kopeck rate again consumed half an hour and put me in a bad humor about these 'damn fools' and their inefficiency, 'dubs', 'What a lousy country, anyway!', while R.K., also in a bad humor, told me I was a typical American who expected to find everything just like at home.

We got back to the hotel quite cold and tired, had dinner in the dining room and said goodbye to Platon, who told us he had never received the stenographic notes of our interview from VOKS. R.K. had an acquaintance here who was the wife of the manager of Kurzal, and we went to see them in the evening. They were in the big building where a concert and movie were going on. We listened to the music awhile and then went to their house, a pretty cottage in the park. Although he was the manager of this big concern which had put the place in repair after the revolution and last year netted a profit of 200,000 roubles, he had only three rooms in the cottage, and his wife's mother, and I don't know how many more relatives, occupied one of the rooms which we passed through to get to their rooms. They lived quite cosily, served us tea with jam, pastries, candy, apples while we engaged in a heated discussion of communism. Here was another religious fanatic, was a mechanic before the revolution, now received the Party maximum for this district of 190 roubles on which he had to support his wife and three children. He was enthusiastic about the development of the country, believed that in time the people would have everything, and that the population would not outgrow the productive power of the country as a more cultured people would practice birth control. About the war communism they had had, he said it was simply a measure of the government during a period of great want to commandeer all supplies and ration them equally. His wife was a silly woman, very talkative, heavily made up, who evidently has ambitions for better things, but says the workers are very critical of them if they try to fix up their home. They walked down to the hotel with us. The stars were shining, the air was clear and bracing, a wonderful winter resort. The government should divide the yearly vacations of the workers so there would not be such a rush in summer.

Dec. 25-1927-En route between Mineralni and & Baku. Sun on Mts—
Birds flying against the flow of light—
Snow striped hills & snow peppered ground—a glory of grayness—rich &
thrilling like a fine grey seal
Like children who believe in Santa Claus, we rose very early Christmas morning, at 4 o'clock, as we wanted to catch the fast train to Baku which was supposed to leave Mineralni at 7:25. It was still

Theodore Dreiser
sees the
sights of Stalin
through the
auto window

Ruth Kennell's sketch of Dreiser bundled against the cold. (From the Theodore Dreiser Collection, Special Collections Department, Van Pelt–Dietrich Library Center, University of Pennsylvania, Philadelphia) dark and chill as we rode to Mineralni, a time to think of home. We stopped so long at one station while the crew had breakfast that we were nervous about missing the train, but no danger, the train was late. We sat in the buffet and prepared ourselves for a siege. We drank tea, and then a little later milk and then still later, although I had been suffering severe pains in the solar plexus, I developed a craving for cold turkey. So I ordered a portion at one rouble, D. ordered an ancient looking smoked fish also and we had a Christmas breakfast. This experience has cured me once and for all of cold turkey. They also brought a half a pood of the mountains of white bread piled up in a corner of the restaurant. After breakfast, I played solitaire much to the interest of the spectators. In fact, I had already begun to feel at home in this station when the train arrived at 12:30.

We were soon rolling out of Mineralni in an International car. I had thought we had said farewell to the steppes, but here they were again, snow covered, absolutely flat. There was a dining car on this train, the first I have experienced in Russia. We had dinner there; they are very spacious, much wider than an American. The dinner consisted of soup, cold fish with horse radish sauce, roast duck with pickles, apple with rice, coffee and cakes, (not real coffee of course), the cost 5 R.80. It was already dark at four and as we were very tired we went to bed. At about 8 p.m. we were awakened by the fact that the train was standing in one place a long time; this was Gudermas, the station after Grosni and Vladikavkaz. We could hear our neighbors talking about the wreck of a freight train ahead of us. A rail had split and the middle car turned over, the others piling on top, four killed.

26/XII

Slept intermittently until 8 a.m. At 8:30 the train pulled out. Now the country was changing, frozen marshes filled with tall brown grass, wild ducks flying, shrubs in the distance and small clumps of trees—now a range of snow covered mountains and little villages near the tracks—clay huts with thatched roofs and pigs and cows in the dooryard, at the door a woman in a red kerchief sat cross legged and sifted grain in a circular sieve; thatched little houses on poles. Then we came to the remains of the wreck: twisted and smashed freight cars lying along the siding, grain, paper, books, scattered all over and then soldiers guarding the bodies of the dead. A little later, and it might have been our train. . . R.K. imagined such a thrilling story in the American papers that she almost regretted our escape: 'Theodore Dreiser dies in railroad accident on Christmas Day on the Caucasian steppes'.

By noon, all the snow on the prairies had disappeared and could be seen only on the mountains. There were sheep, cattle, herdsmen in the black sheeps wool Caucasian cloaks with broad straight shoulders as though a pole were stretched across inside from shoulder to shoulder, and big fur hats. Out of Petrovsk Port a cluster of dugouts near the tracks with mounds of earth on top.

In the same car was a crowd of responsible Party workers returning to Baku and Tiflis from the Conference in Moscow. There were Armenians, an old Georgian who had worked with Stalin, — Shamshe Lezhava — A White Russian, a Siberian, a Jew. One young Armenian, of the Tiflis Financial Dept., was most attentive, insisted upon my drinking Caucasian cognac, Tiflis champagne and vodka. We had dinner together in the diner and afterward he sat in the coupe and sang Armenian and Georgian songs, a wild, crazy young fellow. Elchebikov.

We arrived in Baku about 10 p.M. It struck one as a wild kind of station, crowds rushing to and fro, the porter running away from us, everyone jabbering in a strange tongue. Baku is the capital city of the Azerbeidjan Republic, has a population of 447,000 and the official language is Azerbeidjan although the equivalent in Russian is printed on signs. Outside, our porter rushed over to one of many swarthy Izvozchiki who were lined up. All of them knew very little Russian. The carriages in Baku were the finest yet, drawn by two horses, the costumes of the drivers long coats of a bright blue, tied about the waist with a red sash, and big fur hat on the head. We drove to the Novaya Evropa Otel (New Europe). This was a new hotel of seven stories, with the tiers of floors circling about the central pit, in which an open elevator ran up and down. We took a two room suite on the sixth floor for 8 roubles. As in all mild climates, it was badly heated and the windows were sealed tight with no fortochka (little window) to ventilate. The service seemed comparatively good, a great fuss was made about getting us to fill out forms, give documents, etc. but we were finally settled.

27/XII

We got up and had breakfast in the hotel dining room, which we found very expensive — 1.60 for a pot of coffee, evidently real coffee. Then we went for a walk on the wharf. There was a fresh sea breeze and a pleasant reminder of San Francisco about the water front. The street along the wharf swarmed with carriers, in ragged clothes with their wooden shoulder pieces slung over the arm, or bent almost double with some load, like boxes or old iron. They were all native, swarthy, and husky looking. There were also strange little wagons on two high wheels, decorated in colored paint, the horse's harness beaded or silver. Long planks could be carried so that half the length hung over the horse's head. There were numerous old ships in the harbor and any number of the rusty remains of iron bodies of vessels. Facing the water was a large, new stone apartment house, which we looked into. In the court we found a young woman who told us that she lived there, that it was only for ship workers, her husband had been lost at sea two months ago and she was left with two young children. She had a room in a two room flat, with a kitchen for the two families and a toilet. She received a pension from the government shipping company of 26 roubles a month and paid 50 kopecks a month rent.

We took one of the beautiful izvozchiki back to the hotel. Davi had been to the Baku Soviet and was self-righteously waiting for us. The Baku authorities appeared not to appreciate me enough to furnish a guide. Davi said that the woman in the office with whom she had spoken had claimed to know all about me. 'Oh yes, I have read all his works. He is my favorite poet'. I must add here at the same time about a man in the car from Rostov who asked if I were John Reed.

We went down to the Musselman Working Women's Club in the name of Ali Bairomova. This was a very large building which had been the residence of a rich Armenian oil magnate. Here were the club rooms, reading room, theater, a Lenin corner built strangely like a mosque, with a bust of Lenin on one side and a picture of him on the other, and on either side of the dome the emblem of the hammer and sickle.

In 1924 the club had 550 members, in 1925 1300 and now there are many more. A large percentage of these women were illiterate, wore veils and had no training for any work. Here are classes in sewing, embroidery, rug weaving, midwifery, music, dancing and for the liquidation of illiteracy. I was dragged into the day nursery which keeps the children of the members of the club during the day. There was a parents meeting in progress. The children greeted us with 'Salome malekov' (How do you do). The little woman who led us around was herself a Mussleman, very tiny, with a dark, pretty face and large dark eyes. All these women are dark with straight black hair, swarthy skin and large dark brown eyes.

On the street leading up to the club house are many little stalls and here are merchants selling their wares; it is a narrow cobbled street crowded with people, most of the women walking with their veils or cotton shawls which envelope them, drawn over their faces, so that their figures might at first glance be picturesque til one noticed the cheap modern shoes and colored cotton stockings. Every other stall is a schashlika, where mutton on sticks is being turned over a fire in an iron pot, or over charcoal. We looked into one interesting looking little place, with steps leading up to it and a little garden at the side. At once the dark, evil looking proprietor called to us to come in, but we wanted to go farther up the hill to the great church which loomed up at the end of the narrow street. This street was full of life and color and the romance of the East, but the church itself when we went inside was like all the other Greek churches I have seen, except that the old priest was wailing the service rather than chanting. When we returned, the little restaurant had already sold out all its shaschlik so we sought out another on a tamer street. It was a typical beer hall, but the proprietor was most accomodating and suggested two portions of shachlik and one of a beaten mutton also cooked on a stick over the spit, also a lobster, beer with dried peas, green onions and radishes and the thin loaves of white bread which is baked in great slabs which look like washboards. As we came home we stopped at a bakery and bought some cakes to eat with our tea in the hotel. Near the hotel was an animal show, the entire front of the building covered with colored pictures of the animals; this not only served us as landmark but always enticed us, so we decided to see it. Inside it was very cold and dimly lighted, but the animals were interesting, wild cats, tigers, lions, bears, monkeys, snakes and birds. We were quite tired and chilled when we got up to the rooms and had our samovar.

28/XII Wednesday.

In the morning we started out to the oil fields by street car, changing twice and passing through several districts of the city where much new building was going on. At the sea, we went to the offices of the State Azerbaydzhanskaya Oil Industry. Fords were flying up and down the muddy streets and in fact, when Davi presented her documents, the management ordered a Ford to take us about the oil fields. It was a chill, foggy day, almost drizzling. Most the of the wells have been sunk in the water and great stretches drained. This group of wells, the nearest to the city, produces 2000 tons of oil a day. There is an eight hour day of three shifts and the average worker earns 70 roubles. The raw product is piped to the Chorni Gorod (Black City) for refinement. It is exported to Turkey, France, Italy and the refined oil to Germany. Only about 10 to 12% is exported because of the home demand. The methods, so our guide, a foreman, told us, compare with American. In this field are 520 workers whose new and old dwellings are in sight of the wells on the hills. Before, everything was sooty from the kerosene which the workers burned, now they burn natural gas. Their living quarters are free. An average family, say of four, receives two rooms and a kitchen. A worker who is discharged or quits working for the concern cannot be put out of his quarters without a decision of the courts, but he must then pay rent. If unemployed he pays 2 k. per cubic meter rent. If acceptable quarters are found elsewhere for him he must move. 9.75 k. is paid each worker who lives elsewhere, but only about 30 people are living here and not working in the industry, because when a man leaves, he usually finds work elsewhere and is provided quarters there.

I asked about the carriers who are so numerous on the streets of Baku. They belong to a trade union, but don't work for wages, as members of the union they receive certain benefits and get find other employment through the union. Their earnings amount to about 90 roubles a month. I began to think that instead of pitying the carrier, he was to be envied for a good lot in life. He looked very healthy and happy and was his own boss.

Before the revolution, each private firm had its territory and kept from one another geological secrets. Therefore, many mistakes were made in exploitation and boring was done needlessly. Here thus far only the rich wells are worked, and small ones are as yet untouched, and this accounts for the large number of people employed

to an area, in comparison with the U.S. They are now experiment-
ing on pumping out water from the exploited territory instead of
filling in, and constructing only roads. It would cost six million to
fill in this area whereas to drain costs only two million. The cost
of exploitation is more than in America, but the products cost less
and we can therefore compete with other countries. Production in
Russia costs so much more only in the mechanical industries where
machinery must be imported. When the Soviet Government took
over the oil fields they were in a terribly dilapadated condition; now
conditions have been brought up to pre war level, but production is
not yet up to that point. In 1902 the highest output was 520 million
poods, and the plan for 1928 is 480 million poods.
-------- What are all those old iron ships doing out in the harbor?

All of them are more than 30 years old and belonged to individual capitalists. There are about 200 of them which could be used
only by spending much money on repairs and it does not pay. The
largest ships are 1000 tons but we are now building ships of 5 to 6
thousand tons. Our ships go to Astrakan and down the Volga; there
is a small trade with Persia and Turkestan.

Drinking water is a serious problem here, it must be got from
wells 140 km. deep or piped a long distance.

From here we took a street car which went along the wharf and
we saw the many old ships lying in dock rusting away. We arrived at
the Black City, which they claim is not black any more, since conditions have so improved. We picked our way along the muddy streets
where much digging and building was going on, and received at the
main office a permit to visit Plant No. 2. As we were waiting outside
in the court of the plant, RK and I engaged in a discussion aroused
by my remark that I was afraid the new order here would make for
a drabness, due to the lack of class distinctions, and the leveling
down of the standard of living to comprise all. RK claimed that the
intellectual workers in Russia already were creating a higher level
for themselves, that there would always be differences in individual
tastes and temperaments. I said that if all the people must be equally
provided for there could never be heights of beauty and luxury, because the increased population which would follow the better standard of living for the masses would consume the increased wealth.
RK answered that the higher the culture of a society the more it
practices birth control. I said that was the bunk, that the ordinary

man wanted children when he could afford them, and besides the death rate would decrease as conditions improved.

A very courteous guide came along and explained the process of refining the oil. On the hills above were many reservoirs in which the oil piped from the fields is stored. From the reservoirs the oil is piped down to the batteries, where it is heated and kerosene, benzine and different grades of refined oil are extracted, passing through pipes out into troughs. In this plant are 350 workers, 3 shifts. In the whole Black City are 14,000 workers and in the whole oil industry in Baku including all the oil fields, there are 40,000 workers.

As it was already the end of a shift, 3 p.m., as we came out of the Black City, we took an old izvozchik who had just moved some furniture to this neighborhood, in order to avoid the crowded cars.

We had dinner in a very nice little family restaurant near the hotel. In the evening, I went with Davi to a movie, 'A Woman's Victory', which RK had told me was rotten. I quite agreed with her after seeing it. It was a story of feudal times in Russia, how a bandit-baron carries off a girl and forces her to marry him, how she outwits him on her wedding night, and then when soldiers come and arrest him and he breaks down, she leads him out as her beloved husband and all ends happily.

29/XI Thursday

We got up bright and early; the sun was struggling through a fog and it promised to be a fine day. We got an izvozchik and I asked him to drive to a mosque which I had seen from my windows. It stood alone on a bleak hill and we had to drive through mud and filth to get to it. I had expected something finer—it was very plain and shabby, and falling to ruin. There were poor cottages in the neighborhood and peat piled up in high piles along the streets. We descended the hill and drove to another mosque whose dome and praying towers were visible. It was much larger and finer. We were leaving the courtyard when one of the boys asked us if we did not want to look inside. I had thought that no unbeliever could enter a Mohammedan church. However, he opened the door and we looked in. It was a great white interior with modern electric fixtures, on the floor many oriental rugs and a little carved stairway, otherwise quite bare, with a balcony where the women stood.

When we reached our neighborhood again, we decided to go into the fortified wall, which had looked so enchanting from a distance. Here was a new world, or rather an old world, like a page from the Arabian Nights. Narrow, winding streets through which streamed a procession of carriers with packs and boxes and bales of hay on their backs, donkeys likewise loaded, or carrying men who looked ridiculously large sitting on the tiny weather beaten beasts, women holding their shawls over their faces even while they carried buckets of water or babies, stalls of porcelain and chests, meat cooking over little charcoal fires, street peddlars buying their day's stock of oranges from the merchants,—a hubbub of voices in a strange language, dark, friendly faces. A fragment of an ancient gray stone wall, strangely shaped, rising high above the old buildings. We were seeking the Chanski Dvoretz ⌊   ⌋ and wandered in and out of the maze of narrow streets inquiring here and there, but nobody seemed to know it by that name. Then a slender boy of 16 stepped out from a group and pointed and gesticulated in an effort to make us understand at the same time trying to speak, although he was tongue-tied. He decided to conduct us himself and went ahead, looking back whenever he turned a corner in a timid, questioning way, to be sure we were following. In and out we went, climbing up broken stone steps, through dirty courtyards, through narrow passages until we came to a high stone wall with parapets on top. But the wooden gates were closed, and we were told the castle would be open to visitors tomorrow. We said we were leaving today, but the aged keeper, who had a long nose and a beard, shook his head when our guide told him what we said and answered irritably in the native tongue. We looked through the crevices in the wall at the castle, a small, gray stone building which had been standing since the fifteenth century. It is said to have 68 small rooms and the throne room is still intact. Another boy had joined us and he asked us where we were from; when we told him America, the tongue-tied boy made a clicking sound expressing wonder and exclaimed: 'America!' The other boy said if his friend were in America he would be cured of his impediment. To us his home was like finding the scenes of the Arabian Nights, while he thought of America as a wonder land.

A very strange phenomenon among these people is the sight now and then of a red-bearded man or a red haired woman, a red so dark and unnatural that it certainly must have been dye.

We went home, packed, went through the usual procedure of leaving the hotel, including tips for everybody, and taxes on our passports, and drove to the station to catch the 1:40 mail train for Tiflis. Davi went to get the places and after some time returned to announce that all places were taken on this train. We were sitting in the buffet among our extensive baggage; crowds filled the room, waiters were hurrying about with soup and meat dishes—even to see the food in a railway station buffet nauseated us—and I was overwhelmed with irritation and weariness. Nothing to do but return to the hotel—no, we couldn't go through all those ceremonies again at the Novaya Evropa. There was the Hotel Bristol near the station. Davi was sure it was quite near the station. Ah, a chance to economize! She would get a carrier to carry the bags right *to the hotel.*

The Hotel Bristol seemed to be much further than Davi thought. We, RK and I, stopped at the park because we were already tired of the chase. Davi ran on after him, around corners, down main thoroughfares, yelling at him not to go so quickly. He made some speed considering that he had my large suitcase and heavy leather bag and fur coat. She said that when they finally arrived at the hotel she was completely exhausted and so angry at him that she gave him only 50 k. which he, feeling guilty at his evident intention, took without comment. The weather had turned delightfully warm; we sat in the park in the bright sunshine in silence for some time, then went to the hotel. Davi had taken one small room in which the windows were sealed and no heat. I asked for a heated room and was told that one would be free later. I went for a walk along the water front, and the interesting sights and fine air lifted my spirits. We had dinner in a shabby cafe near the hotel which had very funny mural decorations on the walls, ladies and cavaliers walking in gardens. There was the usual borsch and beer. Returning to the hotel, on the road we stopped at a general cooperative store, packed with customers, a long line standing at the cashier's cash register. There were placards on the walls about the value of cooperation.

We strolled down a narrow street and looked in the windows of little shops, jewelers where the large earrings worn by the women were displayed, musical instruments including the tara and a Caucasian drum on which they play with their fingers like on a piano, the instruments were inlaid with mother of pearl and tara or balalaika covered with silver. We came to a row of shops showing Caucasian silk stockings manufactured on a frame in the shops, for 3 roubles a pair.

Returning to the hotel, we moved into a larger room with an iron wall stove which they promised to heat. We had coffee served by a very human landlady who regretted that we were leaving so soon and could not sample her sister's good cooking. We went to bed very early, and the clatter and talking in the buffet annoyed us; sometime in the night someone came and made a fire in our stove out in the corridor.

29/XII–30/XII

The wind was whistling madly around the corner and rattling the windows of our room and the doors of the balcony, but when we rose in the dark at 4 o'clock, the room was warm from the fire. As we had slept without undressing we were soon on the street. A chill, stiff wind still blew, the stars were gone, and it was snowing in scattered, wet snowflakes. Arriving at the station, we heard that the train was three hours late. Checking our remaining bags, we returned to the hotel and were permitted to occupy our room until seven a.m. During this time, we slept fitfully, rose again and went to the station. The corridors and waiting rooms were packed with people. We got our baggage and piling it in a free place in the corridor at the head of the main stairs, we sat down on the bags and waited, watching the ebb and flow of humanity. I have never in my life seen such wretched people, little boys in filthy rags, old men scratching themselves beneath their tatters, poor women sitting patiently on their blanket rolls with their children, a population which was previously almost entirely illiterate, and is still to a great extent. Now and then a little boy with a black face from grime, rags and tatters hanging from his bare arms and shoulders, perhaps half covered by an old straw mat, bare feet, matted hair, would come close to me and beg for money. This was a signal to watch my pockets more closely and hold on to my bags. After two or more hours of waiting, our porter who had a number and therefore could be trusted, led us along with the crowd out to the platform, at last we were seated in an international car again on our way to Tiflis. In the rush to the train, an orange was taken from RK's pocket.

On the road to Tiflis the railroad followed the Caspian Sea to the south a few miles. On the other side of the tracks was a brown waste, with low brown hills near at hand. All along were herds of sheep and herdsmen's villages of dugouts. 'I'm afraid there's no Lenin corner here', said RK. Now we were coming to wider and more desolate stretches, camels were grazing, or caravans were moving across the plains, with faded striped coverings, and packs on their backs. Now we had left the sea behind and the railroad veered slightly to the north in the direction of Tiflis, through level grazing country, and villages somewhat less primitive—new clay houses with thatched roofs, a red tiled roofed building in the center which might be the local Soviet! Against a background of clay houses a woman's figure stood motionless, watching the train—a gray veil enveloped her form and face so that she might have been a symbolic figure on a stage. Further on, a woman in bright red garments is walking carrying a tall earthen jug. The houses were built on high poles. Near the track a caravan of oxen drawing wagons moved along. One caught a flying glimpse of a tractor in the field. The aspect of the country gradually became more prosperous and civilized. There was much new building in the towns, a new bridge across the river and a new railroad track under construction.

We arrived in Tiflis, the capital of Georgia, at 11 p.m. This station struck one also as a bit wild. Our porter had no number and raced like mad out into the street. The air was certainly not balmy, but there was no snow, at any rate. Conveyances were at a premium at this hour. Our porter found a wretched old automobile, the fat driver started the engine and we had to bargain with him above the deafening clatter. He asked five roubles to the Hotel Orient. We had to accept and rattled along the streets to the hotel. When it came to paying him he asked 7, saying that he charged two roubles for the baggage. We refused to pay it. He bellowed, although the engine was not going. We referred the case to the hotel man, and finally he accepted the fee five roubles. The hotel was quite attractive looking, with a charming Turkish hall, but our rooms were not very good. However, this proved to be at least a 2-sheet hotel.

31/XII

The window of my room looked out on the main street. In the morning, I was astonished at the beautiful view. Directly across the street stood a great stone church, in cream and brown, the brown stone running like stripes around the walls. It had a large central dome and four smaller domes, the whole a perfect and compact symetrical structure looming up against a background of mountains gardens and streets lined with tall cypress trees. On top of the mountain stood a white building and there was a railway running straight up to it. Automobiles were spinning by, the street swarmed with well dressed people; Tiflis seemed to be a modern and properous city. Wet snow was falling, and when we went out we found the streets slushy, the air damp and chill. We went to the post office, and found only a package of Soviet charts from Serge. When we returned to the hotel, Davi was waiting with a program from the local Soviet. The museums were near at hand—a collection of old Georgian paintings, copies of mural decorations in churches, etc. and some new pictures, then a natural history museum with beautiful settings of wild animal life in Georgia and the surrounding Caucasus: wolves, wild cats, birds, flamingoes, a great tiger killed near Tiflis, wild boars, mountain goats; a collection of lovely butterflies and bugs. We walked through the mire down the main shopping streets. It was the day before a holiday and the stores were crowded. We bought a couple of pieces of Caucasian silk just before the shops closed at three o'clock.

When we returned to the hotel, I felt very miserable; evidently the damp and fog had a bad effect on my chest. We had tickets to the opera, and I got up and went. The opera house was a fine looking building inside and out. The corridors and halls were far more beautiful than the interior of the theater itself. The walls were decorated in quaint designs like the old palace in the Moscow Kremlin. The piece was a new comic opera, 'Life and Joy', written by a Georgian, and was in the Georgian language. The music was good, the costumes quite colorful, but the plot was old: a gay young fellow is given a sleeping potion and when he awakes finds himself in royal clothes and being crowned czar. He falls in love with a charming lady but finds that a frightful looking czarina goes with the throne and runs away. It was a short performance over at 10:30. It was interesting to watch the people, for the Georgians have very strong characteristics: an energetic, virile, capable people, the men tall, handsome and dashing, (Tiflis seemed to me a city of Stalins)[12] and the women well

---

12. Joseph Stalin was born in Georgia.

dressed in silk gowns and with quite an air about them, although the dark heavy features which make for masculine beauty are too hard in a woman.

Tiflis was meeting the New Year in cafes and in our hotel restaurant. When we went up to my room, the Armenian Communist whom we had met on the train to Baku came; he had been telephoning the hotel and asking for us for the last two days. Davi had blown herself on a bottle of wine; I went to bed and she and RK took the young fellow to the other room, where they must have had a gay time as RK's head was still turning from at least two glasses of wine the next morning.

1/1/28

When I rose New Year's morning, the city was beautiful in the bright sunshine, and the snow covered mountains were shining in the sun light. At quite an early hour for a native, our Armenian friend appeared to take us out. We went to the cafe Germania, a little German confectionery, again for breakfast. We had already given our orders when a policeman came and told the proprietor he must close his shop because it was a holiday. However we were permitted to finish our breakfast, although the whole police force seemed to be patrolling the shop to be sure no other customers got in, and the harrassed looking German proprietor went out several times to reassure them.

We went into the grounds of the headquarters of the Sovnarkom (Soviet of People's Commissars of Tiflis). The garden was charming, formal beds of plants, cypress trees, old vines climbing over the buildings, red earth on the paths. Here many soldiers from the barracks nearby were strolling. There was a pond with one lone swan in it. Adjoining stood the church which I like so much. Our guide said it was now a Pioneer Club. In the courtyard are sport grounds, and when I remarked on the incongruity of such a use of this noble edifice, our Armenian said there had been a project to tear the church down and erect a new building on the site. I said I thought a better use would be to turn the church into a mausoleum for the country's distinguished dead. We had now come to the government garage and were given a car to drive about the city. We drove first to the old section of the city; above on the hills stood an ancient fortress, only a wall and tower remaining. Here was the old Tartar section, many old buildings, narrower streets, markets. We crossed one of the eight bridges which span the River Kara. The churches were numerous but added nothing to the beauty of the city, for the Georgian style of church is ugly—a rectangular dome or three domes painted silver or made of inlaid silver, severe and plain in outline and of a dirty gray stone.

We began to climb the mountain road and at each higher curve the view became more wonderful. Tiflis lies in a valley and on all sides rise mountains. We climbed to a considerable height and looked down on the city. I could make out my church, there was a very large hospital, a macaroni factory of red brick, red roofed houses, gardens. Above, at a height of 1,500 m. was a colony of cottages for children who are delicate or tubercular. It is called the 'children's city'. Descending we stopped at a pretty central park and went into the picture gallery. Here was a fine small collection of Georgian paintings. Two large paintings of streets in Samarkand, in Asia, pleased me. Here were the street bazaars being held in the shadow of beautiful ruined mosques whose domes and towers reminded me of the blue mosaic work of the mosque in Leningrad. The artist was Gigo.

We had no dinner as all restaurants were closed. Our train was to leave at 10:40 p.m. for Batum. Our Armenian friend saw us off. There was only one 'myaki vagon' (soft car) on this train and it seemed from the crowds that about a thousand people were trying to get places. We had some arguments about our places, as someone else claimed one of them. However, the G.P.U. man who is always on the job at stations intervened and we settled down in a four place coupe with a young Red commander who tried to be very helpful to us. This was the worst car I have traveled in yet, with the exception of the Maxim Gorki.

2/I/28

In the morning, a real winter scene met our eyes—a landscape simply buried in snow, and a little stream running swiftly through the snowy banks; thick snowflakes were falling. RK in the berth above had taken out our guide book and was reading the description of Batum.

As we rode along the snow gradually disappeared, and a heavy fog or drizzle took its place. In another two hours no snow at all, but rain, marshes, strange foliage, crops hung on trees to preserve them from the damp, thus giving a very queer shape to trees, houses built on piles, fresh green grass. The custom of the country seemed to be turbans on the heads of the men. The villages were primitive looking, and the better houses were on brick piers evidently to raise them from the marshes. In the background were low mountains. I asked the Red commander some questions about the army. There are 450 men in his regiment. In battle, the commanders are at the very front; in private life they sleep and eat with the men. The eight hour day applies to soldiers also; in fact, they often work less than eight hours. Much of the time is given over to education. Before, under the czar, the soldier was very much restricted and abused. There were signs on the boulevards and street cars, 'Soldiers and dogs not allowed'. The soldier gets a month's vacation every year and everything is free to him. With his higher officers he claimed he was socially on equal terms, but on duty of course subordinate. The officers cannot discipline the men harshly, never scold or yell at them, discipline is attained more through instruction and training than through punishments which are now abolished. Before punishments were terribly severe. Illiteracy is being abolished through the army. He claimed that the living conditions of the soldiers are very good and they do not complain. If a relative comes to visit a soldier, he is given a room, and at all times relatives can come to entertainments in the camps of the army.

Our train was already three hours late, now we heard that there had been a wreck ahead, and we had to stand still one hour at a desolate station, waiting for a train to come back from Batum and take us on. Our train then moved on slowly for a few miles and stopped in a wild place. We got out, and as no one was allowed to pass along the tracks where the wreck lay, we had to make a circle about, along muddy roads with heavy baggage to the train standing on the

What wretched looking natives! Clad in ragged clothing, with cloths tied about their heads, turban fashion, they followed us begging for a job of carrying our baggage. We hired two of them and a girl besides. A couple of carts drawn by oxen (*a very pretty girl with black curls under yellow kerchief driving*) also carried some of the baggage. After wading for about a mile through the mud, we came to our train and got on. The wreck lay all over the tracks, overturned oil cars, a freak accident—the brakeman had slipped in the mud, his lantern had struck against an oil car and broken and the oil had caught fire. He was completely burned up. The chief conductor further back, seeing what had happened, uncoupled the other cars and saved 26 of them. The guard who related the story to us claimed that the conductor, who had black hair, had turned white with fright. The train was now traveling close to the Black Sea, black sand, tangled undergrowth along shore and mountain woods on other side of tracks. We passed the large botanical gardens outside Batum. We arrived in Batum about five o'clock in gray, chilly weather.

It seemed a provincial town. We took an izvozchik to the pier, and learned in the waiting room of the Sovtorgflot (Soviet Trading Fleet) that we could buy tickets only at nine o'clock, steamer leaving at midnight. So Davi went into town to get some money from the bank, while we sat and waited in the buffet. There was a wretched collection of humanity sitting about the metal stove. When Davi returned we went into town, first to the telegraph office, but no telegram from Serge. Then to the restaurant nearby. A cheerless dinner which cost 4.80. RK inquired about the possibility of getting her typewriter repaired. The waiter led us about trying to find the residence of the mechanic who runs a typewriter repair shop in town. He kept saying, just a little bit further and kept leading us on and on down lonely streets, around corners, asking occasionally for information. At last we tracked him down, the mechanic agreed to repair the machine and bring it to us at the steamer. Hours more waiting in the buffet, I felt very sick, my chest was paining. Crowds stood about in the room. At 11 we went on the steamer.

3/I/28

At about 3 in the morning of the 3rd, our steamer of the Soviet Trading Company, 'Pestel', named after a Decembrist admiral on the Black Sea, left Batum. I was so glad to be on the last lap, but my stateroom was a shabby affair with five beds. If this were summer I would have to room with four other men! The women's and men's cabins are entirely separate, the former being above and altogether more comfortable. This is a one-sheet boat, no bath, and only a blanket if requested. No water excect the usual small bowl with two gallon tank attached. I resigned myself to a week of face washing. The sea was very rough. The boat rolled and pitched and the waves dashed over my porthole.

At seven in the morning we reached a small port called Poti.

This was a small dreary shipping station inside an artificial harbor. Snow, rain, a cold raw wind. I think only of Constantinople and the south. Eggs with wretched coffee and watered condensed milk in the dining room, which was a confortable type of ship dining room. The Baku officer whom we met on the train talked with me. He was on his way to Sochi. I made the best of the morning playing solitaire and looking out at the loading. It was a slow process. We did not get off before 1 p.m. By then the clouds were breaking to the north, revealing as we went west the line of mountains that edges the north shore of the Black Sea! The clouds of gulls as we go out—they flew high looking like silver specks in the golden light to the north. The sea was rough but obviously calming. I was interested by the group of sailors who are on their way to Sebastapol to attend naval school—their gayety in their heavy clothes. One of them, a tall, ungainly fellow with a typical fair Slavonic face, followed me about with his eyes, and asked RK for my books. A bookstand on the boat displayed 'Sister Carrie' and a volume of short stories called 'An Unusual History'![13] In the evening we arrived at Sukhumi, but remained some distance from the shore. It looked a very attractive place in the darkness with lights shining on the water. It was cloudy with a cool breeze but the air was mild.

4/I/28

The sea was calmer this morning and I walked on deck and watched the dolphins and sturgeons leaping out of the water as we steamed west. The sun broke through and lit the sea to the north. To the south and east it is somber and bleak. Wild ducks by the hundreds, also mud hens, and northern loons—I never saw more. It has grown warmer and still. At 12 noon we came to Gagra, considered the most beautfiul of the Caucasian resorts. It has the mountains behind it and consists of many large fine buildings, most of which no doubt are sanitariums, hotels and bath houses. We did not dock and the unloading took place in small boats. I noted the second and third class passengers, as Asiatic and dreadful as ever. The huddled masses of them gave me a sense of nausea. Russia is permanently spoiled

13. *Sestra Kerri*, trans. unknown (Riga: Academia, 1927); *Neobyknovennaia Istoriia Drugie Rasskazy* [*Free and Other Stories*], trans. T. and V. Ravinskiĭ (Leningrad: Mysl', 1927).

for me by the cold and dirt. Bukharin talked of building a paradise. But when? In fifty or a hundred years. I will seek mine while I am still alive. Further down the coast lies the town of Adler, where the railway line which follows the sea shore to Tuapse begins. Today it is quite calm and sunny. We were still cruising at the base of these great mountains, which as we neared Sochi became higher, in the background rising two or three very high snow-covered peaks. All along the shore were scattered houses, some of them very large and beautiful, evidently sanitariums; near Sochi are the famous sulphur baths 'Matsesta'. As our boat came into Sochi, it was already four o'clock and the sun was setting. Behind the front ranges of lower mountains rose the snowy summits of the higher peaks, turned rosy by the reflected glow from the sunset, their profiles purely cut like pink cameos. One did not know on which side to look for loveliness: on the shore side the beautiful city with its fine buildings and bath houses against the mountains and on the other the sun setting in streaks of red gold on the sea. But in a few minutes the radiance had all passed, the mountain peaks turned a cold pure white, and at once the moon, already for some time palely visible above the mountains, began to shine on the water.

5/I/28

Early in the morning we docked at Novorossiysk, a leading port city of 62,000 population. As we walked off the boat, near at hand stood a line of izvozchiki with a new style of drosky—flat on top with a mattress or carpet folded on it, on which you sit and hang your legs over the side, resting your feet on the dashboard. We rattled along. It was a bright, frosty day. The town was new and drab looking. At the center we got out and looked in vain for a restaurant, so we strolled up a slight hill past soldiers drilling (those same three soldiers I meet everywhere) to where the town ended in meadows. Nearby were two or three fine looking buildings. We had hoped to find a good restaurant in Novorossiysk, something that would be a relief from the ship food, but we looked in vain. We wandered through the bazaar where peasants were selling all sorts of foodstuffs; I wanted some hot milk and told RK to go and buy some plain cookies we had seen in a booth on the other side. She was cold and cross, and couldn't see the sense of doing it, but after some time with reluctance bought a few cookies and we ate them with hot milk, standing up at the counter in the midst of melting snow and dirt. We went then to the main street again, and saw that the main dining room was now open, but when we went in the smell was nauseating. We escaped with a glass of tea, and my companion had to admit that the bazaar at least was in the open air. Along the main street, were people carrying pretty little fir trees, for it was the day before the old Russian Christmas, and the devout persistently celebrate the old date although the new (25th) is observed along with the new calendar in Russia. This really makes two separate Christmas holdiays and with New Year's Day in between on which the modern Russian celebrates, *so that* the winter holidays are quite extended. We looked up a bank and changed some American dollars for roubles—of course, they were tickled to death to get the dollars, but they paid me only 1:93. We walked back to the boat feeling disgusted with the city in general. I talked with RK about her leaving Russia; she rallied to the defense and spoke of the advantages of living in Moscow, the personal freedom, lack of strain of keeping up appearances, workers' benefits, like free medical services, so that even if the standard of living is low, it is possible to live on a small income. I kept scratching myself all along the street. 'Think I've got lice', I said, feeling furious at the idea. Near the wharf, we met Davi and her cabin-mate and they took us to a restaurant nearby. Same old lay-out, buffet, potted plants and palms, dreary, pungent. Some returned Russians who had brought a ship from New York were sitting at the next table and talking in loud tones in execrable broken English, just to show off. We ordered fried chicken and bread and butter—chicken not so bad, but butter rank and those great platters of thick white bread! RK, even on land, never free from a feeling of seasickness, was very much depressed and I was in a worse mood. We returned to the boat and I went to bed early in the chill, dank cabin.

6/I When we once got started again, it was very rough. At seven a.m. we arrived in Feodosia on the shore of the Crimea. I did not go up for some time. Met Davi coming back from the town. 'Oh why didn't you go—wonderful place, I even saw the art gallery.' RK and I walked off, got an izvozchik for a rouble and rode about town; the street facing the sea was beautiful—one beautiful home after another, formerly the residences of the rich and now clubs, rest homes, and sanitariums for workers. Greek architecture predominated, showing, it seemed to me, that the Greeks must have been here at one time and influenced the place, or that natural characteristics influence architecture. One especially beautiful palace, of grayish stone with mosaic work, and a pagoda in the garden had been built by a tobacco magnate and not quite finished when the revolution came. So he never lived in it, but fled abroad. It is now the sanitarium of the Soviet Commercial Employees Union. Turning up one of the side streets we came to an Art Gallery of the artist Aivazovsky, a collection of beautiful marine paintings, one enormous canvas of the sea occupying one whole side of a wall. This artist loved Feodosiya best of all; he had lived here as a boy, and used to go down on the wharf where trespassing was forbidden and sketch; he would be driven away, even arrested, or punished by his mother, but nothing could keep him from the seashore. There were also some new paintings by artists of the town. Altogether the gallery was very charming.

Of course, like a good izvozchik, ours must show us the bazaar; the streets were muddy, it had probably rained recently for the weather was mild and cloudy.

To the next stop, the sea was pretty heavy. Everybody took to their berths, but I did not feel a quaver. At 9 p.m. we arrived at Yalta, where the earthquakes have been most severe. At first I did not want to go ashore for nothing could be seen from the boat except the lights of the shops along the beach so RK and Davi went off without me. Later, I decided to go. I strolled along the dimly lighted street, noting the new frame houses evidently erected for the refugees. Not an inspiring street, but the streets leading up into the town past walled gardens, where cypress trees stood sentinel, looked attractive. I went up a dark street. Suddenly a large section of a brick wall crashed down to the sidewalk not twenty feet ahead of me. I jumped into the street; people came running and talked and gesticulated. So I experienced something of the earthquake. Here also the weather was mild, the roads very muddy. We left Yalta very late in the night, but I went to bed early.

7/1/28

At 8 a.m, Sebastapol, the famous port over which many battles have been fought. I again hoped to get some decent food. We hired an izvozchik to show us the town. We jogged along up the main street and down to the sea again—a mild looking place, with naval academies lying on the outskirts and many marines on the streets. At the pristin was a monument to an admiral who had saved the port from the Turks in 1853.[14] 'Drive on,' we said, and our izvozchik turned back up the same way. 'Why not another?' we asked. 'There are only two streets in town,' he answered, 'and we've already been on both'. Up at the corner, he began industriously to point out the places of interest: 'There's the street car that goes to the railroad station', he volunteered. 'Wonderful,' said I,—'and up there is the bazaar', he went on hopefully. 'Let's get out here,' I said, and we looked up a restaurant. We found a kind of dairy lunch, we hoped at least to find some wholesome food. Hot milk, eggs, butter, white bread. . . 'I'm too far gone,' said RK, looking very miserable, 'for anything to help now'. We returned to the ship. The group of sailors were leaving here to go to the naval school. I bought copies of my books on the boat and gave them to the tall fellow who had looked at me so curiously all the way up. He was much surprised and grateful. 'It will be a great memory', he said.

At five p.m. we anchored some distance from the shore of a small shipping point. The sea was very high. I went on deck and watched a tug trying to come close enough to take passengers off. It bobbed about like a cork and any moment might have struck our side. Another boat which had already been loaded with cargo floated nearby waiting to be towed back. It was dark, the wind was blowing—a wild scene—but finally the passengers were off and after some time we were on the way again.

Our last night was the roughest yet. It was impossible to rise until we had almost reached Odessa, because it was too rough to pack. I remember saying as I lay looking at the five life belts hanging on the wall: 'Probably all rotten. I'll bet if a fellow put one on he'd sink right to the bottom.'

8/1/28

At about eight in the morning of Sunday we reached Odessa. It was cold and foggy, with slushy snow. There is a fine harbor. We took the Passage Hotel automobile. The Passage stood on the main

14. A *pristan* is a dock.

square facing a great cathedral, a very old hotel, but my room was not bad, and I rather liked the old black upholstered furniture and the mahogany wardrobe. This was a no-sheet hotel. Guests either had to provide their own, as I understand is the custom, or you pay extra for the linen and blankets. The bed was hard with a straw mattress. But the view from my windows of the square and the church with the dome and steeple was interesting. We looked up a place to eat, a sort of family dining room in a court; the food was not so awful, but it was a stuffy place. We spent the afternoon riding to the end and back of various street car lines. Odessa is a very old city, the buildings have once been very fine, but are decaying and gray. The official language is Ukrainian, but the Russian words are always given also on all notices. It was a raw, foggy day. We came home in the evening and got Davi and went again to our family restaurant for dinner. Although the proprietor gave a home atmosphere to the place by playing the violin to a piano accompaniment, the food seemed just as bad as ever, same old borsch, same old schnitzel, cutlets, Hungarian gulash which would make Bela Kun start another revolution, same old perozhki—oh, my God! In the evening there was nothing to do but go to bed.

9/I

On Monday morning we went to Derutra to find out about the steamer. To my horror, I learned that there is no boat to Constantinople before the 18th, the Italian line, and the 19th the Russian. But as the Italian takes five days and the Russian only 36 hours, it would be better to take the latter. Then it occurred to us that it might be better to cancel the Constantinople trip and then I could go straight to Paris through Poland. I got all the information from Derutra, they examined my passport and said I would have to get a Polish visa, and also my Russian visa renewed. We went to the visa department and learned there that I had no exit visa at all and would have to make application and pay 21 roubles. We got very much excited, and protested, saying that I was a guest of VOKS and that they should have attended to the matter in Moscow, to which the visa man agreed.

I wrote a request to be granted an exit visa through Poland without charge, and the request was granted. Derutra said that they could get the Polish visa in two days after the Russian exit visa was ready. I sent a wire to Constantinople informing about my change of plan.[15] My one desire is to get out of here as quickly as possible and back to America.

I took a long walk late in the afternoon down to the waterfront. It was a sunny day. I found the steps on which the firing took place in 1905 which is pictured in the film 'Potemkin'. There are 200 steps which I walked up and down.

10/I

On Tuesday when we went down to Derutra we inquired about examination of baggage, and I learned that I could not take any printed matter or writing out of the country without special permission. I was very indignant. We then asked about money—also necessary to get special permission to take sums over 300 roubles, and as I had almost a thousand dollars which had been sent me in Moscow, they said it might be difficult to get permission. I came home and packed up all my papers, including these notes, all my English books, personal letters, etc. They quite filled my bag. At this point, a young reporter from the local paper came to see me. He wanted to know what I thought of Russia, spoke English, so I made him a long speech about what I thought of conditions, that it was an interesting experiment, but—they had a long way to go before they could try to put the system in other countries. I had no objection to their trying it out here, but they should not try to change other countries until they had proved the system here. I said also that before they send any more money abroad for strikers, etc. they should take the children off the streets. He said they had only a hundred left in Odessa, that most of them were in homes now. We hurried down to Derutra with the bag which they took possession of and began to examine, making a list of the contents. It made me boiling mad, and then the discussion about the money still madder.

I asked Davi for the papers from VOKS which she had been using for the trip, in which it is stated that I am the guest of the Soviet Government, as I thought it would be useful in getting over the border. She refused to give it to me. I then used some strong language about the lousy organisation and about her, and about the whole god damn business. I took the paper and went out on the

15. This wire was probably to Helen Richardson, who, as planned, had gone to Constantinople to meet Dreiser.

street. RK had been making a list of the papers, and now she followed me and said that Derutra must have the VOKS paper to get the permission. I handed it over to them.

This was the final split with Davi. She went home and we had dinner in the Bristol Hotel restaurant, where we had eaten a fairly good breakfast of pancakes, ham and eggs, and cereal coffee. I was inveigled into trying 'wild duck' which we found on the menu, being reminded of all the ducks I had seen flying in this part of the world. Also some stuffed cabbage. The duck was awful, so was the cabbage, and we went away quite discouraged.

After the scene in Derutra, RK and I took a long walk down on the water front in another direction. We passed many fine old houses that had no doubt been the residences of the rich, and probably now were occupied by about 60 families. Some of them were very charming. Here again we met divisions of soldiers marching and singing—there seemed to be barracks nearby.

In the evening, without seeing Davi again, we went to the opera, at the great opera house: 'Sadko', one of the best known Russian operas by Rimski Korsoka.[16] The first act was terrible, the setting bad, the voices bad, the chorus bad. RK was very much disappointed because she had seen it done so much better in Moscow. She persuaded me to stay for the second act in which there is the 'Song of India'. The second act was so much better that I was glad we stayed. The deserted wife had a nice voice and the home scene was effective. Sadko himself was such a big bull with a bad voice that he spoiled every scene. In the market place at the wharf a crowd had gathered to see Sadko off on the boat—here were foreign visitors who stepped up and wished him luck on his journey to the kingdom below the sea. One of these was in Indian costume; he stepped quietly forward and with folded arms sang the 'Song of India'. It was very effective. We went home at the end of the second act.

11/I

Today we filed permission for taking the money out of the country and were granted it, also received permission to take out the papers. Davi and I are in open warfare, with RK as mediator.

16. Nicolai Andreyevich Rimsky-Korsakov (1844–1908) was a composer and conductor who wrote operas, choral and orchestral works, and chamber music.

We had breakfast at the Bristol, pancakes, jam, smetana,[17] cereal coffee and 8 eggs fried with ham although we asked for four—that was simple, they gave two portions, four each. It was a cold, sunny day. We came home. I had received a telegram saying that my telegram to Constantinople had not been delivered, so I telegraphed to Cook. Returned to hotel feeling rotten. It was cold in the room and I put on my fur hat, fur coat and fur gloves and lay down on the bed while I dictated the rest of my article to RK. Write-up in the morning Odessa Izvestiya about me today with picture. I didn't have the heart to go out on the street again, we had tea in the room and I went to bed for want of anything better to do.

12/I/28

In the morning we went down to Derutra for further information. They were still waiting for the Polish visa which was expected next day. I sent through them a telegram to Constantinople to trace my niece.[18] We then had breakfast at the Bristol and sat at the table next the goldfish who kept coming up to the top for water, as if the water in the tank must be very stale. RK said it looked as though they were saying 'Bla-bla' all the time. We got into a disagreeable argument on the old subject of communism and individualism, she defending the dubs and the 'svines' maintaining that it is better to lower general standards at the expense of the few if wretched poverty of the mass can be eliminated thereby. We were as usual passing compliments to one another; I said very well, she could have her communism, we would part good friends and each go his separate way. This hurt her feelings very much and she wanted to cry right there, so we decided it would be better to go home and do that. I suggested that a trip somewhere might raise her spirits and she very coldly assented. We went to the railroad station, a dreary place, and found out that we had missed the train to a village. We then took a street car to a summer resort called 'Fontan' some miles out of the city. It was dreary weather for our dreary mood. A thick fog hung over the city, so that only objects in the immediate foreground could be seen from the car

17. *Smetana* is heavy cream, often used as a topping or added to soups.
18. This is a reference to Helen Richardson, who was in fact distantly related to Dreiser. Kennell is preparing this entry; probably Dreiser did not wish her to know the nature of his relationship with Helen.

windows. But such objects! Mile after mile of ruined buildings, only fragments of stone walls standing on the desolate plains. It was as if an army had battered everything down in its march on Odessa.

We arrived at Fontan on the seashore, no doubt a nice enough place in summer. Now it looked desolate in the chill fog. There were little summer cottages of cement and the ruins of fine homes standing up on the heights. Here stood the scrap of a wall and a stone gate and on the gate a rusty plate: 'Datcha (cottage) of L. Kermachov'. A number of ferocious dogs came running into the road and a fellow struck at them with his whip and drove them back. We made our way down a slippery hill where the boys were coasting to the beach where a number of large fishing boats lay and nearby nets hung drying. A few nice houses were still standing, one the datcha of the Soviet Commercial Employees Union, another of the food workers, a pavilion now boarded up and a nice looking stone building, evidently a theater. We wandered down a gully. Down on the slope was a little white clay cottage with a brush fence about it and a little porch with dried weeds put up as a wind brace. A little old woman on the porch called to us: she said we could not get out that way and that she would show us the road to the car. We returned, and RK, scenting an opportunity for some local color, engaged her in conversation. She invited us to come in and warm ourselves. We went inside. The house had three tiny rooms in a row, the middle room just off the porch was evidently the living room. There was a brick stove, a table, two or three chairs and a shelf; straw on the stone floor, a lamp on the window sill. The panes of the small latticed window were composed of innumerable pieces of glass cemented together. The bowl of the lamp looked like an ink bottle and I said when I got home I would make a lamp out of an ink bottle. RK said that would certainly be a great economy. On the freshly whitewashed walls were one or two quaint religious pictures, in the room to the right were religious pictures and an altar and several milk cans. It was deadly chill, for here they kept the milk which they sold to the townspeople. In the room on the left was a wooden bed covered with some old rags and sheepskins, and also unheated. We sat down in the living room and the little old woman began making up the fire which had gone out. She wore an old black skirt and a white woolen sweater, over which she had put a man's vest, giving a sort of quaint bodice effect. She had a sweet, refined face, and as she had been ill for some time, moved with heavy sighs, murmuring now and then: 'Bozhi moi' (My God). Her husband was a little old man of 68 with a pathetic comical face, out of which his little dark eyes peered shyly. He wore an old padded canvas coat and felt boots. He sat huddled down on a low stool next to the stove while she added peet to the fire and fanned it with her skirt, explaining that it was hard to make burn in the foggy weather. We asked her for hot milk and she put a saucepan on the stove. He had been a gardener before the revolution for the rich who lived in the fine houses, but now as they had all been destroyed, there was no work for him. He owned his little house, having built it himself years ago and was exempt from taxes because of his years. He was entitled to an old age pension of 15 roubles a month but said it was necessary to go throughso much red tape to get it, that he just didn't bother. He also sighed everytime he stirred. The woman brought a loaf of white bread and cut a slice for the cat who devoured it as if it had been meat, uttering growls as she tried to swallow it. They had a cow and sold milk. In summer they moved out into the yard and rented their rooms for 150 roubles for the season. Yes, he supposed he could get land to farm from the government if he agitated enough, but most of the land had already been distributed by the local Soviet, and they would not want to give such an old man land. They were Polish, had come thirty or forty years ago to Odessa, had no children, and all through the war and famine had lived in this little gully unmolested. During the famine, he said, the cat would not have survived—yes, of course, they ate cats. We asked about the ruined buildings. These had not only been destroyed by the fighting, but also by the people themselves during the famine, when they actually tore down the deserted dwellings of the rich who had fled or been killed and sold the materials in Odessa for food. There anything could be bought for enough money. He had not fared so badly because he was working for the local Soviet and received a payok.[19] When they found out we were from America, they asked how the people lived; she wanted to know, did we have the Soviet system there now?

When we had finished our hot milk, which was very good, we paid her, said goodbye and went on, looking back now and then at the little cottage, which somehow reminded one of a hut in a fairy tale, and they of the old couple in the legend 'The Miraculous

---

19. A *payok* is a ration.

Pitcher'. We went down to the street car station and, quite unprepared for an hour's wait, walked up and down the road feeling miserable and cold and unable to think of anything worth while talking about. In the window of a house on the street a woman was looking for lice on the head of a little girl, probing with a fine comb. Finally the car came and we rode home; the room was cold, we were cold, and so we ordered hot baths which at least would warm us up.

In the evening we had dinner at the Bolshaya Moskovskaya, came home to the room which was still cold as the heat had not yet come on, and I dictated an article for the Russian press on my general impressions of Russia. Davi left on the 5:40 and I felt at once a sense of relief. 'Rebecca Kopeck' was gone.

13/I/28

Telegram received from Constantinople, visa received, everything ready to go on 5:40. We walked down to the steps, and went into an archaeological museum where a large collection of remains from the Greek occupation along the Black Sea, several centuries before Christ. An artist who looked like a priest showed his special collection of paintings and pottery from this district, especially Bessarabia. His name was Chernyavski. He said he had a hard time now, not even money to buy paints, 'We are not needed' he said.

I thought his paintings of local scenery and of an old fortress near Odessa from which much of the pottery and stones in the exhibit had come, were charming. I liked his sense of color, his skies. And yet how wretched he looked—long scraggly hair falling from beneath an old fur hat about his sallow, thin face, a long shabby black robe. 'There is a new form of art coming up' he went on, 'no one is interested in the old art, or in art at all. We artists simply exist.'

Another chill, foggy day. We returned to the hotel and longed for tea to warm us, but the maid announced severely that there was no kipyatok (boiling water) until after six. By telephone we learned that the Polish visa had come and we could leave today. The train would leave at 5:40 and on this same train RK could also go with me to a certain station where she would change for Moscow. Derutra had arranged for their agents to meet me at Shepatkova, on the border, then at the Polish border and at Warsaw. We seemed to have found some efficiency at last, now that the trip was ended. Of course, they charged me enough for the services. I came home in excellent spirits—at last I was going to leave, yes, literally crawl across the border. 'I'd rather die in the United States than live here' I told RK. She did not retort, evidently feeling that I was a hopeless case, anyhow (her defenses were pretty well battered down by this time. She said that my mission in coming to Russia was to win her back to her native land). For the first time on the trip, I came out twice on solitaire. 'You see,' said RK joyfully, 'your luck is changing'. At five o'clock a Derutra man came and took us to the station. The manager was also there to see us off. The accomodations were pretty bad, half the car soft coupes and the other half hard, no electricity, only candle light. The stupid looking little conductor was made to feel by Derutra that I was very important, 'personally conducted', and he hung around looking at us stupidly out of bleary eyes, and asking if there wasn't something we wanted. We knew what he wanted; these people think we are made of money. He brought us tea in a white coffee pot. RK said any Russian would proclaim it excellent 'kipyatok'. I got out my cake, bread sticks, lemon and cheese and we had a feast. It was quite dark when the train pulled out and the flickering candle filled the coupe with soft shadows. Every minute our unctuous conductor pulled open the door, shuffled in and asked if we wanted something, were we ready to have the beds made up (he was afraid the gentleman would find the bedding very uncouth). We told him at least half a dozen times that we did not want the bedding yet. Then finally when I did want it, he was not to be found. Just ahead of our coach was an International coach bound for Moscow. RK decided to go straight onto it at five in the morning when it would be necessary to change cars, where she could pay there for her place card instead of buying at the station. But our conductor insisted that 'soft' was just as good and that he would buy her ticket himself at the station. We lay down, but had no peace. Every few minutes, that little rat scratched at the door—had she decided yet about the myakhky or international? Yes, she had decided to go International. A mistake, he thought. Then when did she want to change. Not until we reached the station where the train divided, she said. We slept, but woke in the early morning and looked out at the snowy world and the frosted woods. I said that already this was better than the mild cold of the south. We talked about the museum of old Greek remains that we had been to that day, about the enduring perfection of Greek civilisation, as yet unsurpassed. About the Greeks as traders on the Black Sea coast. Our little rat scratched again at the door. Did she want to go into the international car now? No, she did not. She would wait until we reached the junction. He had evidently been drinking too much. His eyes were still more bleary and he looked at us sleepily. We dozed, — again the door. Did she want to go in, now, he would take her. How long, she asked, before we reach the station? An hour and a half. Then she would wait. In another half an hour, he came again. Our candle had long ago spluttered out. The coupe was quite dark. RK decided to transfer, as there would be no peace until she did. I got up and went with her, because I did not trust the drunken conductor. With the baggage, we crossed a dangerous place between the two cars. Inside the international were bright electric lights, cleanliness and warmth. What a shame we could not have spent the night here! We said goodbye and I went on back. In a few minutes, a tapping again on the door. What, that fool again — then RK's voice. I opened it. She explained that the conductor had just told her he must take the bedding at the next station because he had borrowed it from the International car. I told him to take it and get out and leave me in peace. RK told him not to come around again, that I wanted to sleep. If she had not come and explained to me I probably would have killed him when he came and tried to take the bedding. She stayed with me until the conductor came again and said that we were nearing the junction. Again farewell. . . .

FAREWELL

14/I/28 (Supplement of Secretary on her way to Moscow).

I have now so badly got the habit of writing notes on everything that I think this journal will go on forever. I can't realise that my job of personal secretary is ended.

When I left you at last I stood in the corridor and watched our coaches being uncoupled and how yours went off in the darkness. And it seemed as if it were a physical separation of just us two, as if you were cut away from me, or worse, that only a part of me had been cut away from you and the rest had gone on with you in the darkness in that other coach. I went into the empty coupe and felt so desolate. I didn't want to pick up the broken threads of my individual life again after having so completely merged myself with you for the past two and one half months. Your overpowering personality still envelops me. No one has ever so completely absorbed my individuality—but at the same time you have been such a tremendous intellectual stimulus. We couldn't have given nearly so much to one another if we had agreed in our philosophy. However, we both reason in the same way, and since you reason better because you have a really great intellect you broke down my arguments. Just the same, I think you are wrong in your ultimate conclusions about life and specifically about the social experiment in Russia. Yes, I agree with you altogether about human nature being just the same here as anywhere, but I maintain that this is the beginning of a social system which will supplant capitalism just as capitalism succeeded the feudal system. Naturally it is not so individualistic as capitalism because it is founded on a social theory that all should work for the common good (therefore eventually giving more freedom to the individual). There is only as yet a tendency to carry out this theory in practice. Russians temperamentally, as you say, are more inclined to do things together than westerners. This may still be due more to their primitive state (which would make them herd together for mutual protection) than to any conscious application of Marxian theories.

Perhaps you are right in thinking that the individual is more suppressed in Russia today by this new system, but I think this is only temporary. You can't keep the individual down and he will come up all too soon and fight for the best of things—but meantime perhaps the concerted effort will have created better *general* conditions for him to develop in. I think the Soviet system as directed by the Communist Party will prove to be the best system to develop

Russia. It may be slower than capitalist exploitation, but in the long run there may be less waste and a more enduring system. This seems to be just about all that has survived out of my faith. . . .

- - - - - - - - - - - -

When I reach Moscow, the first thing I shall do is to look up Rebecca Rachel K. and convey to her your farewell message, i.e. that you had no letter of thanks to send to Madame Kameneva, that your opinion of those svines, lice and dubs, and of this lousy god damned country is unchanged, and that you crawled across the border on your hands and knees, stopping now and then to put your thumb to your nose and shout feebly: 'What a lousy country. What a bunch of svines. When I get back home I'm going to stay there for the rest of my life. And may the lord punish me if I ever complain again'.

14/I/28 (Supp. No.2 — my salary as your sec. is really paid to Moscow and I must earn it.)

I keep thinking about you, how you are faring on the road to the border. You have already reached the first border by this time. My traveling companion is a merchant. I am trying to benefit by your remarks and behaving quite properly and coldly so as not to encourage him. When I am reading or typing, I only see the outline of his figure across the way, and quite unconsciously I feel that it is you. In the afternoon, I slept a little; he was sitting reading, and in my half-conscious state, I continued for some time under the impression that you were playing solitaire. Such a pleasant, comfortable feeling that everything was all right — together in an International coupe on our way somewhere. And at that very time, no doubt, you were nearing the border, with a prayer of thankfulness on your lips; 'Thank God, that's over'.

Snow, snow and then more snow, but the weather is mild. At Kiev it was so foggy I could see none of the landmarks. I was dying of hunger this evening and there was no food to be bought along the road. The merchant produced bread, ham caviar and apples, we ordered tea and we had a feast. (The lord does provide.) He agrees with you about the deadness of the cities commercially due to the absence of private trade and private initiative. 'But' he says, 'why should the government want this lively competition? Whom does it benefit?' I asked him about interest on deposits; banks pay all the way from six to eight per cent depending upon the conditions of deposit.

I have just finished reading 'Dark Laughter' and liked it very much.[1] When Anderson gets away from that jerky reminiscient style of the first few chapters and down to the story, it is very interesting and charming. <u>You</u> may love the American business man, but Anderson doesn't. At Kiev, I telegraphed O'C and hope there will be some sort of reception for me at home.

And now farewell, a long farewell, to my dear boss. I hope I can live down my loneliness, but if I don't, won't that prove the endurance of human affections—once in a while, at least?

CONCLUSION

15/I/28 (Supp. 3, Moscow)

I slept very well on the train, although I was somewhat troubled by the illusion that I was on the boat and that you were lying in the other berth. I warned my companion not to be alarmed if I had a nightmare—this after I had aroused him once by jabbering something in English—lucky, perhaps, that he couldn't understand English.

In the morning when I looked out, there were the beautiful forests of Moskovskaya Gubernia, deep in snow. We were due at 9:35, and would you believe it, I was already passing through the station when the clock pointed to 9:35. An ill fate pursued you, and now you are gone, everything works nicely. Moscow weather was gray, it is true, but warmer than Tiflis; the snow was melting a little. Everything seems topsy-turvy this year.

Arriving at the Lux, I looked about me as a prodigal son might after a long absence, expecting to see great changes. But no, there was still that sign on the elevator 'Lift ne rabotayet' (Lift does not work) and the man at the desk said O'C had not yet been given a room there. But when I saw O'C a little later in my room (Varya had cleaned up the place so that it looked quite decent and my roommate greeted me pleasantly) she announced that she is going back to England this week. Nothing seems to have been done about my

---

1. Sherwood Anderson's novel *Dark Laughter* (New York: Boni & Liveright, 1925).

place in the library. I would go with her, if I dared be so unfair as to leave so soon, if they still want me. I shall know tomorrow. Serge did not know I was coming, and when I called up he was not at home. . . . . Rebecca K. called up and was quite solicitous about your departure. I hope you didn't have trouble about your papers at the Polish border—O'C says she had.

In the evening I met Serge in O'Cs room; as usual he is terribly busy, just rushing from one appointment to another. He said he thought we would be in Odessa only until the 29th, and therefore did not have time to write. He took the agreement and will send you a copy.

Postcard created by the Soviet government to advertise Dreiser's visit to the Soviet Union. The translation reads as follows:

Theodore Dreiser

In Russia I saw a nation capable of thinking. It is precisely in Russia nowadays, rather than in any other country in the world, that all the great revelations both in a sense of practical reforms and in the sphere of thought are destined to appear. In any case, I believe so. We live during a turbulent epoch when our Western world is dashing around in search of a way out of the deadlock. And now, when Russia is able to give us something new, is it really possible that common sense doesn't suggest to us that we need to help her to create all that she is capable of.

Theodore Dreiser

(From the Russian State Archives of Film and Photo Documents, Moscow; translated by Marina Tchebotaeva)

DREISER'S FAREWELL STATEMENT

Before leaving Soviet Russia, Dreiser dictated a statement summarizing what he had observed and learned on his journey (see p. 275). This statement, taken by Ruth Kennell, was released to the press. Kennell evidently kept a copy for herself; this version she published as an appendix to *Theodore Dreiser and the Soviet Union* (pp. 311–15). The text below, with its headnote, appeared in the 6 February 1928 *Chicago Daily News* (pp. 1–2). It differs slightly from Kennell's version: hers is addressed "to the Russian public," for example, and uses "you" and "your" instead of "they" and "their" in the subsection entitled "Laws Cannot Make Men Clean." The Kennell version also contains a few apparent typos, such as "places" for "spaces" in the second paragraph and "importance" for "impotence" in the second sentence of the subsection "Praises Actual Achievement." Neither text is without flaw—the subheads in the newspaper version, for example, were surely added by desk editors—and both descend at equal remove from a lost typescript with (one assumes) carbon copies. Kennell's text, however, is available in her book, so it has seemed more useful to reproduce here the *Daily News* text, which has not been reprinted since its original publication. The headnote gives a good picture of Dreiser on the eve of his departure from Russia.

Theodore Dreiser Finds Both Hope and Failure in Russian Soviet Drama

Theodore Dreiser, the noted novelist, just before leaving Russia dictated his impressions of the country and its government. Junius B. Wood, The Daily News correspondent at Moscow, sends the statement and the following comment: "Though his optimism and penetrating philosophy were indomitable, Mr. Dreiser was far from comfortable physically, coughing with bronchitis and trying to keep warm under the blankets in a swayed backed bed of an unheated hotel on a bitterly cold Russian morning. To aid the heating he had pulled a fur cap over his ears, wrapped himself in his fur coat and even donned fur gloves and galoshes—a picturesque sage philosophizing to a muffled, blue-fingered stenographer. He had just completed an unusually rough six-day trip in a little steamer across the Black sea from Batum without losing appetite or spirits, only to meet an enforced wait of a week in Odessa because the Society for Cultural Relations with Abroad which sponsored his trip, had forgotten that a visa was necessary for one wishing to leave the country. The delay compelled him to forego his expected visit to Constantinople and to start for the United States. In addition to seeing factories, new residences, officials and the other stock exhibits of soviet Russia, Mr. Dreiser saw the actual life of the country as have few other visitors in such a short time. He whiffed the million odors of a Russian hotel bedroom hermetically sealed for the winter, rode a night in a "hard" car to Yasnaya Polanaya with peasants' boots dangling around his ears and passed a night in the railroad station at Constantinovka because the officials said the train might come at any minute, but did not come in for twenty-four hours. An irascible policeman thumped any who dozed, some pampered Moscow bureaucrat having prohibited sleeping in the station. He waited another day amid the squalor and filth of the Baku station for another lost train, but saw sunshine through the gloom and hope for humanity in the soviet effort."

BY THEODORE DREISER.

SPECIAL CORRESPONDENCE
Of The Chicago Daily News Foreign Service.
Copyright 1928. The Chicago Daily News, Inc.

Odessa, Ukraine, U. S. S. R., Jan. 13.— After a two months' visit in soviet Russia I should like, before I leave for the United States, to give my first statement of my general impressions:

As a westerner, accustomed to the comparatively mild climate of the United States, I can only look upon Russia as a boreal world that would try any save those born of its very soil. Russians ought to be hardy because they survive so much that people of milder climes could not endure. To me, at times and in places, it seems to possess a kind of harsh beauty born of biting winds and vast spaces. That man should find it necessary to conquer it at all seems almost pitiful.

Yet dotted as it is with so huge a population, hitherto restrained by such untutored conditions, it seems not a little astounding that it should be the scene of the latest experiment in human government. Personally I am an individualist, and shall die one. In all this communistic welter I have seen nothing that dissuades me in the least from my earliest perceptions of the necessities of man. One of these is the individual dream of self-advancement, and I cannot feel that even here communism has altered that in the least. On the other hand, after the crushing weight of czardom and the unbridled capitalism that one sees in places, I can sympathize with the emotions of those who swung from oppression of the mass to their unlimited emancipation and authority.

Individual Comes First.

It is so plain that just now not the individual in general, but the individual in particular, as an artisan and little more, comes first. Everything is to be done for him; the intellectual—assuming that the laborer has the mentality so to do—is to be used by him as a servant of his mass needs.

Naturally, as an individualist this makes me smile, for I see only the most individualistic political leaders of Europe trying to guide him to an understanding of what this means. That even now he grasps or fully believes it, I doubt. More likely it is the shimmering array of material benefits dangled before him that interests and enthralls him and what he actually believes is that great and powerful individuals are now kind enough to aid him in his struggle for a better life. And he is grateful to them for that. And so am I.

But that the right of the superior brain to the superior directing and ruling positions has been done away with I question. Really I do not believe it. In Russia as elsewhere I am sure you will find the sly and the self-interested as well as the kind and the wise slipping into the positions of authority, executing for the rank and file the necessary program which guarantees their comfort. And as time goes on, if not now, with a much larger return for their services. It is a survival which I for one am sure will never be completely abrogated.

Praises Actual Achievement.

Now as for what this superior group of idealists have done for Russia so far I have only praise. For one thing, and to my immense delight, they have swept dogmatic and brain-stultifying religion from its position of authority and cast it into the background of impotence where it belongs. Furthermore, they have given to the collective mentality of Russia freedom to expand, and while perhaps this expansion is a little too much colored by the new dogmas of communism, I do not really object, for exact communism is not by any means in force here now and I doubt if it will be much so in the future. For unless I miss my guess, the Russian mind is at bottom a realistic mind and it will see life for what it is—a struggle not to be too much handicapped by the incurably incompetent any more than it is to be too dogmatically ruled by the self-seeking and indifferent materialist.

I am pleased by the enormous housing program and the material evidence of its fulfillment in every part of the Union. It is wonderful to see the new factories, the new schools, hospitals, clubs and scientific institutions which are now already dotting the land.

I sincerely hope that this vast enthusiasm for the modernization of Russia and the introduction of western facilities of every kind will not slacken until the land is the paradise which this most amazing group of idealists wish it to be. It certainly is a land that needs and deserves a brighter day and a gayer spirit. And I, for one, would do nothing anywhere to counteract the fulfillment of this program.

Pleads for Homeless Children.

On the other hand, there are certain obvious defects in either the Russian temperament or the fulfillment of this program, or both, which I think should be attended to now. One of these is the immediate care of the thousands of homeless children whom one encounters in every part of Russia. It is useless to say, as many do, that the government as yet lacks either the means or the facilities for their assumption and care. The trade unions, I notice, do not lack means for their new homes and their new clubs, and new theaters. But they had better suspend action on some of these material comforts for themselves until they have done the needful thing for these children, and it is a shame and an outrage, a commentary on the Russian temperament itself, too dark to be endured for one minute if the nation has that dignity and self-respect which it so consistently claims.

Another thing that strikes me as not only irritating but discreditable is the national indifference to proper sanitation. One hears so much of what is to be in the future, but there is so much that could be done right now with little more than the will of the people to be cleaner than they are. The Russian house, the Russian yard, the Russian street, the Russian toilet, the Russian hotel, the individual Russian's attitude toward his own personal appearance, are items which convey to the westerner (and particularly to a traveler from America) a sense of something neither creditable nor wholesome, and which cannot possibly be excused on the ground of poverty. There are as many poor people in Holland, Germany, France and England as there are in Russia, but you would never find them tolerating the conditions which in Russia seem to be accepted as a matter of course.

Laws Cannot Make Men Clean.

Cleanliness is not a matter of national law or fiat, or even prosperity, public or private, but of the very essence of the individual himself. Either he loves and responds to cleanliness or he does not. If he does, he will make untold sacrifices to keep himself free of disorder and filth; if he does not, no law this side of a bayonet will aid him. And it seems to me that the Russians whom I have seen, from the Baltic to the Caspian, are far more indifferent to the first essentials of sanitation than any of the more progressive nations of whom they now claim to be one. It will not do, as some insist, to say that all this is a matter of prosperity and equipment; it is not, I insist it is not. And unless the international slur in regard to this is to remain, the Russian, individually and not nationally, will have to bestir himself and purify as well as decorate his immediate physical surroundings.

Their hotels, trains, railway stations and restaurants are too dirty and too poorly equipped. They do not wash their windows often enough. They do not let in enough air. They either overheat or underheat the chambers which they occupy. They live too many in one room and are even lunatic enough to identify it with a communistic spirit. I rise to complain. And I suggest in this conection that more individualism and less communism would be to the great advantage of this mighty country.

Sees Need of Efficiency.

Now as to the future of this great program I think that it will succeed providing, first, that the program which the government now has of introducing the latest labor-saving devices in every phase of the national life is fulfilled, and second, that the discrepancy between the cost of manufacture and the wages of the worker is bridged. For as I see it, as yet there is too much effort to make the laborer comfortable and too little to make him thoroughly efficient. Really there should be no talk of the seven-hour-day until the workers are earning enough to pay for the latest type of machinery which would make such a day possible.

In the next place, one of the staggering problems which confronts this government is that of the peasant and the land— 120,000,000 peasants, the enlightening of whom in regard to modern agricultural methods is still incipient. It is true that there are a large number of what in America would be known as agricultural stations, with all the latest information and machinery in regard to farming and stock-raising. But it is one thing to take this information to the peasant and another to make him accept it.

Mostly, unless I am maliciously informed, the peasant desires nothing so much as to be let alone, to be allowed to go along in the way he had hitherto gone. The problem of interesting him has barely been touched and I see that his indifference is one of the severest trials.

Make Farming an Industry.

Now my solution would be for the government to divide the land into departments and according to its peculiar possibilities; that it place at the head of each department an agriculturist or board of agriculturists whose business would be to develop it quite as any commercial or financial prospect anywhere would be developed. The government should provide machinery and whatever other equipment might be necessary and then employ farmers, quite as a factory employs hands. They should be organized in unions, paid so much a day, limited to so many hours of work and allowed to look after their own welfare quite as trade unionists now look after theirs. By this method their efficiency might be standardized; farm schools could be operated at the source of the crop supply.

The literature, the equipment and the practical methods would all be at the door of the farmer-unionist, and by that method the entire possibilities of the enormous agricultural area of Russia be brought into full force. If this could be done, most certainly Russia would leap into the forefront of nations, economically stable and powerful. Also, she would be the first to solve this disconcerting and depressing problem which now faces every nation, capitalists or otherwise, the world over.

In spite of many difficulties connected with this trip, I have appreciated the opportunity given me by the soviet government of witnessing the details of this great experiment and I have only kindest thoughts of and the best wishes for its eventual success.

EMENDATIONS

This table lists significant editorial emendations in the text of Dreiser's Russian diary. The page-line reference in each entry is followed by the emended reading from the published text, then by a left-pointing bracket, which should be read as "emended from." To the right of the bracket is the reading from the original diary.

Emendations in the Text

31.8   *enough? No Bolsheviks."*] *enough?* ¶ *"No, Bolsheviks"*

39.30   *C5 at*] *C5 with at*

41.33   *each eat*] *eat each*

44.5   *now are*] *now is the*

56.12   *did not*] *did*

61.1   *into*] *in*

61.37   *for how*] *for*

103.14   *him as short and homely*] *as short homely*

108.27   *His old*] *This old*

136.7   *good*] *go*

138.7   *hang around*] *hang*

147.34   *Did*] *What did*

148.36   *Are the*] *And the*

152.14   *each*] *each should*

161.29   *some ways*] *some*

167.24   *recognised by*] *recognised*

178.29   *would not*] *would*

Emendations in Dates

113.9   Nov. 19th,] Nov. 18th,

143.17   *Nov. 27*] *Nov. 26*

146.37   *Nov. 28*] *Nov. 27*

182.26   *1927*] *1928*

183.24   *1927*] *1928*

195.25   *Thurs.*] *Wed.*

252.1   Wednesday.] Thursday.

254.22   Thursday] Friday

INDEX

The University of Pennsylvania Dreiser Edition